A note from the publisher

The book you are holding was nearly lost to time. When we discovered it was no longer in print, Two Hoots Press was born. We simply could not allow the work of John Parris to be forgotten. For almost four decades, his brief, illuminating non-fiction essays comprised his Asheville-Citizen-Times column, "Roaming the Mountains." A selection of Parris' columns was first published as this book in the 1950s. They quickly became popular in Western North Carolina homes but sadly went out of print.

Parris wrote with the crispness of Hemingway and the grace of Thomas Wolfe. Indeed, he was a war correspondent like Hemingway and a decorated hero for his work with the Belgian underground during World War II.

The book's original publisher, Robert Bunnelle wrote, "Western North Carolina is a many storied country of wondrous mountains and valleys, so rich in beauty, in history and in folklore, that it needs a very special chronicler. Such a chronicler is John Parris, to whom nothing in the mountains of Western North Carolina is an old or jaded story…it is all new and fresh and wonderful."

As Western North Carolina rises to meet the changes and challenges of the 21st century, these stories are more vital than ever. They remain as "fresh and wonderful" as the day they were written. With every word John Parris reminds us that we are stewards of these mountains and their history.

Two Hoots Press is honored to publish this Heritage Edition of *Roaming the Mountains with John Parris,* making his beloved book available for generations to come.

Marty Keener Cherrix
Publisher

Amy Cherrix
Editor

ROAMING THE MOUNTAINS

With JOHN PARRIS

CITIZEN-TIMES PUBLISHING COMPANY, ASHEVILLE, N. C., 1955

Two Hoots Press
P.O. Box 15496
Asheville, North Carolina, 28813

ISBN 978-0-9975069-0-7

Printed and bound in the United States
First Heritage Edition, 2016
10 9 8 7 6 5 4 3 2 1

twohootspress.com

Our books may be purchased in bulk for promotional, educational, or business use

Please contact Two Hoots Press at twohootspress@gmail.com.

To Dorothy whose love and devotion and encouragement through the years have made this book possible, and whose mountain flower sketches are scattered through its pages.

Foreword

WESTERN NORTH CAROLINA IS A MANY STORIED COUNTRY of wondrous mountains and valleys. So rich is it in beauty, in history and in folklore, that it needs a very special chronicler.

Such is John Parris who was born in the Western North Carolina mountain town of Sylva in 1914. He worked his way as a newspaperman of distinction from Raleigh to New York, to London, to the beaches of the North African invasion, back to London, back to New York and then completed the circuit by coming home to his mountains to write.

I first met John Parris when I was heading up the European operations of the Associated Press. I was impressed by the constant freshness of his viewpoint and he later came to work for me.

In his diplomatic and United Nations assignments he regularly walked with kings and prime ministers, but he never was half so impressed by any one of these as by his grandfather in Sylva, who is now 96 years old. The grandeur of The Mall in London and the sparkle of the Seine and its environs in Paris for him never quite came up to the grandeur of the Nantahala gorge and the sparkle of the Tuckaseigee River.

The London blitz, the North African invasion, Whitehall—none of these ever had for John Parris one-tenth the glamour of his present assignment—roaming and writing about his native mountains.

Nothing in the mountains of Western North Carolina is an old or jaded story to John Parris. It is all new and fresh and wonderful. And he writes about it in a sensitive, nostalgic style which has made his column for the *Citizen-Times* one of the most popular and widely read of all newspaper features.

This book, which *The Citizen-Times* is proud to publish, is a collection of some of the best of the stories John Parris has written of the land which we who are privileged to live here cherish and revere.

ROBERT BUNNELLE
Publisher
Asheville Citizen-Times

Preface

THIS BOOK GREW OUT OF A THOUSAND NIGHTS AROUND THE hearth-fire and out of a thousand days among a people whose heritage is as old as the hills.

It is the story of a unique region, its history and legends and folklore, its tall tales and traditions and ballads. It is the story of a distinct and often misinterpreted people whose lives have been molded by the mountains wherein they dwell.

Much of it I heard from my father and from my mother, and from my grandfather whose memory is an amazing and wonderful encyclopedia that covers almost a century. The rest I collected by roaming the mountains.

Actually, the seed for it first was sown on a winter night when I was seven. For it was then that my father introduced me to the mountain world he had known as a boy, telling of the days when panthers screamed on the ridge above his home and of that unbelievable morning when the first wood-burning train came puffing into the little town of Dillsboro to awe and captivate the people of a region where isolation and loneliness walked arm in arm.

In the nights of the years then yet to come, he impressed upon my mind the things the ordinary folks had done and thought and dreamed since first they settled here in Western North Carolina. The kind of things that go to make up the history of a people but things which seldom find their way into the history books, because few historians ever seem to realize that the simple, human, every-day things that men do is history, too.

The fascinating and ever-enchanting story he began has continued to develop for me through the years because mountain folks are born storytellers with tales to tell and because of their affinity for the old ways and the old customs.

When Robert Bunnelle became publisher of *The Asheville Citizen-Times* in 1954 he began concentrating on broadening and expanding the regional voice of the newspapers. I had worked for him in London when he directed the European operations of The Associated Press and he shared my love for the mountains, their people and the people's way of life. He suggested that I roam the mountains and tell the story of the region in terms of what it was like then and now.

So it was that a few months later *Roaming The Mountains* was born as a column. From the beginning the response has been both enthusiastic and generous.

It is usual at this point to thank all the people who have had a part in this book. That is impossible, for they are legion. To name them individually would require a volume larger than this. Yet, to each who has taken the time to stop and talk, to suggest ideas, to pass on words of encouragement, I wish to express my thanks and appreciation.

For many favors, for his unusual interest and help in making "sit-'n'-whittle" sessions productive, I want to thank personally Reuben B. Robertson.

Finally, to Robert Bunnelle, who gave me the assignment; to my publishers for their confidence; to my mother, for her long and devoted years of whetting my curiosity and leading me back into yesterday; to my grandfather, who has shared with me his storehouse of memories, all gratitude and praise are due.

John Parris

Sylva, North Carolina
November 23, 1955

Contents

	Page
Foreword	v
Preface	vii
In the Good Old Days	1
Molasses Pulling	4
The Whiskey Rebellion	8
The Morris Hearth-Fire	12
The Gander-Pulling	15
The Typical Hill Man Is a Myth	18
Mountain Idiom Fading	21
Persimmons, Possums and Politics	24
Hot Biscuits and Sourwood Honey	27
The Valley of Independence	30
Beau Sabreur of the Frontier	33
Tall Tales About Old Ways	36
Nathan Dempsey, Fightin' Man	39
The First Tourists	42
Memories of Bone Valley	46
The Brown Mountain Lights	50
An Untamed Jungle	53
The Gingerbread Man	57
The Madonna of the Hills	61
The French Broad Is a Gypsy	64
The Drovers' Road	68
The Axeman Came First	72
The Whipping Post and the Branding Iron	75
Old Bill Williams, King of the Mountain Men	78
The Blockaders' Roost	82
Majestic Old Man Dominates Region	85
Horn Lured Dan'l Boone	88
The Eternal Flame of Friendship	91
A Story For Mother's Day	97
A Man With Tales to Tell	101

Page

The Vanishing Gristmill 105
Other Springs in Other Years 109
The Ballad of Kidder Cole 112
Frankie Silvers 116
Post Office Is Link to Past 120
The Apostle of Grandfather Mountain 123
The First Gold Dollars 126
Sir Alexander's Swindle 129
Readin', 'Ritin', 'Rithmetic 133
There's Nothing Like Cherry Bounce 136
Tom Wolfe's Month 139
The Spool-Thread Banjo 141
Minstrel of the Appalachians 144
The Old-Time Drummer 148
An Old-Timer 151
The Corn Shuckin' 154
King of the Sorghum Makers 157
Quiltin' Woman 162
The Pioneer Iron-Makers 166
Road of Shattered Illusions 169
The Fiddlin' Ballad Woman 172
Bear-Huntin' Men Know the Feeling 175
Origin of Mountain County Names 179
Prophet of the Long Trail 183
In Calvary Churchyard 187
Tinkle of Bell Team Fades 190
The Legend of Tom Collins 194
The Sisters of Loneliness 197
The Beef Shoot 201
The Ballad of Tom Collins 206
Chestnuts: Only Memories Stand 209
Yugwilu, the Magic Bait 212
Frog Hunting 215
Old-Timy Recipes 219
The Fairy Crosses 223
Ghosts of Yesterday 226
Yellow-Jacket Soup 230
Hog-Killin' Time 233
Before Sutter's Mill 236
The Mountain Dulcimer 239
A Christmas Long Ago 242

In the Good Old Days

Sylva

ON WINTER NIGHTS THE OLD MAN AND HIS GRANDSON SIT beside the log fire, and the old man tells how it used to be when this was a land of do it yourself or do without.

The old man is older than Time but his eyes still shine like a bright, new dime, though three generations have sat upon his knee and listened to his tales.

He is the last link to a pioneer past, and as he sits beside the fire his youth returns, like the rains of Spring, and he remembers how it was on Cartoogechaye and Burningtown and Hog Rock.

The words that fall from his lips are strange words—toddick, piggin, puncheon, rooftree, twistification and ruction; pallet, poke, ash hopper, feather-bed, salt-gourd and biddie-pecked.

Time was (said the old man, pulling at his pipe) when a man could get along here in the mountains if he had a good sharp axe and a rifle; maybe a woman.

Of course, he had to have a strong back and a good pair of hands, and he had to have gumption to figure things out, else he would starve.

Now, with an axe and a rifle a man could just about fill his wants. With his axe he made the things he needed and his rifle provided meat.

Your great-grandfather (said the old man) was just a boy when he come into these mountains from over the Blue Ridge. His pa drove an ox wagon and they settled on Cartoogechaye in Macon County.

They camped out while they felled trees and built their cabin. They had no nails so they used wooden pegs. They rived oak shakes for the roof.

Their furniture was all handmade. Their table was rough-hewn walnut. Their chairs were made with hickory dowels fixed hard in green maple, and seats of split and woven oak.

Your great-grandmother had a spinning wheel and a loom. It had been her mother's and she learned to weave from her. She made all of our clothes. I was a grown man before I had my first store-bought suit.

Folks here in the mountains (said the old man) wore homespun until fifty or sixty years ago.

My uncle made wool hats. It was every bit done by hand. And they were fine hats, too.

Speaking of hats, they had what they called a beaver or a bee-gum. These were high hats and anybody who owned one had to pay a yearly revenue tax on it.

Every man was his own blacksmith. He made his own hoes, plows and horseshoes. He was a tanner and a cobbler, too. He made his own axe helves, made 'em out of hickory, and you couldn't beat 'em. Why, a homemade helve would outlast four axes unless a feller used it as a prying-bar.

Things like salt and sugar had to be brought in from Walhalla in South Carolina and Macon in Georgia. Folks would set out in a body with their horse and ox teams. Usually made one trip a year.

But if a-body didn't have sugar they used molasses for sweetening.

Matches were scarce and costly. Everybody had a firebox to fetch coals from a neighbor's when his fire went out.

We made our own candles, and sometimes we just had tallow-dips or a thing we called a "slut." To make a "slut" you took a saucer and filled it with fat. A piece of cotton cloth was put in it, allowing one end to hang over the edge. This end of the wick was lighted.

Cooking was done on the hearth or over the fire in the fireplace.

We made some use of just about everything that came our way.

For bedding, ticks were filled with cattails or oak leaves until enough corn or wheat was raised to fill them with shucks or straw.

But feathers made the best bedding.

A man was real proud when he got to own a feather-bed. But it took a long time to collect enough feathers to fill a tick.

You don't find feather-beds any more. But every house had them in the old days. And when there was a storm and it was lightning, the safest place you could be was on a feather-bed. They keep away lightning.

Folks were neighborly, too, in those days.

Why, everybody helped everybody else. They helped each other raise their houses, build their barns, string their beans, shuck their corn.

The womenfolks joined each other in making quilts and coverlids and in canning.

Cider and molasses were made on the shares.

Everybody worked on the roads. It was a law that every able-bodied man had to give a day a month to working on the roads.

Womenfolks did a lot of work in the old days. They helped to plant, hoe corn, gather fodder. Sometimes they even plowed or split rails.

There was a tub-mill in every community. We took our corn there to be ground into meal. There were just certain days when the mill run. From every turn of corn ground, the miller got a toddick of meal.

What's that? A toddick? Why, that's a small measure. Everybody had to leave a portion of the meal as a toll. I don't know how it got started.

Those were the good days (said the old man), and a-body lived right well, too.

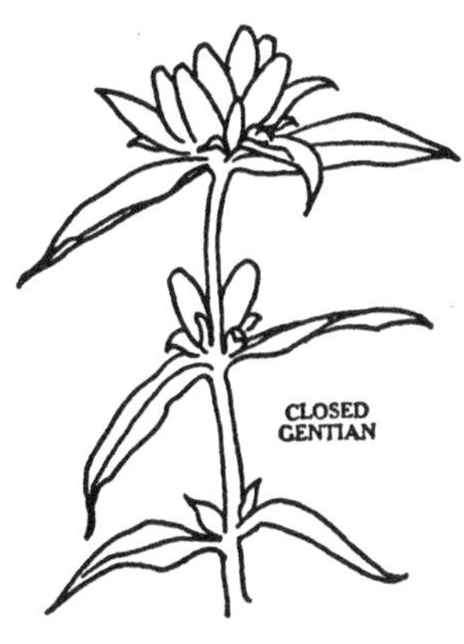

Molasses Pulling

Webster

BACK IN THE DAYS OF THE SEDUCTIVE PRIMROSE PATH corset and the limb-concealing Bonton petticoat, molasses pulling soirees set the pace of the winter social whirl among the young folks here in the mountains.

Unlike corn-shuckin's, which gave a chance to mingle work with play, the molasses candy pulls were designed strictly for developing that most tingling of entertainments—courtship.

They afforded the means for courting couples to pair off and pursue their romance, and many a June wedding grew out of a winter night of pulling molasses.

The nearest thing approaching the molasses pulls as a contrivance for promoting an opportunity for a hug and a buss were the hay-rides, but the wagon-in-the-moonlight soirees were confined to summertime.

So, when the frosts began to walk down from the hills, molasses pulling socials crowded the calendar and provided a form of gay companionship in an area where loneliness was sometimes a desperate thing.

They started off with the first batch of molasses to come from the sorghum mill and rolled along week after week through the winter.

Perhaps one of the prime reasons for their popularity—aside from the romantic potential—was because a molasses pulling required no elaborate preparation.

"Why, a molasses pulling was the easiest thing in the world," my mother recalled. "About like a coke or coffee get-to-gether by young folks today. Of course, some of them were pretty big affairs.

"But as a usual thing, a group of young folks would all meet up at somebody's house and just have a molasses pulling. The big affairs were big socials with lots of games that ended up in a candy pull."

When she was a girl here in Webster the old homeplace was a popular gathering place for the young folks who dropped in about once a week to pull molasses and show off their beaux.

"Always at such times," she said, "mama took charge and gave we girls a chance to look after the company. She would go back to the kitchen and put on a kettle of molasses to boil."

Sometimes, my grandmother would swing an iron pot filled with sorghum over the hearth fire to bubble and boil while she sat in the corner with one eye on the cooking molasses and the other on the young folks who were looking for a chance to sneak a buss.

In due time, my grandmother would ladle out some of the molasses and drop it with a spoon into a dipper of cold water. If it hardened just right she knew the sorghum had boiled long enough.

Then it was poured into buttered plates to cool. If butter was scarce, then lard was used.

When the molasses—some called it taffy—had cooled so it could be lifted up in the hands, the fun of pulling it began.

"The girls buttered or greased their hands," she said. "The smart ones didn't put too much grease on their hands, and for good reason. But the unsuspecting boys covered their hands well with the grease. Then the girls all paired off with the boy of their choice and started pulling the molasses.

"In the beginning, the molasses were stiff and hard to handle. But once you got started they were easier to work and you worked them into a sort of rope. Your beaux would grab the rope of molasses in the middle and pass on the end to you."

Of course, she said, a twinkle in her eyes, the girls all managed sooner or later to get all mixed up in the rope of taffy.

"That was because enough grease was not put on the hands," she explained. "You can imagine what happened. Nothing can be as sticky as molasses."

She laughed, perhaps at a memory.

"It was one way," she said, "to get a feller stuck on you."

For, when this happened, there was no better way for a young feller to get his arms around the girl of his choice.

"You see," she said, "the boy had to stand behind you to help free your hands from a wad of taffy which could be as treacherous as quicksand but not as fatal. Though sometimes it was the thing that set off the spark for a wedding."

A girl all tangled up in molasses taffy gave us one of our most popular phrases. Who said it first, no one remembers, but being "stuck on a girl" had its origin at a molasses pulling.

Theoretically, the object of the pulling was to make the taffy more brittle and more tasty.

Be that as it may, there was many a young swain and his girl who pulled molasses and ate sparingly and daintily of the finished product.

Those without any romantic interest in the proceedings—and they were as rare as an absence of a mother from her fireside chair on such a time—pulled molasses to see who could get theirs the whitest.

"Of course, nobody paid any attention to how white the taffy turned out, except as a sort of customary ritual to satisfy our elders that we were interested only in the way the candy turned out," my mother explained.

When at last the molasses was pulled into white ropes it was again coiled on buttered plates.

"We had fun coiling it into fancy designs of hearts and links," my mother recalled. "Some of the girls got bold enough to spin it out into the initials of their beaux. But that was rare, and when it did happen we knew that a wedding wasn't far off."

The taffy was left to harden on the plates until it could be broken into pieces with quick tap of knife or spoon.

"When the taffy was ready for breaking up," my mother said, "the courting couples paired off together and helped themselves when the plate was passed. Then everybody went home."

When and how the molasses pullings originated as a social pastime in the mountains is one of the lost mysteries of a part of the old American way of life.

As a matter of fact, sorghum was not brought to America until 1840. It was used first to make molasses in the late frontier years of Missouri and Arkansas.

By the time the Civil War came on, molasses-makin' was being practiced as an art here in the hills. And then somebody discovered how to make taffy candy from sorghum.

It caught on right away among a people who were always looking for a bit of diversion from the every-day chores of a never-ending life of industry.

They made molasses pulling into a gay social affair that marked the mountains' none-too-gay 'Nineties and spilled over into another century where folks learned to laugh and play.

But with the advent of the automobile and good roads, molasses pulling began to die out along with the buggy and the bustle.

Only a few folks in the mountains still pull molasses, and that's a shame.

For, to hear my mother tell it, molasses pulling can be fun.

"Sometimes," she says, "I think the old things should be revived so that the young folks can know that there's enjoyment even in the simplest of things.

"Folks are always looking for new things to do. And you are always talking about giving visitors something with a mountain flavor. Well, why not bring back the molasses pulls?"

Sounds like a good idea, but if it means a return of the Primrose Path corset and the Bonton petticoat, I want nothing to do with it.

The Whiskey Rebellion

Highlands

OLD MAN JOEL LOVIN LIFTED THE SIEGE OF THIS MOUNTAIN town during its whiskey rebellion with only a prayer and a threat.

It all happened back in 1883 when the blockaders of a Georgia community declared war on Highlands and engaged the townsfolk in a three-day pitched battle.

The men who fought it are dead and gone, and there's not even a monument to show that a crusade against whiskey was started here 16 years before Carry Nation went on a rampage with her hatchet.

Probably the only man alive remembering the affair is Judge Felix E. Alley of Waynesville who, as a boy of ten, watched his father and four brothers ride out of nearby Whiteside Cove to the defense of the embattled town.

"I remember the occurrence in all of its details, as if it were yesterday," Judge Alley recalled recently. "I heard the story from my father and my brothers, and from the lips of Uncle Joel Lovin, as brave a Confederate veteran as ever lived and who was the real hero of the affair."

In those days, Highlands was a "Yankee" town. It had been built and settled in 1875 by Northerners, mostly from Massachusetts.

These settlers were a very temperate folk, and were uncompromisingly opposed to the use of intoxicating liquor.

Adjoining Highlands Township was Moccasin Township, just across the state line in Rabun County, Georgia, where blockading flourished without fear and little hindrance.

It was the "moonshine" capital of the Southern Appalachians and many of the blockaders found a booming market for their corn juice among the young men of Highlands.

With the whiskey traffic threatening to make a Gomorrah of their town, and with Georgia officers seemingly unable to stop it at the source, the folks here called upon the federal government for help.

Revenue agents swarmed into the area, destroyed distilleries and secured indictments but made no arrests, thus leaving the blockaders free to make and traffic in whiskey until their trials.

It was not until several years later that any attempt was made to arrest blockaders and hold them without bond.

Rabun County started cleaning up the blockaders with the election of John B. Dockens as sheriff. He was a fearless man who arrested all blockaders or traffickers in whiskey who failed to leave the county for good.

But there was a hard core of blockaders, led by four brothers named Billingsly who had a mean-mad reputation and placed little value on life, figuring that with their rifles they were a law unto themselves.

Finally, a man by the name of Henson was arrested with a load of whiskey in Moccasin by federal agents and brought to Highlands since it was the nearest town.

There was no jail in Highlands and Henson was confined in a room of the Smith Hotel, which is still standing, to await trial.

Without saying anything to the Billingsly brothers, one of Henson's friends rode into Highlands with the avowed purpose of rescuing the imprisoned man. He succeeded in getting into the hotel but before he could use his gun or reach Henson, he too was arrested and placed under guard.

News got back to Moccasin and to the Billingsly brothers who called a council of war and mapped out their campaign.

One of the brothers scrawled a declaration of war and sent it off to Highlands by messenger. It informed the folks of the town that an army was preparing to push on Highlands. The declaration of war set a date for the attack.

On the day named, the Army of Moccasin, some 18 strong, marched on Highlands.

The townsfolk, taking their rifles down from pegs on the wall, barricaded themselves within and behind the Smith Hotel where the prisoners were confined, while the Georgia band bivouacked behind an old store building directly across the street.

For three days and three nights the opposing forces engaged in snap-shooting, every head appearing behind either building drawing a shot.

The men of Highlands did not yet dare send a messenger into the surrounding country for reinforcements because they figured whoever tried to leave the hotel would be shot down.

Finally, Tom Ford, a native mountaineer, took a ladder and climbed to the roof of the hotel. He inched to the edge of the roof, got a man by name of Ramey in his sights and fired. Ramey fell dead.

The shooting stopped. Suddenly there was a heavy stillness over the town. The Georgians withdrew and returned to Rabun County to bury their dead.

But as they withdrew they left a letter, however, declaring that as soon as they had buried their dead they would return with reinforcements and wage their war to the bitter end.

Highlands sent out runners to Whiteside Cove, Cashiers and the adjoining communities to alarm the countryside and ask for help.

"That was when my father, my four brothers, and all the neighbor men, and all the boys old enough to use a gun, from Whiteside Cove, Cashiers Valley and Hamburg, rushed to Highlands to defend the town against the second threatened attack," Judge Alley recalled.

"They waited two or three days, every one being armed to the teeth, but Moccasin did not return to renew the assault. Instead, they sent a messenger with a letter, in which they stated, among other things, that they knew Highlands had to transport their food and all the necessities of life from Walhalla, South Carolina."

The letter also pointed out that the only road leading from Highlands to Walhalla passed through the center of Moccasin Township, and that instead of returning to renew hostilities on North Carolina soil they would kill any and every man from Highlands who attempted to pass over the Georgia road.

Meanwhile, the larders of Highlands became empty. It was necessary that the wagon trains should run uninterruptedly in order to keep the needs of the town supplied.

At first no man would attempt a test of the blockade and the threat of death.

And then old man Joel Lovin, the wild blood of the Irish in his veins, volunteered to make the run.

He was in his seventies but he was a big, hulking man, and he wore chin whiskers and a mustache. And he knew how to use a rifle. He had been through the bloody battles of the Civil War and he had become a legend because of his sharpshooting.

He was a native of Graham County and had moved to Highlands where he made a living as a teamster.

So old man Lovin hitched up his team, and with his rifle in one hand climbed onto the high seat of his wagon and started out.

When Lovin reached the vicinity of the settlement where the Billingsly brothers lived, right at the Chattooga River and at the forks of the road on Pine Mountain, he saw them coming up the road.

The brothers marched in single file and each carried a rifle.

Old man Lovin knew this was the show-down and he worried his mind what to do—shoot first or let the Billingslys make the first move.

The old man had never had much faith in prayer but he reckoned it wouldn't hurt any to do a little praying.

So he prayed:

"Oh, Lord, if there is a Lord, save my soul, if I have a soul, from going to hell, if there is a hell."

The Billingsly brothers kept coming and the old man kept driving.

Then he recalled a prayer that his old father had used when he had asked a blessing at meal time, and so he muttered it:

"Oh, Lord, make us thankful for what we're about to receive."

Still the Billingslys came on.

By now the old Rebel spirit was aroused in the old man.

Holding the reins with one hand and taking a firmer grip on his rifle with the other, he said:

"Oh, Lord, if you won't help me, don't help the Billingslys, and I'll shoot the damnyankees like I used to do endurin' of the war!"

The Billingsly boys passed by, never raising their eyes to the old man, and old man Lovin went on his way.

This ended the trouble between Moccasin and Highlands.

The wagons rolled again and food flowed into Highlands. The whiskey traffic stopped.

But old man Lovin said he never could make up his mind whether his prayers or his threat saved him from the Billingsly brothers.

The Morris Hearth-Fire

Green Creek Cove

THE HEARTH-FIRE UNCLE BILLY MORRIS HOPED WOULD burn forever is only a memory now on which to hang a tale.

It died, just as the old man predicted, for lack of a flame-keeper.

And although it was the last living symbol of the nation's early birth-pains, its passing a few years ago attracted hardly any notice and little mourning.

For 160 years the Morrises—from the patriarch of the clan down to the great-great-niece—had tended the fire, keeping it alive at first through necessity and then, finally, as a flaming memorial to the kin who had gone before.

The Morris hearth-fire was almost as old as American Independence.

The first Morris, lured into the rugged highlands by the trail marks Daniel Boone had blazed, started it after he had taken his axe and grooved together a cabin here in the hills that are now Polk County.

He had sparked it into life with flint and steel a few months after George Washington was inaugurated president of the new republic.

Both Sam Houston and Davy Crockett came this way, and I like to think that maybe they sat by the Morris fire, Houston spinning his dream of Texas, and Crockett fretting because of an icy winter rain that had kept him from bear hunting.

Down through the years the Morris clan saw to it that there was always someone to care for the fire and keep it alive.

But the members of the Morris clan kept dying off until there was only Uncle Billy left.

And by 1947 the old man had come to the conclusion the fire would die when he died.

Uncle Billy was a bachelor and a dozen years past the allotted life-span promised man by the Bible.

He was the last of the flame-keepers, the last of the Morris clan, though he did have a niece. But she was getting along in years, too, and he figured she wouldn't care much whether the fire lived or died.

On winter days the old man would sit alone before the fire, a troubled pinch in his weathered old face. In his mind he could see the flames spend themselves and the embers turn to white ash.

"The fire will go when I go," he would say.

For more than thirty years he had kept a lonely vigil over the fire, feeding it daily in good weather and bad, with never a worry until his last years that it would go out.

Then one day in the winter of '48 he became sick and they had to take him to a hospital in Tryon. He died there.

The niece, Mrs. Ida Owens who was seventy-two, promised as they laid Uncle Billy to rest in his Friendship Church grave that she would keep it going as long as she lived.

She tried but the fire was destined to die, too.

She became blind, her husband died, and she had to go live with a son in Spartanburg, S. C.

The fire burned to ashes like the old man had predicted.

The old cabin became just an empty house.

Not long ago the property was sold and passed out of the hands of the Morris heirs, and now there is to be a resort development there.

Nobody outside Saluda paid much attention to the fire until Bill Sharpe, now publisher of *The State Magazine*, wrote a story about it back in 1937, which attracted nationwide attention.

Uncle Billy became a celebrity and went off to New York to appear on a nationwide radio program.

After that a lot of folks came this way to see the fire.

Then some ladies of the Daughters of the American Revolution came to visit Uncle Billy and to make him a proposition.

They wanted to move him, his fire, his two collie dogs and his mule into the Great Smoky Mountains National Park and see to it that the fire never did go out.

Uncle Billy listened to them until his patience got a little sore, because nobody could tell him how he was going to make a living in the Smokies.

So the D.A.R. ladies left and Uncle Billy went on with his farm work and his fire mending.

Eventually, folks stopped coming up Green Creek Cove, and that was all right with Uncle Billy.

After all, he had his fire, his dogs and his mule.

And for entertainment he had a fiddle which he played at night or whenever the notion struck him.

He would sit there in his cabin and play to the fire, sawing out tunes that were older than either the fire or the cabin.

Such old songs as *Barbara Allen* and *Lord Lovel,* songs the Morrises had played and sung back in England.

Once a week the old man walked four miles to town to do his trading and get his mail. And he walked the four miles back.

He had rather walk, he used to say, than ride the mule which had "an infernal gait."

Up until the last years of his life he cooked on the hearth, but finally he got him a wood-burning stove and used it to prepare his meals.

Uncle Billy grew most of the things he needed.

He farmed back of the cabin, breaking his soil in the spring with a plow pulled by his mule, which some folks said was even older than the fire.

But that is all history now, all memories.

The cabin is empty, the fire dead.

And Uncle Billy sleeps in his Friendship Church grave.

Some folks guess he is restless, knowing that his fire has turned to ashes, too.

The Gander-Pulling

Cartoogechaye

NOW AND THEN THE OLD MAN RETURNS TO THE HILLS OF his youth and when he does, his memory walks familiar paths and gives voice to times past.

"Over there," he said, gesturing with his cane toward the tree-rimmed meadow, "was where we used to have the gander-pulls."

The old man chuckled, gleefully aware of the questioning look in his grandson's eyes.

"I can tell you never heard of a gander-pull, boy. They don't have 'em any more. But when I was coming up more'n eighty years ago a gander-pull was rare sport."

As the old man described it, the gander-pull was a sort of tournament on horseback among frontier knights in homespun.

"Folks would come from all over. All the politicians would be there. If it was an election year, you could count on every last candidate showing up to get in some electioneering. The women-folks brought baskets of food and everybody had a big time, except the gander."

A path was laid out on the rim of a big circle about two hundred feet in diameter. Usually it was picked where a tree draped its limbs over the path.

But if such a spot was not available, then sapling posts were set about a dozen feet apart on each side of the path and a slack rope hung from pole to pole.

"Most of the time," said the old man, "the gander-pulls were held where there would be a tree that could be used. I never went to but one gander-pull where they had to use sapling posts.

"Well, when the path had been laid out, a live gander was produced. Everybody had geese then, so it wasn't hard to get one.

All the feathers had been picked off the gander's neck and head. A gourd of goose grease was handed up to the feller with the bird and he dobbed that goose grease on its neck until it was as slippery as an eel.

"Of course, the gander was a-flapping its wings and a-screeching and a-hissing all this time, and folks was a-milling around and making jokes and laughing and having a time, just waiting for the big fun to begin."

The bird then was tied by its feet to the overhanging limb, head down, with enough rope so it would sway in the air and just low enough so that a rider, standing in the stirrups, could barely reach the gander's neck.

"There'd be a dozen or more riders," said the old man. "And they all had good mounts. Riding horses, we called 'em. They were horses that never had been turned to the plough, and the boys had 'em all slicked up, some with their tails plaited and some with red ribbons tied in 'em.

"A lot of the fellers pranced around and showed off and cut their eyes at the girls and boasted what they were a-going to do. A feller wasn't much popular with the girls on such a day if he didn't go for the goose."

The community blacksmith usually was the master of ceremonies. Folks referred to him as the manager. He was the umpire. He stood to one side of the path where the gander hung, armed with a whip of many thongs.

When the preliminaries were out of the way, the gander hung, the manager shouted, "Mount up!", and the knights in homespun sprang into their saddles, then filed slowly around the prescribed space once, twice.

During this "riding the ring," final bets were made and the crowd of men, women and children quieted and waited expectantly for the signal that would send the first rider out on the track to try his skill at snapping the gander's neck.

Then came the signal, "Blaze away!"

As the rider passed beneath the branch from which hung the gander, the blacksmith laid his whip upon the flank of the horse to keep it from slowing down for the grab.

Despite the wild and sudden plunge, the rider rose in his stirrups and clutched the greased neck of the swaying gander, which resisted, and then the rider was away, the tough old bird shrieking.

Only an expert rider on a well-trained mount could even grab the gander's neck. Hardly anyone could hold onto the slippery neck while going at such speed.

The riders continued to make their passes, one after the other.

"I've seen it go on for an hour or more," said the old man. "The gander is a tough old bird and he's got a tough neck."

But usually it took only a few severe wrenches to put an end to the gander's wails. And as they ceased, there would be a cry from the crowd, "He's a gone goose now!"

Which leads to the premise that the expression, "a gone goose," had its origin at the gander-pulling.

Yet, even after the neck was broken, it was some time before the gander's head was pulled off.

The rider pulling off the gander's head was declared the winner, and the goose was his trophy. But his real prize was a portion of the money that had been paid to the blacksmith as entry fees.

To participate in the gander-pull, a rider paid twenty-five cents and was allowed to keep on making passes until a winner was declared.

"That was a lot of money back in those days," said the old man. "Folks had little money then, and if a man worked for wages, maybe he'd get as much as fifty cents for a whole day's work.

"The feller winning the gander-pull would come out two or three dollars to the good most of the time, but chances are if he had a girl he'd get rid of a good part of it before the night was over.

"Most times after a gander-pull there was a box-supper. A feller who had won the gander-pull was fresh meat for the losers. They'd see to it that he had to bid way up to get his girl's box."

The origin of the gander-pull is lost in forgotten history, but it probably grew out of the days when knights jousted on the fields of England.

It was a popular sport on the American frontier as early as 1837.

"The last one I heard of here in the mountains," said the old man, "was somewhere about 1880. There was a lot of folks that didn't take too well to gander-pulls and I reckon maybe they kept on until it stopped altogether.

"But the gander-pulls weren't no worse than bear-baiting or coon-baiting. Which reminds me. . . ."

Now and then the old man returns to the hills of his youth and, when he does, his memory walks familiar paths and gives voice to times past.

The Typical Hill Man Is a Myth

Sylva

THE TYPICAL MOUNTAINEER IS A TALL, SLOUCHING, BEARDED clansman with a squirrel-rifle in one hand and a jug in the other.

He is a barefoot, tobacco-chewin' hillbilly who spends all his time a'fiddlin', a'feudin', and a'fightin'.

He's a distiller of corn likker, and, brother, hold on to your hat.

He's the overlord of a one-room log cabin with a dozen mouths to feed and a passel of hound dogs in the yard.

He's a giant of a man named Thomas Wolfe who rocked the literary world with his matchless prose and said you can't go home again, albeit he did.

He's a distinguished gentleman with calluses on his hands.

He's Snuffy Smith, Quill Rose, the Shepherd of the Hills, the Representative Talking For Buncombe, Eugene Gant, Gov. Zebulon Baird Vance, the Rev. George Truett, and Judge Felix E. Alley.

He's a myth and a fancy.

He's the hero of a thousand stories and a thousand legends.

He's Charlie "Choo Choo" Justice and Billy Joe Patton.

He's a cartoon out of *Esquire* and a painting by Corydon Bell.

He is all these things, and so, he's none of them.

He is a farmer, a mechanic, a trader, a doctor, a lawyer, a banker.

He is an engineer who changed the face of the Mississippi River.

He's a man in a wool hat straight out of a university with a business degree.

He's a boy who went to work for fifty cents a day and ended up owning stocks and bonds and one of the most famous resort hotels in the South.

He's got hayseed in his hair but he's sharp as a briar.

He's a Democrat by heritage.

He's a backwoodsman who has hob-nobbed with kings and queens, albeit his ancestors fled Europe to get away from same.

He's a fellow who doesn't know all the words of the National Anthem but he's the first to grab a gun when that star-spangle banner is threatened.

He's a man who fears the law but does not always respect it.

He's a sparkin' fool with the ladies, a defender of womanhood.

He's a bashful fellow, shy and almost timid.

He's a man quick to anger, but he speaks softly.

He's all these and none of them, typically, either.

He is a homespun wit who speaks Elizabethan or Chaucerian English and doesn't know it.

He dances to hillbilly music on Saturday night and listens to a symphony the next.

He's the father of a son in Harvard and a daughter at Vassar.

He walks tall and he tells tall tales.

He knows the feel of silk sheets and the taste of champagne but he prefers cotton and bourbon.

He drives a Cadillac and has an air-conditioned office.

He wears tailored suits and buys his wife fashioned gowns.

He's a member of the country club, Rotary, the Lions.

He's thrifty as a squirrel but he will give until it hurts if he agrees the cause is a good one.

He doesn't read many books but he can hold his own with his neighbors who are professors, writers, musicians, scientists, and financiers.

He's a man who likes to sit by his own fire, but he knows London and Paris and Rome.

He's all these things, as we've said, and so, he's none of them.

You can't catalogue the mountaineer any more than you can the city dweller.

He's what folks want to make him and how they see him.

Typically, he's no more lanky or bearded than the folks in New York City.

In fact, I've seen more lankness and beards at a United Nations session than you can see here.

Some years ago there was a young lady at the University of North Carolina, fresh from South America, who never could be convinced that I was a mountaineer.

"But you're wearing clothes just like people at home," she argued. "You don't talk like a mountaineer."

I never did find out how she thought a mountaineer should talk.

I tried my best Snuffy Smith dialect:

"Stop thar! What's you-unses name? Whar you-uns a-goin' ter?"

She shook her head.

"The words seem right," she finally admitted, "but you haven't got that—that certain twang."

"So, I hung my head. I'd let the clan down. Better get back to the mountains, I said, and take a few lessons from my grand-pappy before he found out the truth and beat the daylights out of me."

So I pinned up the front of my hat with a thorn, stuck a sprig of cedar—there wasn't any balsam around—in the band of my hat and galloped off for my bottle and pistol to tilt against whatsoever might dare to oppose me.

And I threw away my shoes.

After all, who ever heard of a mountaineer wearing shoes?

I only wish my South American friend could see me now.

Maybe I would qualify as a genuine, honest-to-goodness Mountaineer.

Qualifications?

A hill of corn I've propped up with a rock to keep it from falling down-hill.

A squirrel-rifle from a New York antique shop.

And I've bought my wife a double-bitted ax with which she does a fair job of cutting wood.

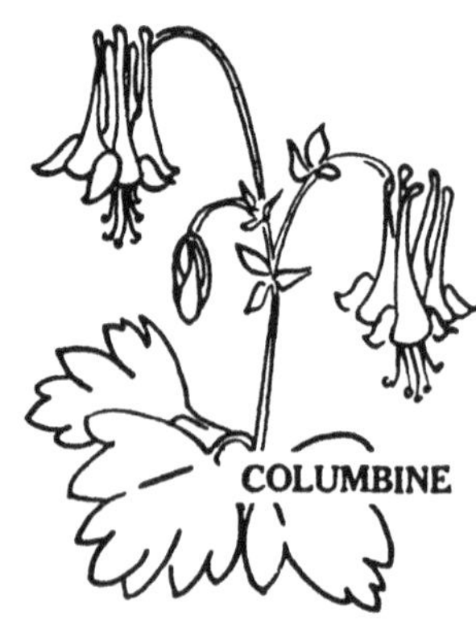

Mountain Idiom Fading

Balsam

THE HOMELY IDIOM OF THE MOUNTAINEER IS GETTING TO be as rare as gritted-bread and the granny-woman.

Jive-talk is replacing Elizabethan.

The juke-box, the newspaper, radio and TV have killed off the balladeers who were not only singing reporters but sort of singing historians.

Be that as it may, there are a few of the old-timers left whose talk is fresh as she-rain.

If you want to know the old customs, the old ways, drop in on them for a settin' spell and you'll get a lavish of it pure as fact.

It is only off the beaten path, back where the cabins nestle among the rhododendron and the balsam, that you will find the dialect used with any integrity.

And don't get the idea that because they say fetch, ham-meat, p'int-blank, yander and nary that they are illiterate.

Read your Shakespeare, brother, and your Chaucer!

Afore, atwixt, awar, heap o' folks, peart, up and done it, usen for used—all these were contemporary with the Canterbury Tales.

Don't laugh when a mountain man talks about how he "feathered into them," a phrase that passed out of standard English when saltpetre replaced the long-bow.

Dauncy is "mincy about eating," which is to say fastidious or over-nice.

Doney-gal means sweetheart, an expression British sailors picked up in Spanish or Italian ports and preserved by backwoodsmen whose ancestors for two centuries never saw the tides.

When maize has passed the roasting-ear stage, but is still not hard enough for grinding into meal, the ears are grated into a soft flour and baked into pones called gritted-bread.

Beans dried in the pod, then boiled "hull and all," are called leather-britches. Green beans in the pod are snaps, and shelled beans are called shuck-beans.

Apple sauce is called sass.

A smidgen is little more than a mite, and a heap is a rimption.

If a man is tired, he is worried. If he's in a hurry, he's in a swivvet. If he's nervous, he has the all-overs. If he's feeling puny, he's on the down-go. If he's undecided about how he feels, he is middlin', or fair-to-middlin!

Slaunchways means slanting, and si-godlin or anti-sigodling is out of plumb or out of square.

The toad is called a frog or a toad-frog, and a toad-stool is a frog-stool. The woodpecker is a peckerwood.

The hemlock tree is called spruce-pine, while spruce is he-balsam, balsam itself is she-balsam, laurel is ivy, and rhododendron is laurel.

Evening begins at noon, and daydown is the pink of evening.

A man who jumps and runs has "lit a shuck for home."

A mountain man sharpens his ax on a grindin'-stone or whet-rock. He whets his knife on sole leather.

He doesn't throw a stone—he "flings a rock."

To him your name "ain't much common" and his "old woman's aimin' to go to meetin'." He had "it in the head to plow today but hit's come on to rain," and he's "laid off and laid off to fix that fence." And he'll say "you cain't handily blame her."

The mountaineer named the peaks and rivers and streams to commemorate some incident.

The Shut-in is a gorge; the Suck is a whirlpool; Squeeze-Betsey is a narrow passage between the cliffs.

Calf-killer Run is where a meat-eating bear was using. Meat-scaffold Branch is where venison was hung up for jerkings. Still-house Branch was a moonshiner's retreat.

His spirit lives in such places as Fighting Creek, Shooting Creek, Gouge-eye, Vengeance, Four Killer, and Disputanta.

His humor holds forth in such place-names as Weary Hut, Frog Level, Shake a Rag, and Chunky Gal.

Signs of his times are etched in such places as Defeat and Desolation branches of Bone Valley, Needmore, Poor Fork, Long Hungry, No Pone and No Fat.

His literalness shows in Black Rock, Standing Indian, Water-rock Knob, Sharp Top, Twenty Mile, Naked Place, the Pocket,

Punkin Town, Tumbling Creek, Briar Patch Mountain, Buckhorn Bald, Cedar Cliff, Hogback, Potato Hill.

Incidents of his lonely life are Dusk Camp Run, Mad Sheep Mountain, Drowning Creek, Burnt Cabin Branch, Broken Leg, and Raw Dough.

The mountain man is never at a loss for a word, a phrase.

My grandfather is one of the old-timers who has retained the speech of the mountaineer.

Not long ago he and I were watching a dance and when the intricate steps had been completed in the old time square dance, he observed, "That was quite a twistification."

A perfectly good descriptive, though a few hundred years old.

And to him, icicles always will be "tags of ice."

But for him and a few others like him, the quaint, colorful speech that once was the mark of a distinct and interesting way of life here in the mountains would now be extinct.

Curiously enough, the language of Shakespeare and Chaucer has lived here longer than it has in the British Isles.

There, too, the homely idiom of Elizabethan times has vanished.

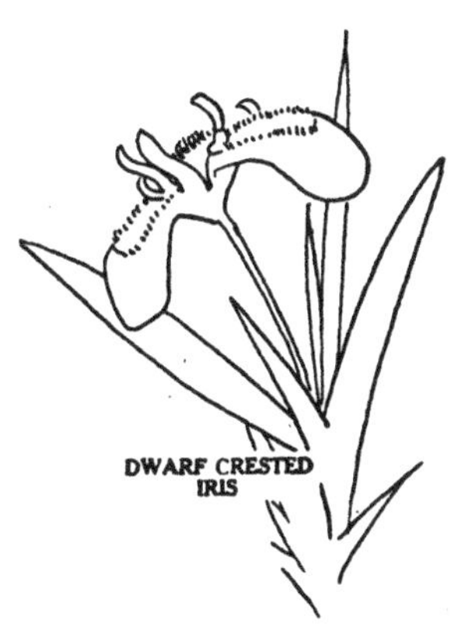

Persimmons, Possums and Politics

Sunset Farms

THERE WAS A NIP OF AUTUMN IN THE AIR AND THE TALK got around to persimmons, possums and politics.

Politics got mixed into it when somebody remembered that Zeb Vance once recommended persimmon brandy as a speech-shortener for long-winded Congressmen.

Of course, if the katydids hadn't been crying in the night, we might never have learned of this tantalizing suggestion, for the katydids prompted the talk about persimmons and possums.

Some of the branch-head boys were gathered on the porch at Ed Bumgarner's lodge here in the hills above Wilmot where there is always good talk and good food.

A teasing wind played in the eaves and plucked at the coloring leaves on the trees, whispering a prophecy and taunting the arguing katydids as they shrilled their nocturnal cry "Katy did, Katy didn't."

"Won't be long till frost," said Ed Bumgarner. "Not if what the old-timers say is true about the katydid. They say you can count on the first frost three months after you hear the first katydid let loose a holler. I heard the first one this year about July 12th.

"That figures out about four or five days before the possum hunting season starts and means the possum and the persimmon will be ready for plucking about the same time.

"Of course, it looks like it's going to be a bad year for both. From what little browsing around I've done these past few days, the persimmon crop is going to be mighty thin. That late freeze last spring just about killed 'em off. And the automobiles have sure killed off a lot of possum these last few weeks."

There was a whine from one of Ed's blue-tick possum dogs.

"He's getting restless," Ed said. "But it's going to be slim pickings for him this fall. This morning I counted five possums that had been run over by automobiles between here and Sylva. Counted four yesterday morning and six the morning before."

The dog whined again, and Realus Sutton spoke up.

"That's the possum-huntin'est dog you ever saw," Realus said. "Don't reckon there's his equal in all the mountains. He'd rather hunt possums than to eat. Tell 'em about him, Ed."

Ed reached down and patted the dog.

"He's supposed to be a coon dog," Ed said, "but I couldn't make a coon dog out of him. He strictly had a nose for possum. He's as sensible a dog as I've ever had. Why, when it's a good night for hunting, he'll come to the door and scratch on it until he gets me up. And then he'll run out there and false tree, trying to make me think there's a possum in the tree."

Somebody then mentioned persimmon beer and persimmon pudding and persimmon cakes.

"That reminds me," said Ed, "of the story I heard about Zeb Vance and persimmon brandy. Now, I've never tasted persimmon brandy but I hear tell it's quite a drink.

"Well, anyway, Zeb was making a speech once. It was a long time after he'd been governor and while he was serving in the U.S. Senate. He was making a lecture up in Boston. He got to talking about when he ran for governor back in 1864 and how folks had to make do with a lot of things.

"He told 'em how folks had to find something else to make their pearting juice out of because of a scarcity of grain which forbid its use for distillation. Said they turned to potatoes, rice, pumpkins, turnips and even persimmons.

"Zeb said as to the brandy made from the native persimmon, he could vouch for its good traits. He said he could especially commend it to oratory.

"Then he told how during the 1864 governor's campaign he made a speech under the refreshment of persimmon brandy. Said his admiring friends had declared it the best speech he had ever made, because the astringent drink had tended to shut him up and that he had said less than usual.

"Well, at that point, Zeb told his audience that Congress could not do wiser than to purchase a quantity of the beverage for its own use."

Ed paused, grinning a big grin.

"Don't reckon Congress ever got around to taking the suggestion to heart," he said. "Never heard of any of 'em shortening their talk when they got a chance to speak out to their constituents."

Somebody said the price of corn liquor being what it is, and pretty bad corn at that, it looked like maybe some enterprising feller might do a little experimenting with persimmons.

"I don't think I'd like to try it," Ed said. "Everybody knows what a persimmon does to your mouth when you bite into one if it isn't dead ripe.

"Well, folks have got a way of rushing things these days, and nine chances out of ten if there got to be a market for persimmon brandy you'd find fellers picking 'em green and whipping up a drink that would yank a feller's insides right out."

One of the branch-head boys wondered out loud if anybody still knew how to make persimmon beer, which was quite a popular drink here in the mountains until a few years ago.

"Strange as it may seem," Ed said, "I never tasted persimmon beer but I've heard the old-timers talk about it and I know a couple old-timers who make a little every year as a sort of medicine to sip on when their stomachs get upset.

"The way to make it is to beat the persimmons into a pulp, mix in some locust pods. Then you take a barrel and put in a layer of this mixture, then a layer of straw, another layer of the mixture and so on until the barrel is about two-thirds full. Then you dump in corn meal on the top layer and fill the barrel with water.

"Now you cover the barrel and let nature take its course for about two or three weeks. Then you've got persimmon beer."

Ed looked off into the night, off toward the lower pasture where his persimmon trees grow.

Finally, he said:

"They're yours for the pickin', boys, except for a few I'd like for a persimmon pudding. The only thing I ask is just wait till they get ripe."

The wind whispered a prophecy and the katydids shrilled in the night.

And somebody said:

"That's enough talk of persimmons, possums and politics for one night."

Hot Biscuits and Sourwood Honey

Bunches Creek

HOT BISCUITS AND SOURWOOD HONEY!

"Now, that's real choice eatin'," said the man known as the Master Beekeeper of the Smokies. "A man ain't tasted nothin' lessen he's put his tongue to sourwood honey. It's the pure stuff."

A heap of folks will agree quick as a bee-sting with Wallace Bradley, an old-timer of 82 who set up his first bee-gums here at the turn of the century.

To the epicure, a dish of sourwood honey is like sampling the choicest wines from the vineyards of Europe. And it's just as hard to come by, for the demand is greater than the supply.

Usually the local demand takes the entire crop at prices above the open market. It practically never appears on the market at all and can only be had by those who journey far for it.

For pure flavor, it's a prize-winner among the world's most famous honeys, such as the wild thyme of Greece, the rosemary of southern Europe, and the heather of Scotland.

"Yes, sir, it's a dish fit to set before a king," said the old man, "but I reckon ain't none of 'em ever tasted sourwood. Not real sourwood, anyway.

"There's honey on the market that's claimed to be sourwood, but it ain't. If a man's ever tasted real sourwood he'll know the difference. It ain't as heavy of body and it turns grainy-like before you've dipped into it two or three times. It ain't got the same color, neither. Real sourwood's medium-light in color and it's slow to get grainy."

The old man had been splitting locust rails out by his bee-gums back of the house when we arrived. He laid aside his ax and we got to talking about his bees and sourwood honey.

"This has been a good sourwood year," he said. "Guess I got

about 250 pounds of honey out of my hives. That's as good as I've done in the last ten years.

"I've only got about thirty gums now. That's enough to tend to, what with everything else I have to do about the place. Time was, though, when I had as many as 110 gums.

"Bees didn't swarm none this year. The honey came early and they didn't have time. It started along in June. The bees got rich on poplar and basswood and dog-hobble—and locust.

"Then the sourwood started and they didn't have time to stop for nothin'. They worked like everything right in the rain, just as if it weren't rainin'. Yes, sir, they worked right in the rain. And I watched 'em in the rain.

"Yes, the honey came early this year. I had honey in June and the last about two weeks ago. I knowed it was gettin' late and I got out to see about the bees. I ain't caught 'em makin' any honey in about a week now.

"They're just as still as they can be. Sort of like they're plumb tired out. Won't do a thing but sting you. I was up there among 'em today and they made me set down two or three times. A bee'll hardly ever sting you if you're still. Just set still and they'll usually go away and not bother you."

The old man paused and looked off toward the hill where his bee-gums trooped along in orderly rows.

"When I moved in here back in the spring of '98," he recalled, "I fetched in six gums. Carried 'em in on my back from over the mountain. By fall I had ten gums and kept adding to 'em. Made 'em out of hollow logs, out of basswood, 'cause they don't season or crack."

When his bees swarm, he just lets them go. But that means he has to go out and look for them and get them back in the hives.

"Why, I've hunted bees all over these mountains," said the old man. "You've got to hunt 'em with stink-bait. You set it out and some of 'em go to work on it. A few minutes later you can see 'em go straight to the tree where they're holed up.

"Me and my daddy used to hunt 'em. We'd run 'em two or three miles, a hundred yards at a time. We'd set the bait, move up and set it again. Just kept following a little at a time and after a while we'd get to their tree.

"Then we'd cut down the tree and put the bees in a tow bag. They'll sweat and die if you put 'em in a gum and tote 'em back. I don't never put 'em in a gum. A tow bag is the best thing to use.

"When they swarm and light on a bush you can just cut the

limb and put the limb, bees and all in the bag and tie it at the top and they'll keep in there two or three days, easy.

"To get the bees in the bag, you lay your sack on a log or on the ground and prop the mouth of it open with a stick and dip the bees right in—or put the whole limb in.

"You dip 'em in with a piece of bark or with a wash-pan. It's easy. Why, a man can learn more from bees. He can learn from 'em as long as he lives."

Back in the old days, he said, sourwood honey sold at ten cents a pound, if a man was lucky enough to get paid in cash. Now it brings seventy cents a pound and up.

"Years ago I used to tote my honey to Waynesville on my back," the old man recalled. "I bought might near all my meat with honey, pound for pound.

"Hanes Queen used to send his big lard cans up here for me to fill with honey. I guess you knowed Hanes. He run a store and he engaged all the honey I would let him have. Them cans would hold seventy-five and eighty pounds of honey, and I'd fill six or seven of 'em for him."

The old man was silent for a moment.

"You know," he said finally, "folks just don't seem to take an interest in bees like they once did. Why, I know the time when a feller was considered trifling if he didn't have a dozen or so gums.

"It's got so now that everybody wants honey but they don't want to keep bees. If this keeps up there just won't be no real sourwood honey. And that'll be a shame."

Yes, it will be a shame.

For there's nothing like hot biscuits and sourwood honey.

As the Master Beekeeper of the Smokies said, it's real choice eatin'.

The Valley of Independence

Sugar Grove

THE WATAUGA, RIVER OF BROKEN WATERS, COMES LEAPING down out of the Blue Ridge to water a land where native-born Americans first proclaimed their independence of British rule.

It is born in the head-springs of venerable Grandfather Mountain, wheels south of the town named for Daniel Boone, then scampers through lush valleys from which rise mile-high peaks and plunges westward into Tennessee.

This is really the valley of independence, and few of the millions who come journeying down the Blue Ridge Parkway a few miles to the east ever get over this way or know that this was part of a historic settlement.

Only a river and a county still bear the name of the famous Watauga Settlement where, long before the Revolution, mountaineers banded together and told themselves they were independent of British rule.

These were the same mountaineers that, when the Revolution did come, went over the hills with their long rifles to a place called King's Mountain and broke the back of King George.

A little later these same mountaineers organized the State of Franklin, an independent commonwealth as sovereign as North Carolina, and, if John Sevier had not lost a political venture, Americans now would be saluting a flag with fourteen stripes and forty-nine stars.

In its day the Watauga highlands, as lush and beautiful country as the world affords, played host to many men who wrote their names into the history books.

Daniel Boone called it home for a dozen years. John Sevier defended it against the Indians. Andrew Jackson came this way from studying law under Spruce Macay at Salisbury to launch his career just across the hills in Happy Valley. Russell Bean, the rifle-maker, ran his packtrains through its coves and valleys, supplying its settlers with salt and iron, lead and powder.

This was a land where folks didn't value money much.

Russell Bean used to tell the folks down at Morganton that you had to offer the Watauga settlers something useful, such as cow-bells and axes, " 'cause they've got most everything else."

The State of Franklin—it included sections of what are now Watauga and Ashe counties—was born out of the turbulence of the Revolution.

When the Revolution was over Congress, deep in financial straits, called on states with vacant lands to cede them to the federal government.

Money from the sale of these lands and from taxation was to be applied to the national debt.

North Carolina gave the federal government a two-year option on her western land, which by charter extended to the Pacific Ocean. Meantime, North Carolina was to exercise sovereignty.

This was a remote region and North Carolina found it difficult to govern.

The folks of the Watauga Association were hard pressed by the Cherokee Indians who were continually making raids on the settlement.

The settlers grumbled and protested and demanded money to wage war against the Indians, but all to no avail.

That's when they decided to break away from North Carolina and establish their own commonwealth.

Early in 1784 they met just across the hills from here in what is now Jonesboro, Tennessee, and declared themselves a separate and independent state from North Carolina.

They drew up a constitution, elected a legislature and established other governmental machinery.

At first they called their state Frankland—land of free men. But later it was changed to Franklin, in honor of Benjamin Franklin.

Meantime, the legislature of North Carolina, alarmed by the attitude of the settlers, repealed the act of cession and set up a governing body for the rebellious territory.

John Sevier was sent into the territory as commander of militia with orders to persuade the folks of Franklin to come back into the fold.

They answered by electing him governor of the new state.

Then both the new state and the mother state installed governments in the disputed territory.

Each was levying taxes and disallowing each other's official acts.

And then John Tipton rose up and really started the downfall of Franklin.

At first a Franklin enthusiast, he broke with Sevier because of a desire to be the head man of the new state and returned his allegiance to the state of North Carolina.

Sevier failed in his attempts to have North Carolina recognize a separate state. He also lost out in trying to persuade Congress to admit Franklin into the Confederation.

Animosity between Franklin and North Carolina reached such a high pitch in the spring of 1786 that civil war broke out.

Tipton led an army of North Carolina State militia against the new state, and in a hard-fought skirmish Sevier's men were routed.

Sevier was arrested and charged with high treason.

Tipton carried him in irons to Morganton to face trial.

Sevier escaped and never was tried.

But that broke the back of the State of Franklin.

It died, and today it is a part of North Carolina and Tennessee.

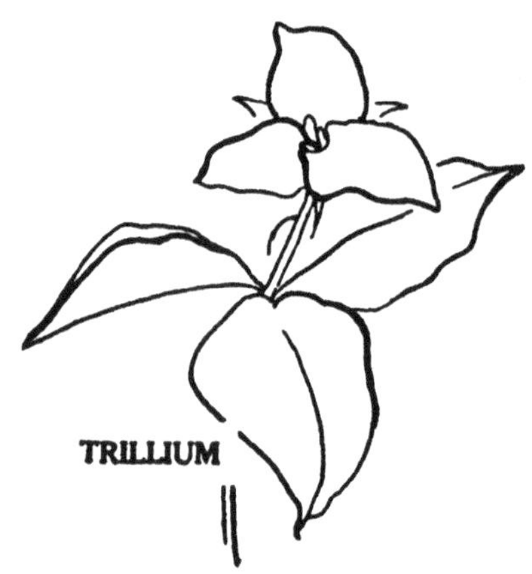

TRILLIUM

Beau Sabreur of the Frontier

Morganton

COME SIT IN CENTRAL SQUARE WHERE THE SUN SPINS golden mists over the Burke County courthouse and re-live that day 166 years ago when John Sevier, the beau sabreur of the frontier, was brought to trial on charges of treason.

Morganton was a budding settlement of log cabins then, seat of government of the westernmost county of the State of North Carolina, and her domain stretched all the way to the Mississippi River.

A square building, somewhat larger than most of the other log cabins of the town, sat in the center of Central Square. It was the courthouse and it stood until 1833 when the present stone structure, now covered with cement, was built.

The town's streets had been named for streets of Charleston, the city to which early mountain dwellers went for their loaf sugar and Jamaica rum, and later for slaves brought from Africa.

The dawn had come up early that morning and the town was overflowing with men, boys, horses and dogs from the backwoods of the Blue Ridge and beyond where Sevier had tried to establish a state independent of North Carolina rule.

Across the square the game-cocks were fighting a battle-royal in the pit and men were shouting their bets and whooping it up as a prelude to excitement yet to come.

There are some who say Andy Jackson was there with his pet fighting-cock, a bird that had licked the best in all the land, and that he was taking all bets.

By midmorning there had been several fist fights and the tavern keeper was beginning to wonder if his five small barrels of rum would hold out against the thirst of the men from the backwoods.

Some had already accused the tavern keeper of watering his stock.

More than a hundred men, heavily armed, bearded and wearing buckskins, had left the cock fights and had crowded into the courtroom until there wasn't standing room left.

If you happened to be one of them, you heard it first like the buzzing of a bee, then the shouts of "Hooray for Chucky Jack" and "We'll see you through, Jack, boy!"

There was a shuffle at the back of the courtroom, and pushing his way to the front was a tall, fair, blue-eyed, brown-haired man of slender build with commanding presence.

This was John Sevier, the man who had joined with other native-born Americans in the Watauga highlands and proclaimed their independence of British rule, the man who had helped establish the first independent republic in America, the man who had fought Indians and now was charged with treason against the State of North Carolina because he wanted a state of his own.

He had been arrested back in Watauga, in the State of Franklin, by his one-time friend and now his sworn enemy, Colonel John Tipton.

Sevier had been brought across the mountains and down the wilderness trail to Morganton in irons, but upon his arrival here he had been permitted to stay at the home of friends until his trial.

The McDowell brothers, Charles and Joseph, had become his sureties until Uriah Sherrill, his brother-in-law, was located and made his bond for his appearance at the trial.

In the crowd that day were a lot of Sevier's frontier friends burning with a sense of injury, who had come across the Blue Ridge with the firm resolve of rescuing him and taking him back home.

The guiding genius of the band seems to have been Dr. James Cozby, a tall and brawny soldier-surgeon, scarred in many a fight, who had served under Sevier at King's Mountain.

They had brought a fine racing mare that belonged to Sevier, which they had left, along with their horses, on the outskirts of Morganton. They had left their rifles hidden in the bushes there, too, and had come into the town with only their pistols hidden under their hunting shirts.

But a little later Nathaniel Evans led Sevier's mare to a point in front of the courthouse door, where she could be seen from within, while Cozby entered the courtroom.

Sevier was seated on a platform at the front of the courtroom and Judge Waightstill Avery sat nearby.

No sooner had the clerk begun to read the charge when there was a clamor, and it was evident the crowd did not intend even to hear the accusation.

At this moment, Cozby began working his way into the room and down toward the front.

William Smith, who was there, recalled the scene:

"Sevier sat as firm and undaunted as when charging the hosts of Wyuca on the Lookout Mountain.

"Slowly he turned his head, and their eyes met. Sevier knew the rescue was at hand, but he was restrained from any outward demonstration, by a significant shake of Cozby's head."

During a pause in the trial, Cozby stepped forward in front of the judge and asked:

"Are you done with this man?"

There was a moment of suspended silence.

Then there was a hub-bub of confusion.

In that second, Sevier leaped from the platform and headed for the door.

The crowd fell away before him, then closed quickly after his passing.

A moment later he was safely in the saddle and away toward the hills of home.

Someone in the courtroom shouted:

"Yes, I'll be damned if you ain't done with him."

The pursuit was only a gesture.

The sympathies of the crowd, perhaps of the court, were with Sevier.

The charges against him were not pressed.

Before long the trend of events were reversed, and Sevier was pardoned. He went to Congress to represent the western district of North Carolina.

After that, honors came thick and fast.

When the State of Tennessee was established, Sevier became its first governor.

Tall Tales About Old Ways

Sylva

THERE ARE DAYS WHEN THE OLD MAN IS FULL OF TALL tales and tall talk.

These occasions are prompted by city folks and flat-landers who wonder out loud how the mountain people have been able to survive in a land where the hills run straight up and down.

"It's a matter of gumption," says the old man, a twinkle in his eye. "Just a matter of plain gumption."

Then he loads up his pipe, sits back and tells them how it was when he was a boy and how it is now.

"Times ain't changed much," he says. "Even with all these new fandangled things for farming, some folks still have to use the old ways.

"Guess you've noticed how some of the planted fields seem to sort of hang on the steep hillsides. Ain't nothing been invented yet that'll stick to them hillsides when it comes to planting and reaping, 'cept a man and a horse. And both of 'em have got to be anchored with a rope to keep 'em from falling off.

"When it comes corn-plantin' time, a feller just gets his shotgun and a bag of plantin'-corn and climbs up on another hillside. He loads his gun with corn and fires it into the other hill that he's got set up for a corn patch.

"Why, I've seen corn planted on hills so steep that a feller had to run a rope around his horse or mule and tie the other end to a tree to keep the critter from falling off.

"And as soon as punkins and squash begin to grow they have to be tethered to the cornstalks to hold them until harvest time.

"I remember there was a feller over in Macon County—that's where I was raised—that had a corn field on a high hill. It was just about the best corn field I ever saw. Shore didn't have to worry none when it came corn-pickin' time.

"Now, all that feller had to do was shuck out his corn and toss it down a natural chute of rock. When it got to the bottom, all his folks had to do was separate the corn cobs from the shelled corn.

"Which reminds me of a place here in the mountains where it was so rough that the folks had no teeth. The reason for this was that level land was so scarce that cabin chimneys opened out close under the slope of the hills, and when the beans were cooked in the fireplace, gravel from the hills ran down into the chimney and mixed with the beans.

"The folks wore out their teeth chewin' 'em.

"There's another place—up Cashiers way—where the folks even to this day look up the chimneys to see the cows come home.

"Yes, sir, as you've noticed we've got some right steep hillsides. And because they're so steep, we've got a special breed of cattle to go along with 'em.

"Maybe when you've rode along in your car you've kind of wondered how them cows are able to stay on the steep hillsides. Well, I'll tell you. Their legs are shorter on one side so they can graze around the hill without discomfort.

"Now, if you don't believe it, take a good look next time you see cows grazing on a hillside. They'll all be facing the same way."

Time was, the old man will tell you, edging back over his 96 years of memory, when it was hard to get around here in the mountains.

"You'd have to see what the roads were like back then," he says, "to believe they could be so bad."

"The streets in Sylva were all dirt back then. And that's not been too long ago. About thirty or thirty-five years ago. In the winter time the wagons would mire up to the axles, and we had to put poles along the sides of the streets to show people how to keep out of deep holes.

"Yes, sir, the mud used to get mighty deep around here.

"One day I was driving my wagon up toward Webster. That's about two or three miles from here. It used to be the county seat. Well, the mud got so deep we just couldn't go no farther, me and the horse and wagon.

"About that time I looked over in the mud and there was a

new hat sitting there. I climbed out on the wheel and reached for it. But about that time a voice said:

" 'Leave that hat be, it's mine!'

"Well, I says, 'Why, where are you?'

"And the voice come back at me, 'I'm down here under it trying to tighten this saddle-belt!' "

The old man's face is grave as he talks. There's a mask of reluctant, rustic eloquence behind his laconic drawl.

"Guess you've heard tell of the razor-back hogs we've got up here in the mountains," he teases, easing into another phase of his yarning.

"There's nothing like a razorback. He's shaped in front like a thin wedge, and he can go through laurel thickets like a bear. Like a man, his eyes won't shine in the dark.

"They say the razorback hog got his start right here in the narrow valleys, and we've got some narrow valleys, as you may have noticed.

"If the razorback got too fat, he just naturally stuck between the walls of the valleys and had to get thin again before he could amble along.

"In fact, some of the valleys are so narrow you have to lie down and look up to see out.

"The narrowest valley I reckon I ever heard tell of was back over in Swain County. I always aimed to get over there for a look but never got around to it. Well, now, that particular valley was so small and narrow that the moonshine had to be wheeled out on a wheelbarrow early every morning, and the daylight wheeled in.

"Which reminds me, some of that corn you see growing on them hillsides has to be brought out in jugs. That's how steep it is. And folks who grow it always figure on how many gallons to an acre, not how many bushels.

"There's a place up near Balsam, right on the highway, that's mighty interesting. Maybe you've noticed that ladder sitting there against the bank leading up into the hillside field.

"Well, they grow potatoes in that field, and the rows run up and down the field, rather than across. All a fellow has to do is stand on that ladder, chop out the end of a row and the potatoes roll right down into the road.

"Next time you're along that way, take a look and see for yourself.

"Yep," the old man says, "all it takes is a little gumption to get along up here."

Nathan Dempsey, Fightin' Man

Burnsville

YOU CAN HAVE PAUL BUNYAN AND JOHN HENRY, BUT we'll take Nathan Dempsey.

He was the fightingest man who ever threw a punch in the Blue Ridge Mountains.

He was a living legend, and his grandson became a pretty good man with his fists, too.

Nathan Dempsey lived in the Kane River section of Yancey County prior to the Civil War.

He was a giant of a man, small waisted, raw boned and tree-top tall. He tipped the scales at better than two hundred and fifty pounds and he stood six feet six. He could swing a ten-pound hammer in each hand. He could pick up a mule and he could throw a horse to the ground.

Twenty years ago there were folks still living who remembered Nathan Dempsey and his exploits. And there were others who had got the story first hand from their mothers and fathers.

All remembered him as a man not easily excited.

They remembered, too, that he was both envied and feared.

He was a hard worker, plying a hard trade.

He was a blacksmith.

But come Saturday and he laid aside his leather apron, his hammer and iron and joined in for the only known sports of the frontier times—wrestling and cuffing matches, running and jumping.

He was unbeatable.

No man was his superior in these sports.

He could clear a seventeen-hand horse in a running jump, take on any two mountain men in a wrestling match, cuff men equally as big as if they were strawmen.

But there was one certain Saturday that Nathan Dempsey lost his calmness and really went on a tear.

As usual, the men had gathered in the public square where a section had been set aside for the marketing of fowl, hogs, sheep, venison, bear meat and wild game.

There was business and pleasure to be transacted. And there was boasting and trading and knife swapping. The fiddlers were there.

The trouble started during the wrestling bouts.

Nathan was judged the winner in bout after bout, with his opponents shouting "calf rope," the mountain equivalent of enough.

Finally, Nathan offered to throw any two opponents at a time.

Again he won, adding injury to insult by bumping his victim's heads together before throwing them to the ground.

This made Nathan a popular man, except with his victims.

As they took the ribs of spectators, they fumed and figured for a way to bring the big man down and regain some of their lost pride.

Meanwhile, a farmer had set up several coops of chickens for barter and sale. The coops had been piled one on top of the other.

Nathan wandered over to give the birds an eye.

While his back was turned, eight of his victims went into a huddle. There were a few whispered words. They had hit upon a plan. They would charge him in groups of fours and slam him to the ground. They would pound him until he yelled for quarter, until he screamed "calf rope!"

From the left and the right they charged Nathan.

He turned, let out a roar and braced himself.

His long, strong arms shot out. He grabbed the first man nearest, spun and hurled him through the air. One after the other he tossed like sticks of kindling wood. And each went flying into the chicken coops. They lay where they fell.

When the last had made his sudden flight, Nathan wiped the sweat from his forehead and walked off toward his blacksmith shop.

Friends gathered around the fallen men, helped them to their feet and carried them to nearby cabins for first aid.

The eight fallen would-be heroes, once out of Nathan's sight, charged that he had battered them with his big ham-like fists without provocation. They whined he had handled them in a most unsportsmanlike manner.

The more they talked, the bolder they got. They announced they were going to have the law on him.

Nathan Dempsey was not arrested, but pressure was brought to bear on the town fathers and a special ordinance was passed.

It stipulated that it was unlawful for Nathan Dempsey to strike a man with his closed fist, which was classified as an "unlawful weapon."

But the measure was quite unnecessary.

For legend has it that from that time onward, no man in Yancey County ever came within striking distance of that unlawful weapon.

With all the fun gone for him, Nathan soon moved away to West Virginia.

In all his life in the Blue Ridge, Nathan was never known to have picked a fight. But he never avoided one. And he always let the other fellow start them and toss the first punch.

Some folks say his grandson inherited old Nathan's punch.

Some who met Jack Dempsey in the ring and left it battered and broken were ever afterward of the opinion that his fists, too, should have been classified unlawful.

The First Tourists

Highlands

THE FIRST TOURISTS STARTED COMING INTO THESE MOUNTAINS 415 years ago.

They were lured by the facetious promotion of a golden city which didn't exist, but it was the kind of bait folks snap at and it seems a pity the natives didn't exploit it.

Mind you, the natives had nothing to do with this promotion which was as puzzling to them as it was fascinating to the folks it attracted.

As a matter of fact, the natives could have made themselves quite a few yards of extra wampum by latching onto the idea and building such a city and then selling off chunks of it as souvenirs to the tourists.

No man ever admitted dreaming up this fantasy of a golden city but it actually was started by a few Spanish grandees who had fallen for Ponce de Leon's Fountain of Youth commercial.

Of course, they admitted they had never seen it and they said the natives had fetched tales of the golden city down from the mountains.

The tales, spun into attractive commercials, reached Spain.

All of which resulted in a flock of folks hopping on a boat for Florida and a tour of the Western North Carolina mountains.

This first tour of our highlands was sponsored by a certain Mr. Hernando De Soto, who, at 36 was worth some $300,000 in gold he had picked up down in Peru.

He had persuaded quite a few wealthy Spanish grandees to join the tour and just before he sailed from Spain he took unto himself a bride whom he left in Cuba to spend her honeymoon while he headed for a land which is now a honeymooner's paradise.

Among these first tourists to Western North Carolina was a notetaking fellow named the Gentleman of Elvas who set a pattern for future travel writers.

He wrote the first travel guide on the area.

He had some competition from some of his fellow travelers who apparently saw a future in the travel guide field, too.

These other travel writers were Rodrigo Ranjel, Ruiz Hernandez De Biedma and one Garcillasso, none of whose accounts agree.

But as a promoter, the Gentleman of Elvas was a bust, for some ninety years elapsed before folks really discovered the mountains as a place to visit and to settle.

This De Soto tour was quite a party.

There were 720 members and 237 horses, so a lot of them had to make the tour on foot, which the travel writers described as rugged to say the least.

Luckily, they brought food along with them, including a herd of some 200 hogs, for De Soto's touring Spaniards found the natives hostile.

Incidentally, some of the hogs strayed from the herd and established the razorback as a citizen of the southeastern United States.

When they ran out of hogs they bartered or just plain stole food from the natives—the Cherokee Indians.

The Gentleman of Elvas reported in his guide book that at one Cherokee village they visited the chief gave them "little dogs that couldn't bark" for food. Actually, they were possums.

The De Soto tourists entered North Carolina from Oconee County in what is now South Carolina.

They came up the Winding Stairs road and onto Highway 107, south of Cashiers, cut around Glade Mountain and came up in the vicinity of Silver run.

The tourists passed along by what is now one of the most famous resort hotels in the South, High Hampton Inn.

Then they struck west past Whiteside Mountain, and some of the party may have strayed up there to carve their initials and a few words on some of the boulders.

Some Spanish writings were discovered on Whiteside a few years ago, all of which goes to show that tourists were the same then as they are today—some of them are name-carvers.

De Soto and his party camped here at Highlands, never realizing that one day a tourist town would rise where they slept.

Out of Highlands they followed the gorge of the Cullasaja down to Franklin, which in those days was known as Nikwasi—the sacred town of the Cherokee.

West out of Franklin, the tourists forded the Little Tennessee and struck a war trail—later known as the Macon Trail—up the valley of Cartoogechaye Creek and crossed Black Gap into the valley of Shooting Creek.

On a flat where Peachtree Creek unites with the Hiwassee, they came upon the Indian town of Guasili, which was the nearest the Spaniards could come to imitating the Cherokee Ayuhwasi, or, as we pronounce it, Hiwassee.

In the tour across Western North Carolina, the Spanish tourists covered roughly eighty miles.

They traveled through the area during the months of May and June.

This is a time when tourists come today, a time when the first flowers are blooming and when the whole landscape picks up its spring dress and begins to weave the blooms of flame azalea and rhododendron and laurel in her hair.

De Soto apparently wasn't impressed by the scenery that since then has drawn hundreds of thousands of visitors a year.

De Soto was looking for the golden city and for gold, and his eyes were forever on the ground over which he passed.

Like most travel tour conductors, De Soto had his troubles.

He wasn't able to keep his folks happy.

Some wanted to go slow, some wanted to hurry on. Others wanted to stop and tarry, and some wanted to be back home in Spain.

But one Juan de Anasco of Seville, mighty of girth and temper, seemed to give De Soto's aides the most trouble, since he seemed reluctant to speak out to the man heading the tour.

At one place along the tour the party came to a swollen stream and Gomez Arias, who was in charge of the horses, was having quite a time getting them across.

Amasco rode up and upbraided him for not making better speed.

Arias spoke a few well-chosen words seasoned with pepper, which are unprintable although Garcillasso dutifully recorded them in his account, and invited Anasco to take over the work himself if he chose.

Out of North Carolina, De Soto guided his tour west.

And a year later, in May, 1541, he camped on the banks of the Mississippi.

De Soto was the first to come touring through these mountains but he was not the last.

He started a movement that is paying off in the gold that he sought but never found.

Some folks think De Soto would have found it if he had ever stopped and lifted his eyes out of the dust.

Memories of Bone Valley

Bone Valley

THE LONG HUNTERS ARE GONE, THE BAND SAWS ARE hushed, and the great forest has been given back to nature.

The sharp ring of the woodman's ax and the shrill whistle of the loggers' train are lost in the winds of time.

The herders' shacks have disappeared, like the wandering cattle and the razorback hogs, and the old settlers' cabins have fallen in ruins.

The little cemetery is weed-grown and the gravestones have been tumbled and scattered by marauding bear.

Only a few remember the sawmill town that lived and died with the trees.

The forgotten herdsman who gave the valley its name picked a prophetic one, never realizing that in time it would mean many things to many men.

For it is only a valley of ghosts and of memories.

But Granville Calhoun knew the valley when it was a hunter's paradise and later when it was the Babylon of the Smokies.

Granville grew up in the valley and saw it change from a land back of beyond into a bustling, feverish community, then change back into a widerness where man never again can heft an ax, raise a cabin or fire a gun.

When he talks of Bone Valley a pageant of memories floods his heart.

Granville has lived ten years past the Biblical promise of man's allotted span upon the earth and in all that time he has never been very far from Bone Valley.

Sit with him on the porch at the Calhoun House in Bryson City and get him to talking about Bone Valley. He will tell you how it used to be when he lived there.

"I guess folks seeing the place today would find it hard to believe that it has ever been any different," he said. "Sometimes I even think it was all a dream.

"First there were just a few settlers. And it was that way for a long, long time. They came to farm and hunt and just live in a place where they had a lot of room.

"Then came the lumbermen. They came because here in the Smokies was the finest timber in all the country. They built towns and put up sawmills and run a railroad right into the wilderness.

"A passenger train ran ten miles into Bone Valley and the log train went sixteen miles. Why, it was just like a revolution. And I guess it was. It changed the valley. Folks who understood a rifle trigger and a fishing pole saw things they had never heard of, much less seen.

"Bone Valley was just like a city. All hustle and bustle. Trains running in and out. Noise like you've never heard. Everybody working. Wasn't much time for hunting or fishing.

"Hundreds of men were in the woods, felling the big trees. Some of them had stood there 400 years and more. There was one poplar tree I helped saw that folks figure was the biggest tree ever to come out of the Smokies.

"It was some tree, and it seemed a shame to cut it. It stood over 110 feet tall. It was seven feet through. A master tree. They sawed 18,000 feet of lumber out of it.

"There were others almost as big, but not quite. Never saw or heard of another poplar to equal that one.

"The big sawmill ran on a ten-hour day and the big band saws could gnaw a hundred thousand feet of timber a day. The dry kilns could take care of a million feet of timber.

"We was cutting on the best stand of timber in the country. The band mill operated for two years, ripping out boards from trees being cut from a 500-acre tract. When the mill closed down there was still good timber and still plenty of it to be cut on that tract.

"I did a little of everything during the seventeen years the Ritter Lumber Company operated in this area. I worked in the woods, run the logging train, was conductor for a while on the passenger train, and operated a store.

"I reckon I liked running the store best. I was my own boss and when I wanted to go hunting or fishing I could go. I was a hunter and a fisherman before I was a logger."

Granville paused, then chuckled.

"I guess I ought to tell you about a bear I killed. More fun talking about hunting than about lumbering. This bear I'm telling you about was the oldest bear ever killed in the Smokies, I reckon. It was forty years old."

He chuckled again, and his eyes sparkled.

"Don't you want to know how I knew that bear was that old? Well, I didn't when I killed it, though I knew it had been here a long time. Wasn't no way I knew of that I could rightly figure its age. How I found out is a story, but I've got to go back a ways.

"Back at the time of the Civil War, old man Dewitt Gormerly started out from the valley with a wagon load of apples. He took apples over to Knoxville and peddled them.

"Well, now, he had a pet bear that he always took along to show off and help sell his apples. This particular time he was going with a load of apples over to Maryville.

"He set out across the Smokies with his apples and his bear. He had the bear in a sort of wooden cage he had made. Just as he reached the top of the mountains his steers stalled and stumbled. They lost their footing and the wagon started to roll back down the mountain. It bounced into a tree, spilling apples and dumping the cage with the bear. The cage broke open and the bear jumped out and headed into the timber.

"That was the last old man Gormerly saw of his bear.

"Well, about forty years later, my father sent word to me one day that if I wanted a bear fight to come on up to his house. So I got my rifle and went up there.

"My father told me that he'd found a bear was wrecking his apple orchard. The bear would come in every night and eat a bushel of apples. So I went out to the orchard that night and waited on the bear. Finally, I saw him. I took a shot and missed and the bear took off with my dogs after him and me after the dogs. We run him five miles and the dogs cornered him and I killed him.

"That was the raggedist bear I ever saw. Its coat looked like hog fur. Its ears were marked, just like you mark cattle to tell they're yours. The teeth were worn down to the gums. Reckon that's why he was so porely. Didn't have teeth to eat with.

"But he was a big bear, anyhow. Measured nine feet from nose to tail. He was a master brute and would have chawed them dogs up if he'd had any teeth.

"Well, a few days later I went up to Bryson City and got to talking to Matt Taylor. Told him about the bear I had killed and how its ears were marked. First time I ever saw a bear's ears marked, I told him.

"Matt grinned and said he knew all about that mark. It's old man Gormerly's mark, he said, the same one he used on his cattle. Matt said he'd heard how the old man lost his pet bear and had never been able to find it. Said the old man had put his mark in the bear's ears and told everybody about it."

Granville paused.

"That was one bear that was shore tough when we tried to eat it. Cooked it for three days. Man might as well have tried to gnaw shoe leather.

"But that was an easy kill. I've had some real bear hunts in the Smokies. Sometime I'll have to tell you about them. Just come sit with me and we'll make a day of it."

We had got a long way from the lumbering days of Bone Valley.

But there was a question that was worrying me.

"Oh," he said. "You want to know how Bone Valley got its name?

"It was before my time, but I heard the old folks tell about it. Back then and even in my time, folks let their cattle run loose in the mountains. Always rounded them up in the fall. There were herders' shacks all over the Smokies. Folks would be out days looking for their cattle.

"Well, one fall a herdsman went out looking for his cattle and spent days looking. Couldn't find 'em any place. He searched the high tops and the balds. Soon it was winter and the snows come on. Still couldn't find his cattle.

"Come spring and some fellers were wandering up the valley here and run upon the cattle. They had frozen to death and there was only their bones.

"After that, they called it Bone Valley."

The Brown Mountain Lights

Wiseman's View

JUTTING OUT OF THE CATAWBA VALLEY LIKE A GRIM prophecy is the mountain that provided the locale for a best-selling mystery novel, *Kill One, Kill Two.*

It is the famous Brown Mountain where mysterious balls of fire gambol across its summit in the night when the moon is down and the stars are too sleepy to wink.

Since time out of memory folks have looked upon the mountain with awe and with wonder, and there are some who say anything can happen there.

The old-timers shake their heads when you talk of Brown Mountain and say there is a spell on it.

Hunters have told strange tales about it. Like how their dogs come whimpering back whenever they get to a certain spot on the long, flat-topped mountain.

For fifty years the Brown Mountain lights have puzzled scientists.

They first attracted nationwide interest in 1913 when the U.S. Geological Survey became interested in the mysterious fire ball capers and sent one of its scientists into the hills to study their origin.

He was here only a short while before reporting that they came from the headlights of locomotives flashing up over the mountain.

The old-timers listened and then laughed.

They had seen the lights over the mountain before a train ever ran through the valley.

Besides, these were balls of fire that popped up over Brown Mountain, and any fool knew that a locomotive threw out a beam.

Then the automobile came along, and the scientists laid the phenomenon at the door of Henry Ford.

In time, there were almost as many theories to their origin as there were lights over Brown Mountain.

In 1922 another government geologist arrived for a more thorough investigation, determined to lay the spooks of the old mountain once and for all.

This was his report after two weeks:

47 per cent of the lights originated from car headlights.

33 per cent from locomotive headlights.

10 per cent from fixed lights.

10 per cent from brush fires.

The old-timers laughed some more and reckoned there was a sight of addle-brained folks drawing down good hard money up in Washington.

Some folks who remembered the 1916 flood in the mountains wrecked the geologists report.

They recollected that the flood put the local trains and the automobiles out of business and that the electric power lines were down, too. It was a wet time, they recalled, and even the devil couldn't have started a brush fire.

While all this was taking place, they pointed out, the Brown Mountain lights still put in their regular appearance.

But the geologist did clear up one point.

Over the years the lights popped up in different colors. One would be orange, another blue, and another white.

The geologist said dust and mist caused the lights to have various tints.

The old-timers reckoned maybe that could be so.

Through the years there have been many explanations given as to the origin of the lights but none has proved correct.

Some have suggested the will-o'-the-wisp, albeit there's no marshy ground on the mountain.

Some have suggested foxfire, the glowing light often seen on pieces of decaying wood. But no one has ever known of a piece that could be seen eight miles away.

A piece of pitchblend was discovered near the mountain and this was offered as the cause until somebody pointed out that the emanations from radium are invisible.

Some wag suggested they were the reflections from the fires of corn likker stills.

Others have suggested they came from nearby towns which can be seen from here. But at night the lights from these towns are steady. They don't stray off, zoom and zig-zag through the sky.

Of course, there are legends to account for the mysterious lights.

One is that it is the soul of an Indian maiden who seeks her warrior brave killed in a bloody battle.

Fall is considered the best time of year to see the lights.

And Wiseman's View is one of the favorite spots to come and watch the mysterious phenomenon.

You'll know when you see them.

Suddenly, as you look toward Brown Mountain, a light pops up on the horizon.

It shines steadily for a few seconds. Then it rises in the air. It wavers as if hesitating which way to go. Then it winks out.

Back in 1940, a friend of mine with the Associated Press in New York decided to write a mystery.

A South Carolinian by birth, he was familiar with the Brown Mountain lights.

So he took Brown Mountain and its mysterious lights and wove them into his novel, writing it, strangely enough, in the AP morgue.

In his book, Andy Anderson put a lodge on Brown Mountain and peopled it with a lot of folks.

Every time the lights started popping up over his Brown Mountain somebody got murdered.

He called it *Kill One, Kill Two.*

But like the old-timers here in the hills, Andy didn't try to explain the mysterious lights.

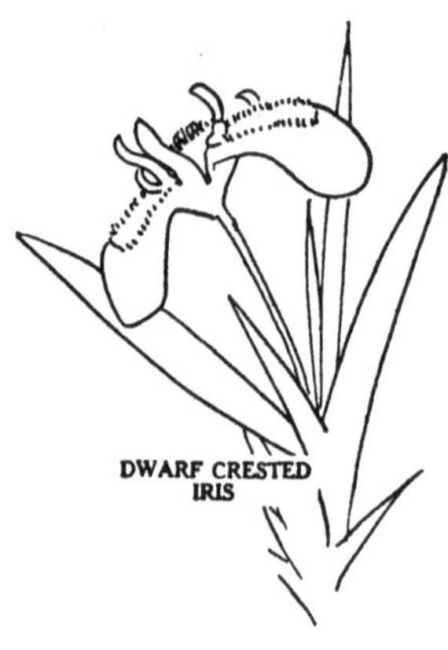

An Untamed Jungle

Bryson Place

THIS IS THE GATEWAY TO A JUNGLE WHERE MEN SELDOM go and where few men have ever been.

Only the adventurous come this way.

For beyond is Eastern America's last great wilderness—a flower kingdom guarded by trees that were saplings when Columbus sailed westward out of Palos.

Yet this untamed wilderness is right in America's front yard.

Nine miles to the south is the town of Bryson City. Ten hours away is Washington. Sixty per cent of the nation's population can reach it in less than two days.

This wilderness area is in the Great Smoky Mountains National Park.

Thomas Divide flanks it on the east and Noland Divide on the west. Deep Creek knifes through the center of the jungle, and riding high above, to the north and west, is Clingman's Dome, black with spruce and balsam.

There are 75,000 acres of virgin trees in the wilderness—the largest virgin red spruce and hardwood forests in the United States. More virgin, in fact, than in all the rest of the East combined.

A few trails skirt the wilderness—none penetrate it.

There are gulfs in the jungle where no man has ever been.

It is no region for the tenderfoot or the amateur hiker.

Men have been known to disappear in the jungle.

There are rhododendron "hells"—a veritable maze of false paths and openings—in which men have been known to wander for days, and it was not uncommon a few years ago to see notices tacked up in the post office at Bryson City telling of someone lost in the jungle.

There are sections that only such men as the late Horace Kephart, the late George Masa, and Kelly Bennett of Bryson City have traveled.

"But there are places," says Bennett, "where no man has ever been and where no man will probably ever go. It is rough, tough country. Beautiful but frightening. There is a certain awe about it."

Within this jungle there are tulip poplars up to ten feet through, their trunks towering like gigantic columns, with scarcely a noticeable taper seventy or eighty feet to the nearest limb.

Spruce trees reach 175 feet and hemlocks—almost twenty feet around—stand sentinel beside the spruce while rhododendron—twenty-five feet tall and gnarled in knots—spread over the face of the jungle.

There are spots where the rhododendron grows so thick that it is possible to walk on top of it but impossible to walk through and difficult to crawl, which is the only way—on hands and knees—it is possible to penetrate.

Animals that know not the scent of man play in its grottoes. Trout leap in its azure brooks with absolute freedom, cloistered from the fisherman who is not allowed this way.

The jungle changes colors like a chameleon during seasons.

The flowering period is a long one, with sometimes only a month or two separating the late flowers, such as witch hazel, from early bloomers, such as streamside alders.

Certain plants that come into flower in early spring at lower altitudes may be found in bloom eight to ten weeks later along the crest of the range that rises out of the jungle.

Arthur Stupka, the park naturalist, says there are about 1,300 species of flowering plants, of which 131 represent native trees—a greater number than is to be found in all Europe.

Among the nonflowering plants there are about 50 ferns and fern allies, 330 mosses and liverworts, 230 lichens, and 1,800 fungi.

From the head-springs of the left fork of Deep Creek on Fork Ridge, where the jungle rises to five thousand feet, down to the gateway to the wilderness here which is three thousand feet, there is a change in vegetation comparable to that which would be seen traveling a thousand miles to the north.

More than half the woody plants growing in the jungle are northern species of the so-called Canadian zone, which reaches its southernmost extension in the Great Smoky Mountains.

The open areas on the ridge crests in the wilderness area are known locally as "laurel slicks" or "laurel hells," or technically as "heath balds."

From a distance they appear to be a smooth, grassy carpet.

"They are in reality," Stupka explains, "an almost impenetrable head-high tangle of rhododendron, mountain laurel and other members of the heath family.

"Probably no individual laurel slick is very old. They seem to have originated from removal of the forest cover by fire, windfall, or landslide, and they are continually being reclaimed by the encroaching forest."

April and May is the time of greatest blooming of the wild flowers of the forest floor, such as violets, trilliums and phacelia.

Early to mid-June marks the height of bloom of the spectacular Catawba rhododendron of the laurel slicks, with the brilliant flame azaleas coming next.

The Turk's-cap lily—it sometimes reaches a height of seven to eight feet—reaches its peak of bloom during the second or third week of July.

Like the plant life, the animal life is diverse.

And the jungle has become a sanctuary for more than fifty kinds of fur-bearers, two hundred birds, and eighty fishes.

Black bears are as prevalent today as when the country was first settled, Stupka believes, and they, along with bobcats, red and gray foxes, ravens, wild turkeys, ruffed grouse, and duck hawks, serve to preserve the wilderness character of the Smokies.

Men who have gone into the jungle have told of seeing and hearing the raven—the first creature Noah liberated from the Ark.

And there is forever the chip-chip-cluck of ground squirrels, the saucy bark of the grays and the great chirruping among the mountain "boomers."

They mock a silence older than Adam.

Cloud shadows troop all day across the wilderness and darken no doorstep, for man never ventured beyond the Bryson Place to build.

Even the Cherokee Indian steered clear of the jungle.

For the jungle held mysteries that even he could not fathom.

Even on the edge of this wilderness there is a brooding, weary silence and inside, as Bennett will tell you, there is a heavy stillness that makes men talk in whispers.

There are spots in the jungle where the foliage is so thick that the sun never shines on the ground.

I spent five days in this wilderness back in 1928 and I still remember with awe how night comes there with a startling suddenness, and that there is a blackness to it for which there is no word.

There is something else I remember, too.

It was a feeling that has come back over the years when I have walked into a cathedral.

And I can hear, too, the night cry of the whippoorwills—"these old hills, these old hills."

This jungle here in America's front yard is one of the few places that man has not defiled.

And only a carelessly thrown match, or an enemy-launched atom bomb, will prevent it from remaining just like nature made it.

Yet, until a road is built to the Bryson Place here on the edge of the jungle, few people will ever have the opportunity of seeing this last great wilderness.

The Gingerbread Man

Sylva

WE KNEW HIM AS THE GINGERBREAD MAN.

He might have been a character straight out of Dickens.

He was a little man with a gargoyle face, and he spoke with a Shakespearean flavor and dressed like a Cockney.

He was a peddler of sorts, a hawker of apples and gingerbread.

He was also a collector of herbs and an herb doctor.

He was the Sage of Little Savannah.

Folks quoted him as faithfully as the Bible and the almanac.

His name was Ira Barker, and for seventy-five years he never missed a session of superior court in the county.

He was a friend of judges and lawyers.

He knew everybody and everybody knew him.

"I've never made the acquaintance of a stranger," he once said. "Everybody is my friend. Which makes me richer than the feller with a countinghouse full of gold."

He had a way with children, and with birds.

"Children and birds were put on the earth by the Good Lord to make people happy," he said. "Show me a feller who don't like children and I'll show you a man with a mean streak."

His mind was as sharp as a meat-ax, and he could expound on any subject under the sun.

"If a man knows his Bible," he would say, "he can hold his own in any company. I've read the Good Book purt nigh a thousand times, I reckon. That's from cover to cover."

He had the uncanny knack of sizing up a jury and a witness in the wink of an eye.

"Set twelve men in the jury box and give me a good look at their eyes and the tilt of their chins," he said, "and I'll tell you what they'll do when they come to vote."

Ira attended his first term of court at the age of five.

"My pa took me and had to hold me on his knee," he once recalled. "And I've been going ever since. Court-time is a time to see your friends and make new ones. And a feller can get an education listening to the lawyers and the judges."

He became a rambling vendor at the age of eleven.

"Found out folks have a hankering to buy things at a court session they wouldn't buy no time else. So I started bringing a sack of apples to court and selling 'em. Then my ma let me take some gingerbread. By the time I got married I had a good trade. Then my wife got to making gingerbread. My ma learned her."

If Ira had been a man with a Midas complex he could have become the gingerbread king.

"I've never been greedy in all my life," he said shortly before his eightieth birthday. "If I had I'd be rich instead of being as poor as Job's turkey. I've never knowingly beat a man. That's why my bed is soft and why I've always slept good."

There were some who bruited it about that Ira had a weakness for the jug.

"I've been taking my toddy off and on for purt nigh sixty years now," he once admitted. "And I can't see it ever hurt me. 'Course a'body can kill theirselves if they drink enough.

"You know, I tell 'em, just take it easy-like and don't try to guzzle it like you're in a hurry to lay down in a pine box. Folks have been makin' 'toxicants since time began and they'll go right on makin' 'em long's there's a feller that can lift a hand and open his mouth.

"A feller's a plumb fool to go to the well and stay. Like the Good Book says, a'body can make a sin of anything. Any time a'body gets hisself full up to his neck, whether it's eatin' or drinkin', he's a'sinnin', and that's a true fact."

We remember the last time we saw Ira.

It was an autumn Saturday twenty years ago, and Ira was standing on a street corner, a sack of apples across his shoulder, a basket of gingerbread at his feet.

"Apples, apples," he hawked. "The finest fruit on the green footstool of creation. Two for five cents."

Somebody stopped to talk with Ira. He let his sack slide from his shoulder, set it down alongside his basket.

"Like I tell 'em," he said to the man. "if they'd stop fussin' about Roosevelt and get out and work this would be a better country. No jobs? Listen, if a feller wants to work he can work.

Look at all this country. Land every place. Stuff ain't goin' to plant itself and sprout up without some help. A feller worth his salt will always make out. He may not eat as high off the hog as he once did, but he can eat if he wants to bad enough."

He paused, sold a couple apples, then a piece of gingerbread.

"The apples are two for five cents," he said. "The gingerbread's a penny a slice."

A crowd had gathered, blocking the sidewalk, and folks wanting to be about their business had to step out into the street and skirt Ira and his listeners.

Pretty soon the last of his apples and gingerbread were gone, and Ira reckoned he could do a bit of talking without being interrupted.

"Made myself about three dollars," he figured, looking at the empty sack and the empty basket. "It's not much but it's an honest living. Buy me and the old woman some meat and salt and sugar and a little coffee that'll last us a spell."

Then he was back talking about the country and hard times.

"No use to kick and grumble," he told his audience. "Could be a lot worse, a lot worse. When you get healthy fellers a'grumblin', well, that's a mighty pore sign they ain't all there in the head. Some folks just got to feel sorry for theirselves and expect it to come a-runnin' to 'em on a silver platter. But let me tell you, them fellers should pull up their reins and give a lot of thought to how well the Good Lord's been to 'em. Think of the crippled, the sick and the afflicted. I tell you, them of us that can be up and about has got a lot to be thankful for."

A boy of twenty, deaf and dumb, walked up and stood smiling. The boy's father explained to Ira about his son. Ira offered the boy an apple, one he had in the pocket of his coat. But the boy shook his head. Ira pressed the apple into the boy's hand, and the boy smiled and nodded and moved on through the crowd.

"I'd pour groundhog oil in his ears," Ira said. "He'd be able to hear then. I've tried it. Groundhog oil is a true remedy for them that can't hear."

Somebody asked Ira how old he was, and the old man cocked an eye at his questioner.

"Some folks say I'm as old as God," he said. "But them are disrespectful folks. If I live another two months I'll be eighty years old.

"Never been real sick in my life. A little puny now and then but never what you'd call sick. Now and then I get the aches in my bones, but that's to be expected. My legs ain't what they used to be, but then I've used 'em a 'plenty. Been walking all my life. Still do. It's four miles to my house and every time I make a trip down here that's eight miles."

He admitted that sometimes he got a ride into town on a wood truck.

"Them things will jolt a man to death," he said. "Ridin' them things will age a man in a matter of minutes. Last time I come off Little Savannah on a wood truck I was so sore the next morning the old woman had to pry me up out of bed."

Finally, it was daydown, the pink of the evening, and Ira picked up his empty sack and basket and started down the street and out of town.

I remember watching him shuffle along, back slightly bent, head bobbing as if he were talking to himself.

It was the last time I ever saw him.

But I still remember him as the gingerbread man who took my pennies when I was a boy and patted me on the head and smiled.

I wonder if anybody makes gingerbread any more, the kind that Ira sold in our town.

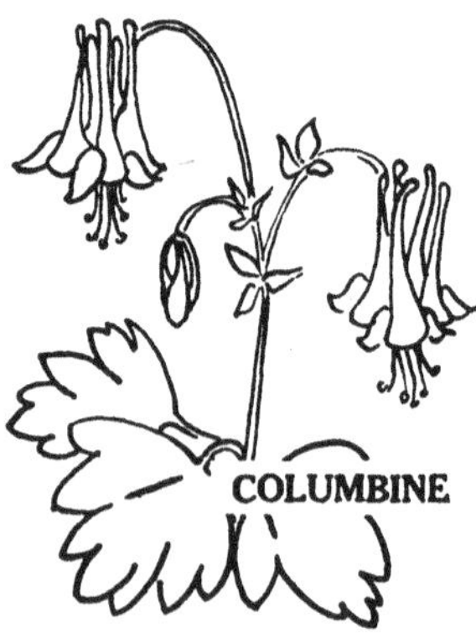

The Madonna of the Hills

Blowing Rock

THE MADONNA OF THE HILLS—SHE'S A LEGEND AND A painting—walked in beauty out of the ageless hills at dawn today.

No man really saw her, but all men who live close to God felt her presence.

Her coming was attended by blue skies and a promise of a bountiful harvest for the folks of the hill country.

There's an old, old legend that on the morning of the summer solstice she walks out of the hills here at the Blowing Rock to greet the dawn.

If her coming is attended by blue skies, fields will yield abundant crops to bring gladness to the hill country.

But if clouds mask the peaks and mists roll out of the hollows to cling about her feet, barren fields and sadness and want are in store.

The old-timers of the hill country know that this is true.

There are some who say, that on this first day of summer, if the scarf of clouds is tight about the Madonna's neck there will be forty days of rain.

If the scarf is loose, good weather is in store and flowers will spring up all around her feet.

The mountain folks had reason today for gladness because there were blue skies and the scarf was loose about the Madonna's neck.

No one knows the origin of the legend of the Madonna of the Hills, but it has been embodied in an oil painting that hangs in St. Mary's of the Hills Episcopal Church on the main street of this famous resort town.

The painting was done by Elliott Daingerfield, the first North

Carolina artist of national reputation, who had a summer home here for almost fifty years until his death in 1932.

Intrigued by the legend, Daingerfield, who was noted for his landscapes and religious paintings, captured the Madonna of the Hills on canvas in 1918.

Appropriately enough, the painting is captioned *The Madonna of the Hills.*

And there's hardly a day during summer that some visitor does not slip into the little sanctuary to sit in quiet solitude and meditation and look upon the canvas that hangs back of the altar.

The richness of the painting stands out like a finely etched stain-glassed window.

It depicts the Madonna of the Hills, tall and graceful, coming in brightness out of the radiance of a great white cloud touched with the gold of the coming sun.

One arm clasps a smiling babe, the other hand holds a white lily of purity.

The changing blues of the hillside over which the Madonna seems to walk is fairly vibrant with the gladness of the summer dawn and one of the shades of blue matches exactly her robe.

Life and light, like a miracle of beauty, follow her coming.

Rhododendron bursts into waxy showers of color beside her, while all the flowers of the fields smile at her feet.

It is truly the Madonna of the Hills of the legend who walks the blue hills each year on the first day of summer.

Daingerfield, who spent his early childhood at Fayetteville in the Sanford House where Lafayette visited in 1825, first heard of the legend when he came here shortly before the turn of the century to make his home and direct the Permanent Art School of Blowing Rock.

There's another legend connected with the famous Blowing Rock, which is an immense cliff overhanging the Johns River Gorge with its valley 2,000 to 3,000 feet below.

Long the legendary haunt of lovers, the Blowing Rock is etched in Indian legend and lore.

There is the story that two Indian braves once stood on the summit of the rock and fought for a chieftain's daughter.

They struggled all day up and down the narrow ridge until finally the stronger warrior cast his opponent over the cliff.

In that moment, the Indian maiden realized that the defeated warrior was the one she loved and she implored the God of the Winds to save him.

The wind caught up the warrior as he fell through space and tossed him through the air to safety.

And since that day, the wind has returned any object tossed over the gorge.

The Blowing Rock got its name because the rocky walls of the gorge form a flume through which the northwest wind at times sweeps with such force that it returns to the sender light objects cast over the void.

This current of air flowing upward prompted the late Robert L. Ripley to call it "the only place in the world where snow falls upside down."

The town of Blowing Rock itself first took on the appearance of a resort in 1875 when William Morris began taking in a few summer boarders.

The fame of Morris' culinary art, or that of his wife, spread and brought his place to the attention of Senator M. W. Ransom who built a summer home here.

Others followed, and soon there were many hotels and inns and summer homes.

Blowing Rock is one of the oldest resorts in the Southern Appalachians and is the only incorporated town on the Blue Ridge Parkway.

The summer folks now begin coming in late spring and stay on through the fall.

And they, like the hill folk, pay particular attention to each first day of summer so they will know whether the Madonna of the Hills, as she comes to greet the dawn, will bring a promise of good weather and a bountiful season.

On this day, this first day of summer 1955, the Madonna of the Hills walked in beauty, and all is well with the folks of the hill country.

The French Broad Is a Gypsy

Rosman

THE FRENCH BROAD IS THE HEAD MAN OF THE RIVER CLAN in Western North Carolina.

He is one of the oldest rivers in America and his sons are many.

He is really the daddy of the Tennessee, which assumes his burden but refuses his name.

It is a pity the Cherokee never got around to giving him a name, for, if they had, the chances are he would have kept his identity right to the Ohio, and the Tennessee would be the brawling brat we know as the Little Tennessee.

But the Cherokee never could decide on a name for him, and some stranger—it may have been Jean Couture, one of La Salle's coureurs de bois, who came this way in 1696—called him the French Broad, which the English never bothered to change.

In their ritual, the Indians called him the "Long Man" or the "Long Snake," but that was what they called all rivers even though they bestowed individual names upon all the others.

There are bigger rivers and longer rivers, but the French Broad is a complex river.

He is a gypsy who had a hard time deciding which way he wanted to go.

And when he did, he flouted nature's law and struck out northeast and then north in what looks like an uphill route to join the Tennessee.

Few other rivers ever picked a tougher, more wandering outlet from the mountains.

The Hiwassee and the Little Tennessee were of the same stubborn mind, but then they are his brothers.

Incidentally, the name "Tennessee" was applied to the Little Tennessee long before it was familiarly given to main stream.

The French Broad has a big family but the Big Pigeon is his prodigal son.

Born only a few miles from where the head man of the clan springs out of the Transylvania hills, the Big Pigeon forsook the chosen path and went his own way but finally turned back in far off Tennessee to pay tribute to his father.

Poets and novelists and makers of ballads all passed him by until Wilma Dykeman, who grew up beside him at Asheville, came along recently and gave him proper recognition among the Rivers of America with a book that bears his name and tells his story.

The only song he ever got is one that nobody ever sings.

In fact, few people ever heard of the song about the French Broad.

And that's a shame, because he is a river that folks should sing about.

"Singing Willie" Walker, who struck his famous tuning fork all over the South, wroté a song called "French Broad" back in 1831 after a trip along the river in North Carolina and Tennessee.

Walker put it in his famous *Southern Harmony* songbook which I never have been able to locate.

Maybe somebody will run across a copy of it some day and give the folks along the French Broad a chance to sing about their river.

It is surprising that no one ever wrote a ballad about the French Broad for he is of many moods and the stuff from which ballads are made.

He has seen the Indian come and go, the forest leveled to make room for cities and towns and factories.

He has been harnessed to the TVA system, bled by power projects, tapped for energy to turn out atomic bombs.

Because he is big and powerful, like the mountains from which he draws his strength, many and varied industries have risen along his banks.

He is a river of industry now.

He is called upon to help make paper and cloth and machinery.

He flows through a land that has been a magnet for settlers since 1778.

Now he is drawing industry.

With the help of his many sons—a hundred and more tributaries —he drains some 2,825 square miles, sopping up the tall walking rain that the Cherokee in ancient times called down out of the doorway of dark clouds.

For the most part the natural wonders along his banks remain the same and the mountains still shoulder each other out into the current.

The Valley of the French Broad is one of the most beautiful valleys in America.

Geologists say the French Broad flowed in its present channel at a time when the land now west of the mountains was occupied by a great inland sea.

His moods change a hundred times in his long run through the very heart of Western North Carolina, knifing as he does from the mountains of Transylvania to the farm lands of Madison where he salutes Paint Rock and slips into Tennessee.

Rising among the very old crystalline rocks of the Blue Ridge, he is one of the oldest rivers in America.

He comes brawling into Rosman from the four corners of the compass, undecided which way to go or how.

There are four prongs that make him the river he is.

Until he reaches Rosman he is known as the North Fork, the West Fork, the East Fork and the Middle Fork of the French Broad.

He takes on the one name here and he is still a maverick among rivers.

He is anything but orthodox as he winds and twists and doubles back through the fertile valleys from here to Brevard.

Then he loafs along by Penrose and Horseshoe and Arden, never complaining at his many sons who load him down with their burdens.

By the time he gets to Asheville he is fat and full and his back is broad and he's got just about all he can carry without stretching out of his channel, which he does sometimes when his sons drink too much.

That happened back in 1916 and he washed away bridges and houses, gave Asheville its biggest, most destructive flood. He claimed many lives too.

When he passes Asheville, where he flows gently now, he takes a deep breath, shakes off his laziness and flexes his muscles.

Then he goes tearing down the boulder-strewn gorge to Marshall, venting his anger against the high walls that box him in for the load he is forced to carry.

He grumbles as he passes through Marshall, the town a mile high and a street wide.

He is in a hurry now to be done with the mountains

He takes on more burdens and grumbles a little more as he twists and turns and charges into Hot Springs.

Then he comes to Paint Rock, salutes the last sentinel along his route in North Carolina, and hies away to Tennessee, at last turning west and south where he loses his identity by becoming the Tennessee.

But he's still the head man of the river clan in Western North Carolina.

The Drovers' Road

Marshall

ZACHARIAH CANDLER STOOD IN THE DOOR OF HIS WAYSIDE inn and watched the dust boil up far down the turnpike.

He knew the signs only too well.

The Buncombe Turnpike, he mused, was beginning to resemble a parade out of Noah's Ark.

As the snail-crawling dust edged nearer, he caught the familiar cry "suboy! suboy! suboy!"

Then a barefoot boy came into sight, scattering shelled corn.

Behind came the first of a plodding, grunting drove of hogs bound for the South Carolina and Georgia markets by way of Asheville.

The year 1826 was proving to be a good year for the stock stand operators along the pike and Zachariah Candler figured close to 200,000 hogs had come this way out of Kentucky and Tennessee.

Why, only last month, he recalled, Hezekiah Barnard at Barnard's on the French Broad had fed 90,000 hogs, while David Vance at Lapland had boasted feeding 110,000 during the same period.

Here at Sandy Bottoms, Candler had sold some 2,000 bushels of corn, mostly to hog drovers, which, based on the required diet of 24 bushels daily for each 1,000 hogs, meant that he had fed around 80,000.

Between Hot Springs and Asheville there were some eight or ten stock stands, or wayside inns with stock yards, at two- to four-mile intervals.

They gave bed and board to the weary drovers and feed to his cattle, sheep, hogs, horses, mules and turkeys that made the Buncombe Turnpike a heavily traveled thoroughfare until long after the Civil War.

James Garrett had a stand about a mile below Hot Springs. John E. Patton ran the White House above Hot Springs. At the mouth of Laurel Creek was a stand kept by David Farnsworth. Samuel Chunn catered to the drovers opposite the mouth of Pine Creek.

At the lower end of what is now Marshall, but then was called Lapland, a stand was operated by Joseph Rice. At the upper end of the narrow village David Vance kept a tavern that was 150 feet long and huddled between the stage road and the mountains.

Samuel Smith accommodated all travelers and their belongings at the mouth of Ivy while Mitchell Alexander was the Boniface at Alexander's.

During the months of October, November and December there was an almost continuous string of hogs from the Tennessee line to Asheville.

It was not uncommon for ten to twelve droves, numbering from three hundred to one and two thousand to stop overnight and feed at one of these stands.

Each drove was "lotted" to itself and "corned" by the wagon-load.

The wagon was driven through each lot with ten or twelve men scattering the corn, left and right and to the rear, literally covering the ground.

The drovers were furnished large rooms which had immense log-heap fireplaces. They provided their own blankets. They would form a semi-circle on the bare floor, their feet to the fire, and thus pass the night.

Many of these innkeepers, such as Zachariah Candler, whose great-great-grandson, Dr. Charles Z. Candler, Jr., now lives at Asheville, kept little stores and bartered or sold everything on credit.

In the fall of the year they would advertise that on certain days they would receive corn in payment of store accounts.

The farmers would begin delivering frequently by daylight and continue until midnight, and their wagons would be strung out for a mile and as thick as they could be wedged.

The price allowed the farmers for corn on their store accounts was fifty cents per bushel.

The innkeepers would furnish it to the drovers at twenty to

twenty-five cents "per diet," meaning per meal for their drivers, asking the whole in lame hogs at so much per pound, or a due bill from the manager of the drive to be paid as he returned home after selling his stock.

Cash was rarely ever paid.

The lame hogs were kept until a suitable time for killing when they were slaughtered and converted into bacon and lard.

The pig pelters were a colorful lot.

Sometimes they frequented taverns where they pulled long and hard from bottles and then whooped it up with a fiddle for hours.

Many drovers camped wherever night found them.

They usually made only about eight miles a day with their droves.

At the stops the drovers would spend their time talking politics and spinning yarns.

And they would listen to the cry of the fiddles telling of young love:

'Twas in the merry month of May
When the green leaves they were buddin',
Sweet William Gray on his death-bed lay
For the love of Barbry Allen.

The first drovers began moving their herds of hogs, cattle and horses out of Tennessee and Kentucky into the southern seaboard regions about the turn of the 19th century.

There were no stock stands at that time and they camped where-ever night found them.

They kindled a fire, spread blankets on the ground and turned in soon after sundown.

The pigs roamed the woods, and morning found the pelters up early. An hour or more was spent daily hunting porkers that had strayed during the night.

Frequently a couple dozen or more strays were left behind, but the percentage of lost pigs was extremely low.

Thunder storms and swollen creeks were the greatest hazards to the drovers.

Like cattle, the hogs stampeded when there was thunder and lightning. They lost their reason and ran wildly.

Farmers who drove their own herds had less difficulty with the hogs than professional drovers.

Trained to come when called or when a conch shell was blown, thoroughly domesticated hogs behaved fairly well on the road.

Autumn and early spring were the best times for droving, since the cool weather not only made traveling easier but also reduced loss of weight.

The Buncombe Turnpike funneled great numbers of animals to Charleston and Augusta, and folks in Asheville got used to seeing the almost daily parade of hogs, cattle, horses and sheep passing through the center of town.

It may have been at David Vance's tavern here in Marshall that a drover, while quaffing a bumper of ale, started the legend that the first pegged shoes were made in the Madison County town, which lies in a narrow gorge of the French Broad River.

The story goes that because the town is so confined, cobblers found it impossible to stretch their thread to arm's length, thus ruling out sewn soles and forcing them to use wooden pegs which they could hammer in by striking up and down.

Such were the legends that grew along the Buncombe Turnpike when it was the drover's road.

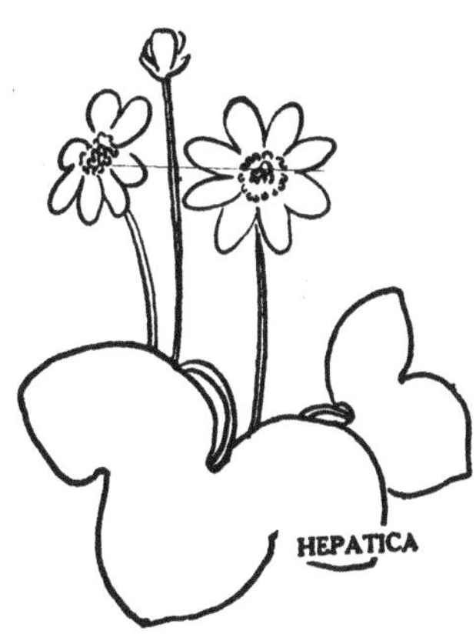

The Axeman Came First

Sunburst

THE AXEMAN CAME FIRST TO GROOVE TOGETHER A CABIN and hoe corn.

He chopped an eyereach straight to the sky and let sunlight in where there never had been sunlight before.

The land was his by law of the rifle and the forests to use by possession. Both were only a means to provide a simple living.

There were more than enough trees to build all the houses the world would ever need and still more to provide the hulls for all the ships that would ever sail the Seven Seas.

Or so he thought.

In time, the lumber barons of the North discovered the forests of Western North Carolina and where there had been one axeman there were a thousand.

The axeman of the 18th century, who had come seeking only wing-room and freedon, suddenly awoke to find his forests being leveled and carted off.

From the Black Mountains to the Smokies, across the Caney Fork and Plott Balsams, the big lumber companies of the North set up their mills whose saws whined from sunup to sundown while hordes of men with axe and saw swarmed through the forests like locusts.

These were the men who only saw in the trees the gold they would bring on the market.

Their attitude was:

"All we want here is to get the most we can out of this country, as quick as we can, and then get out."

They were not the thoughtful thinkers and planners such as Reuben Robertson and the men of Champion Fibre and Paper

Company, who practiced conservation and scientific cutting when they came in.

And Sunburst stands today as a symbol of the old and the new.

The Sunburst Lumber Company operated here in the '20's and it was one of the biggest operations in Western North Carolina.

When the mill closed down and moved away just before 1930, Champion bought the land, and today there is a lake here and the forest has grown back.

Old-timers remember Sunburst as it used to be, and the memory of it fans alive old memories of lumber operations in the mountains.

The present generation know little if any of what it was like then, and the names of such lumber towns as Sunburst, Ravensford, Quinlandtown, East La Porte, Fontana, Cruso and Rainbow Springs, have little meaning for them.

Yet, they played a role in the drama of mountain lumbering just as Fairfield, Corundum Hill and Spruce Pine have played in mining.

Many mountain streams carried great saw logs on their bosoms back seventy and eighty years ago. Thousands were floated down the Tuckaseigee River to sawmills located along its lower course.

Over in Jackson County, logs floated into the Tuckaseigee from smaller streams such as Caney Fork Creek, Trout Creek and Wolf Creek.

Ox teams dragged the logs to the creeks and streams.

To float the logs more easily, big splash dams were built across the mountain streams.

Weeks would be spent in getting them to the streams and rolling them in. Then when rain came and raised the water above its normal level, the water would be released from the splash dams above by means of huge trap doors.

The splash dam release and flood water would create enough force to send the logs far downstream.

Often there would be log jams on the streams and rivers. Some as much as a mile in length.

That's why the lumberjacks wore hobnails in their boots.

For they would have to follow the logs as they went downstream and when there was a jam they would have to climb out onto them and break them loose.

It was hazardous work. One slip and a man could be crushed to death.

Warnings always went out ahead of the splash dam releases. All families below the dams were told well in advance.

Such warnings were especially necessary because the streams, for the most part, were unbridged and wagons, buggies and horseback riders had to ford them.

The pick of the forests went to the sawmills.

Single poplar logs that taxed the strength of three big teams of oxen were taken from the Sugar Creek section of Jackson County.

Logs that were too heavy to float were split into halves.

Oak logs could not be floated to the valley sawmills because most of the streams were too shallow to carry the heavy timber.

Flumes were used, too.

Where there were two or three small streams, boulder-strewn and shallow, a massive flume would be constructed and the waters of these streams turned into it.

Even today the rotting remains of miles and miles of such flumes can still be seen back in the mountains, such as the Balsams.

Probably one of the most fantastic operations—certainly it was unique—was the transportation of logs by incline railway.

The late Robert Long and the late Jeeter Snyder had the highest and longest incline railway in the country for bringing logs from the very top of the Balsams.

The railway ran for more than three miles, pulling logs from out of the valley and along the mountainside and lowering them down into the valley on the other side where they went into a flume.

The incline railway ran up the north and south sides of Waterrock Knob, one of the highest peaks in the Balsam range. It was a mile high and the railroad had an incline of 45 degrees.

Once as a boy, I rode it up the south side of the mountain, hanging on for dear life and then was foolish enough to ride it partway down the other side to the cook shack.

There's only a long gash down the side of the mountain now to show that it was ever there.

And the axemen who chopped the trees that rode it are gone from the Balsams.

The Whipping Post and The Branding Iron

Burningtown

MY GRANDFATHER REMEMBERS WHEN THE WHIPPING POST and the branding iron were instruments of punishment for law-breakers in Western North Carolina.

Rummaging through his wonderful storehouse of memories, he recalled the days when a man could lose an ear to the knife for lying under oath or both ears for malicious maiming.

"Never saw any of it myself," he said, pausing to light up his pipe. "But I have heard my father tell about how it was and I remember when I was seven years old a neighbor of ours right here on Burningtown was flogged at the whipping post."

That was back in 1866, two years before the state revised its ancient and barbaric code of laws and abolished the whipping post, the branding iron and ear-cropping.

"I was too young to attend the flogging," my grandfather explained. "But I remember standing out in the yard and watching the folks gather for it. They flogged this feller not too far from where we lived.

"What's that? Of course I remember his name. Your mother knows who I'm talking about. But there's no good in bringing it up now. I'll tell you who it was but don't put it down on paper. Folks are still living who knew the family and some of the family's still around and about.

"Well, as I was saying, they flogged this feller not too far from where we lived. A heap of folks was there that day and my father said this feller was real shamed, more so because his wife was the one that had him brought up for flogging.

"This feller had a smokehouse full of hams and his wife kept complaining that somebody was stealing them. So one day she decided she would hide back of the smokehouse and catch the thief. Pretty soon she saw her husband come out of the house, look around and then go into the smokehouse.

"When he come out he had one of the hams. She stayed hidden and let him move off down the road. She followed him and he went straight to a house where he had a woman that his wife had suspected him of courting for some time.

"Well, when she saw him go in the house with that ham she struck off across the field to get the sheriff who lived in the settlement. She had the sheriff to arrest her husband and said she wanted him punished.

"And they did, too. Give him thirty-nine lashes on his bare back. That was the proper number. Couldn't give him no more. That was the law."

The punishment in those days for manslaughter was branding in the palm of the right hand with a red hot iron shaped to the letter "M."

A man was branded for the length of time it took him to say three times "God save the State."

The late Dr. J. S. T. Baird of Asheville once described a branding he witnessed in Buncombe County about 1855.

"I saw one fellow taken through this barbarous process and this was enough for me," Dr. Baird recalled. "He was convicted of manslaughter and ordered to be branded."

General Bayles Edney, a fast talker and an eloquent speaker who had a reputation for never getting flustered, was attorney for the defense.

Yet, for all his eloquence, he failed on this occasion to free his client and the wretched man was brought into the Buncombe County courtroom to be branded in the palm of his right hand.

The prisoner was a shy backwoodsman. He was literally shaking in his boots as they strapped his right arm to the rail of the bar. The courtroom was crowded to overflowing.

And to top it off, the prisoner had a slight speech impediment. Some of the spectators wondered if the man ever would be able to utter "God save the State" three times.

General Edney sized up the situation and requested permission of the judge to be allowed to repeat the required phrases for his client.

"This man, your honor, is in no condition to do himself justice, as you can well see," General Edney pleaded. "Please permit me to talk for him when the time comes."

The judge didn't relish the ordeal any more than did the scared prisoner, and he wanted it over with in a hurry.

"All right," he told General Edney. "You're a fast talker. Permission is granted. General Edney may speak for his client."

The spectators detected a visible change in the prisoner. A look of hope came into his eyes and for a brief moment he seemed to relax.

Meanwhile, Sheriff David Tate had gone across the street to a tinner's shop and fetched a little hand stove filled with live coals into the courtroom.

He stuck the branding iron into the live coals and waited until it became a thing of pulsating white heat.

"Now, your honor?" Tate asked.

"Ready, General Edney?" the judge asked.

General Edney took a deep breath.

"Yes, your honor," he said, but the words were like sandpaper in his throat.

The judge nodded to Tate, and the sheriff lifted the smoking branding iron from the bed of coals and moved to the prisoner whose face was beaded with perspiration, his body trembling in a chill of fear and dread.

Tate clamped tight his jaws, pressed the white hot iron into the prisoner's hand.

As the iron bit deep, the prisoner shrieked and then the pain turned him into a groaning, blubbering, writhing gargoyle.

"God—God—God—"

General Edney struggled to get the words past his paralyzed tongue. He tugged frantically at his collar.

"God—"

Again the words choked him.

Finally, he sprang across the room, knocked the smoking iron from the sheriff's hand.

"You've burned him enough," he gasped.

The judge took his hands from his face.

"Release the prisoner," he said.

For a moment he looked at General Edney, shook his head.

No man knows what he thought in that moment, but it seems likely he was thinking that as a fast talker, General Edney had turned out to be a stutterer.

Old Bill Williams, King of the Mountain Men

Skyuka Mountain

THE HEROES WE LIKE BEST TO YARN ABOUT REALLY LIVED, and they were really heroes.

Old Bill Williams, who never seems to have had any youth, was one of these, albeit the years have molded him into a legendary character.

But, on a winter night when the wind is howling and the fire is tramping snow and the talk is good, nobody seems to mind if legend gets mixed in with fact.

After all, Old Bill was a legend, even while he lived.

Old Bill was born here in the Polk County hills, along the base of Skyuka where Horse Creek flows into the Pacolet, but he made his mark as one of the famed mountain men of the old west in the glory days of the fur trade.

Born January 3, 1787 as William Sherley Williams, red-haired and son of a Revolutionary War hero, he had many names, all of which sparked the legend and made him one of the greatest of that "wild and reckless breed of men" who followed the explorers into the west.

The Osage Indians called him Pah-hah-soo-gee-ah, the Red-headed Shooter. The trappers called him Old Soltaire, and before that he was known as "Parson Williams."

He came naturally by his restless, wandering and independent spirit.

When he was almost eight years old, the Williams family sold their farm here on Horse Creek. They loaded their possessions into wagons, and struck out across the mountains toward the west. They went all the way into the Spanish lands and settled near the village of St. Louis.

Bill attended school at Owens Station. He learned to read and write, which was more than some of his companions in later years had done, such as Jim Bridger, who carried around a volume of Shakespeare he couldn't decipher.

They say Bill, while a young man, got all fired up listening to a traveling Baptist preacher named John Clark and decided that was the life for him.

So at 17, he became "Parson Williams" and left his home on the Missouri to ride the circuit, threatening hell-fire and brimstone to the unrepentant, and winning many converts.

There came a time seven years later, however, when he gave up souls for beaver and struck out to become a celebrated mountain man who was noted for his drinking and who was bequeathed to modern fiction by Frederick Ruxton.

Some said he gave up preaching because there was a Sunday when he was in the pulpit and his eyes and thoughts kept wandering to a pretty girl on a front bench.

Be that as it may, Bill went to live with the Osage Indians. In 1813, he married the daughter of a chief and became more Indian than white.

When his wife died eleven years later, Old Bill headed west to become a free trapper and wanderer among the beaver streams and buffalo prairies.

Bill was thirty-seven and he was a rip-roarer, taking his rightful place among such mountain men as Kit Carson, Basil Lajeunesse, Broken Hand Fitzpatrick, Lucien Fontenelle, Bill Meek and Uncle Dick Wootten.

Those were the glory days of the fur trade, when dictates of male fashion decreed that every Eastern gentleman must wear a beaver hat.

Old Bill was a great man in greasy buckskins, and he held his own in the traders' camps, squandering his profits from his fur catches in sprees of drinking, gambling, horse racing, shooting matches, and dancing.

Albert Pike described him as about six-feet-one in height, "gaunt, red-headed, with a hard weather-beaten face, marked deeply with small-pox . . . a shrewd, cute original man, and far from illiterate . . . the bravest and most fearless mountaineer of them all."

He called his rifle-gun "Old Fetchem." He was a giant of a man on a horse, looking too big for the animal as he rode with his knees cocked up under his chin.

Once he wrote a memoir of his life among the Apaches, Navajos and Pueblos, but it was destroyed in a fire in 1872, almost 23 years after his death.

One of the stories they tell about Old Bill was the time he was guiding an English traveler through the western mountains.

Seems the Englishman didn't take too well to Old Bill's spitting habits.

"You spit too much and too inaccurately," the Englishman told Old Bill.

Well, it's like this, the old trapper told the Englishman, in America the white race is divided into two sexes.

"One spits and the other has no call to," Old Bill said. "And those who spit will not be stopped by no Englisher."

It was Old Bill's way of making it plain who won a couple wars from the British.

Once three Blackfeet raiders surprised him while he was out trapping alone. He got an arrow in his thigh, but managed to lose himself in the forest. They took his rifle, horse and pack and left.

Old Bill cut the arrow out of his flesh with his knife, then took out in pursuit of the Blackfeet, finally catching up with them after four days of hobbling through the forest, living on berries.

He found them asleep in their camp, slipped up on them. With his knife he slit one of the Indians throats, then repeated the act to a second. The third he booted awake, and sent him high-tailing it.

When he told the story, someone asked him why he didn't kill them all. Old Bill grinned, then reminded his listeners that if he had killed the third one the Blackfeet never would have known who rubbed them out, or how.

When Old Bill was sixty-two, with the fur trade dwindling and talk of railroads coming in, he set out in the winter of 1848 to guide Fremont's ill-fated expedition.

It was against Old Bill's better judgment that he agreed to guide the expedition.

They hadn't been out too long when Old Bill and Fremont fell out because Old Bill argued against going through a pass that was filled with snow.

Old Bill refused to lead the expedition the way Fremont wanted to go. Fremont dismissed Old Bill. The expedition went into the pass and it was no pass.

While the main party camped in snow caves, Old Bill and two companions headed for the settlements and help.

It wasn't long after that Fremont decided to follow them, for most of his men were dead.

Fremont got out and accused Old Bill of poor guidance, desertion and cannibalism. They were baseless charges and later disproven.

Sometime later, Bill was persuaded to lead Fremont's medical officer, Dr. Benjamin Kern, back along the ill-fated trail in an effort to recover some scientific papers and instruments which had been cached by the party in its flight.

And that was the undoing of Old Bill.

Old Bill and the doctor were camped near the cache on March 14, 1849, when they were fallen upon by some Ute Indians.

There was a volley of shots and Old Bill and Kern fell dead.

The Utes, who had always been friendly with Old Bill, discovered they had made a mistake when they went to scalp the two men. They recognized their old friend, Old Bill Williams, the Red-Headed Shooter.

They were sorry, but it was too late.

They buried him as a great chief and they mourned him forever after.

There's a twin memorial to Old Bill out in Arizona. One is a 9,000-foot peak that bears his name and below it gushes a stream called Bill Williams Fork.

But it was here at the base of Skyuka where Horse Creek flows into the Pacolet that the legendary hero was born.

Maybe someday they'll give him a memorial here, too.

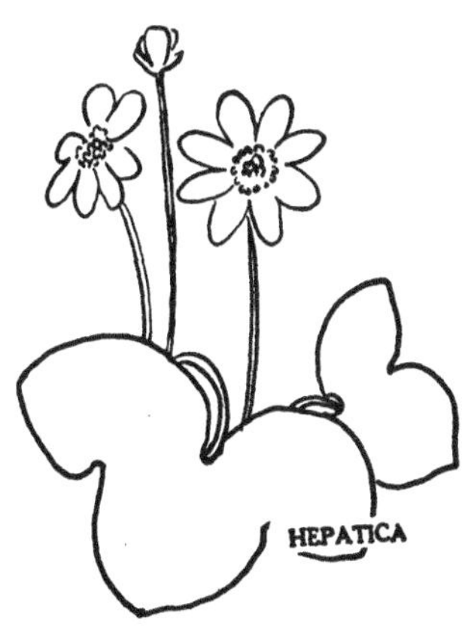

The Blockaders' Roost

Blockhouse Mountain

UP HERE WHERE THE WILD WINDS WHIRL ABOUT THE SAW-tooth peaks of the Smokies there was a time when the buzzards had to fly high to stay sober.

For this was a well known blockaders' roost where mountain men practiced their ancient poteen craft with little hindrance from the revenooers.

These were craftsmen who, taking a cue from their Scotch-Irish ancestors, believed that any man had the inherent right to make and sell whiskey, law or no law.

They hid their stills in inaccessible places, just as their ancestors had done in the savage mountains and glens of Northern Ireland, where it was impossible, or at least hazardous, for the law to reach them.

Of all the wild places in the Great Smokies, this was one of the most wild and hardest to penetrate, and it was worth a revenooer's life to come squirming through the laurel thickets.

Few revenooers ever came this way, and so the poteen craft flourished. In time, the mountain was called Blockhouse and over there to the east they gave a ridge the same name.

Don't get the idea that whiskey was flowing out of here by the barrels.

No, sir. These were small operators who turned it out mostly for their own use, and a few gallons that could be swapped off for hard money which went to pay their taxes.

Some of the old-timers back at the turn of the century used to give bad roads as reason for making whiskey, arguing that the only way they could get the corn they grew out of the hills and coves was in jugs.

Judge Felix E. Alley of Waynesville, who is an encyclopedia

of mountain lore, tells the story of a minister who got bogged down on a mountain road and had to be helped out by a mountaineer.

"My friend," the minister said, "you have a fine country up here, but you certainly have the roughest roads I ever saw. I don't see how it is possible for you to haul over them even the necessities of life."

The mountaineer studied a moment.

"Well, it is pretty hard," he said, finally. "But the worst part about it is, that since we have had this infernal prohibition law they make it so mean that you can't hardly drink the durned stuff after you get it hauled."

Actually, corn whiskey is the most maligned stimulant in America. It is the purest whiskey in the world—when it's made as it should be made.

The only difference between bourbon and corn is that bourbon is the parlor name for corn.

Of course, there's a matter of age, too.

Most mountain folks who practice the poteen craft never have been able to afford the aging process, which takes at least four years.

Quill Rose, one of the most famous blockaders of these parts, was almost eighty years old when he finally was brought before a Federal judge for making whiskey.

The old man entered a plea of guilty, and then the judge asked him if it were true that moonshine whiskey, such as Quill made, improved with age.

"You have been misinformed," the old man said. "I kept some for a week one time, and I could not tell that it was one bit better than when it was new and fresh."

Back in the days when this was a blockaders' retreat, a man took pride in the kind of liquor he turned out. After all, he made most of it for himself and his family.

So he kept it pure, just like his ancestors had made for two-hundred years and more.

First, he chose a good location for his little still. It had to be near running water and miles from any human habitation.

There he set up a still-house which was little more than a shed.

In making spirits from corn, the first step is to convert the starch of the grain into sugar.

It's a slow process.

The corn is placed in a vessel that has a small hole in the bottom.

Warm water is poured over the corn. This process is repeated for two or three days until the corn begins to sprout.

Then the sprouted corn is dried and ground into meal, which is made into a mush and let stand for another two or three days. Fermentation begins at once. The blockader lets the mash stand for a week or ten days. It becomes beer.

When the beer is working well, it is thinned down with water until it is about as thick as buttermilk.

The beer is placed in the still. A hot fire is built under the still, and the containers are then set in place to catch the hot liquid as it comes from the condensation coil, or worm.

The product of this first distillation, called "singlings," is a weak and impure liquid. It must be redistilled at a lower temper-ture to rid it of water and rank oils. When it is run through a second time it becomes "doublings" or "double-footing."

This is where a blockader's skill comes in. If the distillation is not carried far enough, the spirits will be weak and rank. If it is carried too far, it becomes pure alcohol.

Testing is done purely by taking a jugfull and shaking it. If it is good whiskey there will be bubbles or "beads." If the bead rises and is persistent, the blockader nods his head and lets it go.

But if it lacks beads, he shakes his head and condemns it.

The final process is to run the liquor through a rude charcoal filter. This rids it of most of its fusel oil.

Thus, the whiskey is uncolored, And that's how it got its name—white whiskey, or white lightning.

That was the way it was made by the craftsmen who wanted their whiskey pure.

But about twenty-five years ago, folks got to getting slip-shod and turning it out just any way. They got to adulterating it, thus giving corn liquor a bad name.

Some of the blockaders got to adding washing lye. This increased the yield and gave the whiskey an artificial bead. They primed it with pepper, ginger and tobacco, anything to give it a sting.

Out of such distillations came whiskey known as "pop-skull," "bust-head," and "bumblings." Bumblings is a potent run of whiskey that "makes a bumbly noise in a feller's head."

Corn liquor isn't made any more like it was when Blockhouse Mountain was a blockaders' roost.

The stills have gone from the Smokies, for this is a national park now.

And the buzzards can fly low and stay sober.

Majestic Old Man Dominates Region

Linville

MOUNTAINS HAVE PERSONALITIES. GRANDFATHER MOUNTAIN gave me the idea, which I guess is not new.

Looking at the Old Man, the imagery of other peaks in Western North Carolina take shape—Pisgah and the Rat, Standing Indian, the Roan, Wayah Bald, and Whiteside.

But none dominates the region like Grandfather.

He's the geologic grandsire of the mountain clan. Scientists claim he's the oldest mountain in the world.

He was an old, old man when Ararat took form and became the haven for Noah's Ark after the flood.

Nature had etched a likeness of the Sphinx along his brow long before the Pharaohs built those hulking monuments of stone in tribute to their own greatness.

For those who like time spelled out, scientists say the Old Man is 140 million years old.

There are other mountains which are higher than Grandfather but few are so aloof or majestic.

Yet, as you gaze upon the Old Man, you suddenly feel a strange affinity for him that is quite beyond the ken of those who never have lifted their eyes above the horizon.

There is a startling impression that here reposes Father Time himself.

The Old Man so effected Andre Michaux in 1794 that the French botanist wrote:

"Aug. 30, climbed to the summit of the highest mountain of all North America with my guide, and sang the Marseillaise Hymn, and cried, 'Long live America and the French Republic! Long live liberty!' "

Grandfather's great stone face, then as today, "was carved in rock and plumed with ferns, and in the furrows of his face, worn by the lapse of time, clung and crept the most beautiful flowers and vines."

Michaux had to claw his way to the summit of Grandfather, but now there is a toll road to the saddle near the top which can be reached by a mile-high swinging bridge.

There are hundreds of other peaks in Western North Carolina with distinct personalities like the Old Man, many easily accessible, others that you must view at a distance.

To the south of the Old Man, as you drive along the Blue Ridge Parkway, Hawk's Bill juts out of Jonas Ridge, leaving the impression you have just heard his scream.

Somehow, when I look upon Hawk's Bill I have a crazy desire to take a shot at this stone bird.

In the personality class, Whiteside Mountain in the Cashiers-Highlands area along U.S. 64 dominates his region like Grandfather.

Whiteside stands like a giant sentinel, with one side a sheer cliff dropping 1,400 feet into the valley below.

Farther west along U.S. 64 between Franklin and Hayesville is Standing Indian, a stalwart warrior turned to stone, according to Cherokee legend, because while stationed as a lookout he fled his post.

Teyahalee towers over the town of Robbinsville and in winter when snow blankets the peak it takes on the appearance of Fujiyama.

Wayah Bald near Franklin resembles a bride with flowers in her hair when seen during the summer decked in a profusion of azalea, rhododendron and laurel.

The Roan, northwest of Bakersville, is a mountain of contrasts.

Near its southwestern extremity there is a body of rocks that resembles the ruins of an old castle.

Dr. Elisha Mitchell, who lost his life exploring the tallest peak in the Appalachians that now bears his name, described the Roan as "the most beautiful of all the high mountains."

Strangely enough, many peaks in the Balsam and Cherokee area resemble human figures.

Two perfect busts of Indian warriors are plainly visible from U.S. 19-A northeast of Sylva and from U.S. 19 southeast of Cherokee.

Known as the Pinnacle, the peak near Sylva resembles an Indian in repose, silhouetted against the sky, and there are some who say it is Jutaculla, the mythical god of the Cherokee.

Just as you leave Soco Valley and begin the climb toward Soco Gap on U.S. 19, if you look sharply to a great overhanging of rock to your right at the first curve there is a great stone face.

Pisgah, near Asheville, is a quiet, conservative peak that stands like an inspiration, named for the Biblical mountain.

Peaks that need no explanation are Chunky Gal Mountain in the Nantahalas, Cattail Peak in Yancey, Potato Knob in Buncombe, Yellow Face in Jackson, and Big Hogback in Transylvania.

There are 223 peaks in Western North Carolina that range from 5,000 feet to over 6,600 feet.

Each has its individual characteristic, each its lure for one certain person.

There is none of the sudden spectacular of the peaks of the West about them, but once seen there is something about them that forever holds them to your mind.

Perhaps it is because they seem a little more human.

Like Grandfather, the Old Man.

Horn Lured Dan'l Boone

Boone

SOMETIMES WHEN YOU STAND ATOP HOWARD'S KNOB there's a haunting echo in the wind that comes skirling across the high mountains, like a horn blowing in the west.

There are some who say that Dan'l Boone heard it and trailed its promise of freedom and wingroom until the day he died.

You see, this is Boone country.

A half dozen states proudly boast that the frontiersman nonpareil once lived within their borders, but North Carolina was the home of his boyhood, his young manhood and where he chose a wife.

For nine years—from 1760 to 1769—he lived in a cabin in the heart of what is now the town of Boone.

From this cabin, which was built by Benjamin Howard, Dan'l hunted the surrounding mountains for bear and elk, buffalo and deer, with a long rifle-gun he called Tick-Licker.

This, too, was the jumping off place for his trips into the wild, lush lands of Kentucky from which he returned each time with tales folks didn't want to believe but Dan'l had hides to prove some of them.

Kentucky, Boone said, was a land where the meadows were like velvet and the black loam went right down to China.

He said it was the Promised Land.

A lot of folks will argue that Dan'l had been living in the Promised Land right here in the Watauga highlands and just couldn't seem to recognize it.

First, he had lived just a little way across the mountain to the south and east at Holman's Ford near the Yadkin River.

But folks got to pushing in on him, and, too, he kept hearing that sound in the wind which, along with the westering sun, sort of kept luring him across one mountain and then another.

Yet this was the spot that almost kept him.

He came here and started camping out in Howard's cabin until folks got to calling it Boone's cabin.

Howard had built it for herders who watched over his cattle that grazed in the lush valley fast under Howard's Knob, a valley that was destined to grow into a town and a monument to Dan'l in more ways than one.

Using the cabin as a base for operations, Dan'l that first year ventured a short piece over into what is now Tennessee and made a mark every school boy has come to know.

For it was there in the deep forest across the mountains from here after Tick-Licker had spoken that he carved upon a beech tree:

D. Boone
Cilled a Bar
On Tree
In Year 1760.

It became a part of the legend of Dan'l Boone, and in years to come folks would claim the tree and its crude markings for many spots in many places.

But the tree lived long enough to establish the true claim of Tennessee.

It stood on the old stage road between Blountsville and Jonesboro until 1916, the scars of Dan'l's knife carvings still visible.

When it fell, the National Park Service estimated that it was 365 years old, more than two centuries in age when Dan'l carved his famous words on the seventy-foot tree that was some twenty-eight feet around.

Dan'l used to say that all a man needed to get along was a good gun, a good horse, a good wife. He had all three.

When he had come back from one of his trips into the wild blue yonder, somebody asked him if he had ever been lost.

"No, I can't say as ever I was lost," he replied, "but I was bewildered once for three days."

In all his travels into the uncharted wilderness he never carried a compass.

It was John Finley, a Scotch-Irishman who had descended the Ohio River as far as Louisville in 1752, that actually set Dan'l off on axing the Wilderness Trail.

Finley showed up at Dan'l's house at Holman's Ford in 1768 and persuaded the frontiersman to blaze a trail through Cumberland Gap to Kentucky.

So with a party, Dan'l started out from Holman's Ford.

The trail followed the old Shawnee Path on the ridge between Elk and Stony Forks through Cooks Gap, down by Three Forks of New River, through what is now Boone and Hodges Gap, across the Grave Yard gap down to Dog Skin Creek, following the base of Rich Mountain to State Line Gap between Zionville and Trade to the head of Roan Creek and thence over the Iron Mountains.

It wasn't long after that Dan'l came back, packed up his family and moved off to Kentucky.

But he has not been forgotten here.

There are many things to remind you that this was first his stomping grounds.

The location of the Boone cabin is appropriately marked by a monument erected in 1912 which rests on stones taken from the chimney of the cabin.

There is a hotel and an outdoor theatre that bears his name.

And, of course, the town.

But there is something even more significant.

It is the story of Dan'l Boone that is told here each summer, from late June through early September, in Daniel Boone Theatre which stands on the very site where the frontiersman once camped and where his trail ran from Holman's Ford on toward the west.

You can hear that horn there, too, an echoing blast that shouts the title of the Boone story, *Horn In The West.*

And a voice speaking old Dan'l's words:

"*. . . And yet it's more'n that—like a horn of freedom blowing in the west. Seems like I always want to keep goin' into the sunset.*"

The Eternal Flame of Friendship

Cherokee

THE FLAME THAT BURNS ON A HILLSIDE ABOVE THIS VILLAGE will burn as long as man lives and as long as man does not forget.

It flared into being more than a hundred years ago when a race of people had been broken, brought low, and cast out.

But it burns today as a shining symbol that man can forgive and forget.

It burns as a promise of eternal friendship between the red man and the white man.

There is not another monument like it in all the land.

It is called the Eternal Flame, and it burns in a rustic stone mound just inside the entrance to Mountainside Theatre where the epic story of the Cherokee Indian is told in the drama, *Unto These Hills*, each summer from late June through early September.

The theatre is always open and hundreds of thousands of visitors stop by to see the flame, yet few of them know its story and how it came into being.

It is a story you won't find in the history books, although it is one of the great true stories of America.

But, if the flame could talk, this is the story it would tell . . .

The Cherokee had been broken, brought low, and cast out.

And now, in the forest of Tennessee, they paused—a ragged, sorrowing remnant of a once proud and powerful nation, its people stunned by the deceit and greed of the white man and the white man's way of taking what he wanted.

They paused and they prayed. Some—the Christians—prayed to the white man's God. Others prayed to their own gods of a thousand years and beyond—the sun and the moon and the stars.

Behind them towered the Great Smokies, a vast range of timbered peaks that were ancient when history was new.

These mountains were the heartland of the Cherokee Nation.

These mountains had been the sanctuary of the Indians beyond the dates and records and memory of man.

But the white man had taken them with rifle and false promise, and now the Cherokee, except for a mere thousand hiding out in those mountains and sworn to die rather than leave their homeland, were on their way into exile.

Ahead lay a 1,200-mile trail destined to become the saddest in America, a road of misery and heartache, sickness and death.

And when the survivors reached its end there in the rolling hills of Oklahoma, they would call it Nunna-da-ul-tsun-yi—the trail where they cried.

More than seventeen thousand Cherokee had been rounded up by U.S. Army troops under command of General Winfield Scott for the tragic exodus, uprooted and dispossessed from their lands and homes in Western North Carolina, Tennessee, Georgia and Alabama.

And now, as the first company of Cherokee prepared to start the long march into exile, the Cherokee chiefs met in solemn council for the last time in their old homeland.

They met at a place called Rattlesnake Spring, in the forest of Tennessee. The time was late September of 1838 and soon the busk moon, harvest lantern of the Cherokee, would be bowling across the sky above the Great Smokies but the fruit of Cherokee crops would wither and decay in the fields.

From New Echota in Georgia, the fallen capital of the Cherokee Nation, had come the care-taker of the tribe's sacred fire, and there in the twilight he built the council fire for the last gathering of the chiefs in the land of their birth.

From a leather pouch lined with green moss he took a clam shell filled with smouldering punk, wood decayed by some fungus.

Gathering a handful of leaves and then a few twigs, he fed the fire little by little until it was ready for the seven different kinds of wood that tribal ritual ordained must be used.

Onto the fire went blackjack, locust, post oak, sycamore, red bud, plum and red oak.

Then Going Snake, a respected chief whose head eighty summers had whitened, walked slowly about the fire and made his offering of old-man's tobacco, a supplication to the Red Man's god to protect his people on their journey.

Ages had come and gone in the shaping of this symbolic ceremonial, and now it was being performed in the Cherokee country for perhaps the last time.

By ones and twos the chiefs assembled about the fire. In their midst sat the principal chief, John Ross, the mixed-blood scion of a famous Scottish trading family, whose great-grandson was destined to be born in the Carolina hills and become a vice-chief of the tribe.

In the quiet of the forest, the wind ruffed the leaves and the old warriors, some who saved the day for Andrew Jackson at the Battle of Horseshoe Bend, mayhaps heard the faint throbbing of a finger-drum.

But it was only the wind, for the finger-drum was for warriors and the Cherokee had ceased to be warriors.

Yet as they sat there smoking shallow bowls of Indian clay and waiting for John Ross to speak they perhaps were remembering backward and planning forward and hoping a little.

Then John Ross spoke and this is what he said:

"The title of the Cherokee people to their lands is the most ancient, pure and absolute known to man. Its date is beyond the reach of human record. Its validity is confirmed by possession and enjoyment antecedent to all pretense of claim by any portion of the human race."

He paused, and somewhere in the stillness there was the voice of the hidden thrush, talking there with the Giver of Breath.

"The free consent of the Cherokee people is indispensable to a valid transfer of the Cherokee title. The Cherokee people have neither by themselves nor their representatives given such consent. It follows that the original title and ownership of said lands still rests in the Cherokee Nation, unimpaired and absolute.

"The Cherokee people have existed as a distinct national community for a period extending into antiquity beyond the dates and records and memory of man. These attributes have never been relinquished by the Cherokee people, and cannot be dissolved by the expulsion of the Nation from its own territory by the power of the United States Government."

His words went into a resolution and the chiefs adopted it, the last official act of the Cherokee Nation on the soil of their homeland but one that would be pigeon-holed in Washington like so many others.

The fire had burned down to a few glowing embers when the council adjourned and the chiefs turned to the shelter of the forest to lay their blankets and their bodies for the last time upon the earth that had been theirs.

But the caretaker of the sacred fire still sat there and, from time to time throughout the long night, fed split canes to the glowing embers.

The dawn came in gray and brooding and great clouds lumbered up from the southwest. Dozens of tiny fires sprang up through the encampment and soon there was the smell of coffee boiling and bacon frying in the air.

At last came the heart-stabbing order to break camp and begin the long march into exile.

Old Going Snake mounted his favorite pony and, as he moved to the head of the disarrayed column, there was a low sound of distant thunder but the sun was unclouded and no rain fell.

Behind him the sick, the old, and the smaller children, with blankets, cooking pots and other belongings, rode the wagons and the carts. The others trailed along on foot or on horseback.

The caretaker of the sacred fire had once more filled his clam shell with punk which now was smouldering, and he, too, started on the long journey, carrying the fire of his people to their new home.

They traveled through the Cumberlands, up through Kentucky, across Illinois, into Missouri, then Arkansas, and finally into Indian Territory.

The journey had taken six months, and more than four thousand had died along the trail, to be buried in unmarked graves in strange and alien soil.

They settled there in the hills of what is now Oklahoma, but it was strange and unfamiliar country. The mountains of home were a thousand miles and forever away.

All they had were their memories—and their fire.

Back in the Carolina hills, a thousand Cherokee were hiding out, and eventually they were permitted to remain. The Cherokee who live here now are their descendants.

Over the years the Cherokee in Oklahoma tended the fire they had carried from their old homeland.

In 1951, the Cherokee Historical Association sent an expedition, led by four tribal leaders, on a historic journey to retrace the "Trail of Tears."

While in Oklahoma they heard of the fire which was being kept alive in the Blackgum Mountains.

I was on the expedition and we drove deep into the isolated

hill country where few strangers ever go, and there we learned that the fire was being kept alive in at least three places in those hills.

We found the fire in the Red Bird Smith community.

Stoke Smith, a full-blooded Cherokee medicine man and caretaker of the fire, told us its history and how the fire is still used in ceremonies.

When the medicine ceremonies are held each fourth Saturday the fire is brought to the ceremonial grounds where a big fire is built, using the sacred seven kinds of wood.

Participants in the ceremonial fast for twenty-four hours before the fire at the ceremonial grounds is lighted.

"In offering our prayers," Smith explained, "we feed white chickens to the fire. The white deer should be used but it is against the law. Sometimes we use white rabbits or squirrels. Some white people think they are symbols of white people but they are not."

Smith was reluctant to talk about the fire and the ceremonies to me, but he talked at great length with the four tribal leaders from Cherokee.

They talked in Cherokee, which I did not understand, and only the things that he wanted me to know were translated by Arsene Thompson.

Smith said that "God told Solomon that He would be up in heaven and that He would answer Solomon's prayer with fire—that's why we have fire."

After much negotiation, the four tribal leaders from Cherokee were permitted to bring live coals from the fire back to their own homeland.

They filled an alumnium bucket lined with asbestos with charcoal which had been placed in the fire. On the homeward journey they kept feeding new charcoal into the bucket to keep the coals alive.

Once home, in ceremonies at Mountainside Theatre, a pine torch was lighted from the charcoal embers. Then the pine torch was used to ignite a flambeau fed by bottled gas.

This flambeau is encased in stone and fireproof glass so that it never will go out. And there are always two bottles of gas, so that when one becomes empty the other automatically begins feeding the flame.

The flame came into being here when former Chief Henry Bradley and Chairman Harry E. Buchanan of the Cherokee Historical Association ignited the gas jet with the pine torch and dedicated the memorial to "friendship eternal between the white man and the red man."

Thus, a flame that had been carried out of the old Cherokee homeland more than a hundred years before was returned to burn as a blazing symbol that men of two races can live side by side in friendship and peace.

A Story For Mother's Day

Allen's Creek

THEY CALL HER THE MADONNA OF THE BALSAMS, THE mother of the mountains.

She is the most famous midwife in all the land.

And tomorrow, when every mother is a Queen of Hearts, the hundreds of children that Sarah McNabb has brought into the world will pause to pay tribute to her.

She is in retirement now, but for more than forty years she followed the stork wherever it flew.

It's easy to find the home of this fine looking mountain woman who, at eighty-six, has a strong, appealing, sensitive face and who, as she whispers something wise and something humorous into your ear, reminds you of all the mothers in the world.

Inquire of any mountain man, woman or child if you get lost after you turn south from Hazelwood up Allen's Creek and they will put you straight.

Sarah McNabb brought one or two, or all three of them into the world.

She is "Mother" McNabb to them.

She lives in a weathered frame house that is as old as the story of her service to the mothers of the mountains.

The wind sings in the trees along the creek and there's the laughter of children in the land.

"They are some of the ones I brought into the world," Sarah McNabb says. "They are my children."

She has only memories now, but they are wondrous memories.

And as she sits on her porch and rocks away the time, she can look back and know that she was a heroine at least once a month for more than forty years.

"How many babies have I brought into the world? Two hundred, three hundred, five hundred. More than that, I guess. But what does it matter? I always went when called and that is what counts on the Book.

"Not once in all my life," she will tell you, "have I failed to go when called. I feel like God gave me that as my mission on this earth. He gave me strength to rise, even when ill, and do my duty."

And then she whispers a secret, glancing about to see that her daughter does not hear.

"A few years ago I broke both hips and was bed-ridden. My bed was there in the front room near the fire. The others were sleeping in one of the back rooms. Well, one night one of the neighbors up the creek came and begged me to go to his wife.

"Here I was a-bed and could hardly move, but he said he would carry me. So he lifted me out of bed and wrapped me up and carried me out to his car and I went and delivered a baby. He brought me back and the folks here never did know I went out. They don't know it yet."

Nothing ever stayed her from her mission.

She went on foot and on horseback, by wagon and by mule, and at times behind oxen.

The remarkable thing about Sarah McNabb's work is that she never lost a single child or its mother in all the years she was "catching babies."

"But I am not responsible for that," she explains. "A Higher Power is always present at so great an event as birth. It is my firm conviction that Divine assistance is always at hand at the coming of another into the world."

Whenever she crossed her threshold on a mission of mercy she went with a prayer on her lips.

"I asked God to use my strength, my hand, my knowledge to supplement His will, and I continued to pray until I beheld the living, breathing result brought forth in all its loveliness."

Sarah McNabb is a deeply religious woman and she was instrumental in founding the Rocky Branch Free Will Baptist Church. You can find her there any Sunday, in good weather or bad.

"God," she will tell you, "made it possible for me to be so successful in my work. The bringing of babies into the world was a talent that God gave me. I had no education, only what God gave me."

The work she has done in the hills is as fine and as unselfish a piece of true American endeavor as has ever been done in the mountains of any land.

Through the years, Sarah McNabb worked in a land almost without transportation. A land where the women knew the meaning of suffering.

For more than half her life, through rain or snow, day or night, she has been at the beck and call of her sisters in travail.

Herself mountain born, Sarah McNabb knew years ago what those women of the mountain sections of Allen's Creek, Quinlantown, Lickstone Mountain and the Balsams were enduring in agony whenever they brought children into the world.

She knew what went on when young mothers of fourteen and old mothers of twenty came to their hour. Lives hung in the balance.

And Sarah McNabb knew the hills.

So, she saw that life came into the world—life in the form of a bouncing boy or girl. She saw to it that each lived.

"That was my duty," she says. "It was my mission upon the earth. I carried out that mission until I could no longer go. I hope I fulfilled it. Nobody can say I didn't go when I was called."

She is quick to tell you that she was merely an instrument to perform a needed service in the mountains, when the midwife was the most important person in the hills.

Sarah McNabb was born here in the mountains, a short piece from here on Pigeon River. At twenty she was married. At forty-two she had been blessed with ten children, and the years since have brought her forty grandchildren, thirty great-grandchildren, and six great-great-grandchildren.

"I brought all of them into the world," she says with pride.

When she was thirty-five she registered in Raleigh as a midwife.

"But I began catching babies when my own were little," she is quick to explain. "Why many's the time I put my small ones up on the horse behind me and went off to help one of my sisters."

She is proud of her record with the State Board of Health.

"I never registered anything but Grade A on my tests," she said. "Dr. Sam Stringfield—he's dead now—said I was the best midwife in the whole state."

Until a few years ago she was a familiar figure on the streets of nearby Waynesville at Christmas-time.

The folks of Waynesville called her the "Christmas Wreath Lady" because of the beautiful wreaths she wove out of balsam fir and holly sprigs.

"I made wreaths in lots of a hundred for Mr. James McClure of the Farmers Federation in Asheville," she said. "I recall once one of his men came to the house when I was about half way through with one lot of wreaths.

"He asked me what I would do if somebody came for me to deliver a baby before I finished the wreaths. I told him I'd just lay the wreaths aside and go.

"What about all that money you would lose, he said, and I told him money had no price when one of my sisters needed me."

For a moment she was silent, and she looked beyond the creek and into space.

"I loved them mothers and them babies," she said. "And I want the mothers and the children and their children's children to know that my life is glorified because of theirs."

Years ago she had expressed a wish that she could shape her destiny "so that even upon the day of my passing it will be possible for me to assist at bringing into this world life."

"But I reckon," she says now, "that my days of catching babies is over. With my legs and back in such shape as they are, I think too much of them women to do it."

Night had come on as we talked.

A great-grandchild toddled in and climbed chortling to the haven that is ever open to children.

The wind still sang in the trees along the creek and there was still the laughter of children in the wind.

A Man With Tales to Tell

Bryson City

GRANVILLE CALHOUN IS A MOUNTAIN MAN WITH TALES TO tell.

He is the last of the old time hunters and trappers and guides who ranged the Great Smokies when this was a wild and isolated country.

He is an encyclopedia of memories.

He talks in slow words and there is a hint of nostalgia in his conversation.

The years have made a mellow mask of his face. Wind and rain and sun, and the snows of eighty winters, have etched it into a study by Rockwell.

There is a spring in his step and he carries himself tall and straight, a hint of muscles that once were as tough and stringy as the vines of the wild muscadine.

His eyes are as bright as a dream of tomorrow. But when he talks of the men he knew, woodsmen and hunters like Mark Cathey, a far-away look comes into them and they retreat into a time and a place in which only those of his generation had a part.

"This was great hunting country in those days," he said. "A man could hunt just about everything—bear and deer and wild turkey and squirrel."

He shifted in his chair there on the porch of the Calhoun House, and the winds of approaching autumn were beginning to tiptoe down from the high peaks of the Smokies.

Soon the peaks would be turning to red and yellow and brown and it would be bear-hunting time here in Western North Carolina, but not in the Great Smokies where Granville made his kills for years, for the Smokies are now a national preserve where hunting is not allowed.

"The best hunting there ever was," he said, "was back there in the Smokies on Hazel Creek and the country beyond. Once I killed three on a single day's hunt.

"They were big bear then. I killed one that weighed over six hundred pounds. Some said it was the biggest bear ever killed in the Smokies. I don't know. But I do know that the scales wouldn't weigh it. The scales we had only drug five hundred pounds and the scales hit the top mark and almost broke.

"I remember one time when me and my father-in-law, Crate Hall, went out one November to hunt some cattle that had got lost in the Smokies.

"We had a cabin up on top of the Smokies, right on the Tennessee line. We hunted the gorges and finally got up there to the cabin where we found some neighbor boys camping in. Shortly after we got there some fellers from over in Tennessee showed up. There was ten of us.

"We all had our rifles and we decided we'd have a hunt the next day. Everybody wanted a good bear fight. We didn't have much food. So we decided we'd go out the next day and shoot anything we saw and get a store of food before we had a bear fight.

"Next morning everybody left camp with the understanding everybody would bring in something. I went about two miles and run into a flock of twenty wild turkeys. It was the biggest bunch I ever saw. I killed six of them in about an hour. They weighed between sixteen and twenty pounds a-piece, all I could carry.

"We had all agreed to come into camp by four o'clock that afternoon, so if somebody happened to get lost, which wasn't rare in that wilderness, we'd still have some daylight left to hunt them.

"After I killed the turkeys, I went on about looking for the lost cattle and then showed up at the camp on time.

"All the fellows got back on time and we had the biggest bunch of game I ever saw brought in at one time. We had eleven turkeys, a dozen squirrels, a whole raft of pheasants, a bear, a deer, a groundhog and a coon.

"Well, we had a good feast that night and the next morning we all set out on a bear hunt. Some of the fellers had dogs and we looked forward to a good bear fight."

Granville paused and began laughing.

"But the joke was on us that day. We never saw a single bear or even heard one in the brush. We didn't kill a thing. Reckon word got passed around among the bear and other animals that a bunch of true shooters was in the mountains and they all high-tailed it for parts unknown and holed in."

Granville told of other hunts and how he guided Horace Kephart, the writer, all over the Smokies and "taught him all he knew about hunting and camping."

Then he mentioned Mark Cathey.

"Guess you've heard tell of Mark," he said. "Now there was a man who knew the Smokies like they were the palm of his hand. I hunted and fished all over the Smokies with Mark, right up to the time he died several years ago.

"Mark was born down on Indian Creek and spent most of his life there. Mark was older than me and he spent most of his life in the woods. Was out in the woods with his rifle when he died. He was out hunting squirrels and just set down on a log, his rifle across his lap, and his heart gave out. That's the way they found him and that's the way he would have wanted to go.

"Mark was quite a character. I reckon there's more stories about Mark than any man who ever lived in these mountains. I remember a funny experience Mark had with a feller that come in from some far away place to do a bit of fishing.

"This feller that Mark took fishing was all decked out in boots and duck-backs and had the finest fishing equipment money could buy. He had a box full of flies and artificial bait and he had a Bowie knife on his belt.

"They was up on Deep Creek fishing and they had been fishing for some time and neither one had landed anything. Finally, Mark heard a shout from this feller down stream. He shouted he had got a fish. When Mark got to him, the feller had reeled in an eight-inch trout right up to the tip of his pole and was just standing there.

" 'I've caught a fish,' he told Mark and then said, 'What do I do next?'

"Mark thought a minute, then said, 'Mister, if I was you, I'd climb that pole and stob him.'

"Another time, Mark was out on a hunting trip with a bunch of the fellers from around here and they was camped up in the Smokies. Mark had just got himself some new store-bought teeth. There was a feller named Fons Hollifield who also had just got some new store-bought teeth.

"Well, along about sundown, Mark and Fons walked down to the spring near the camp where some of the boys had a jug of peartening juice.

"Mark and Fons decided to take out their store-bought teeth and put 'em on a stump for the night so as to give their gums a rest. That they did and then went on back to camp.

"Some of the other fellers thought they'd have some fun. They switched the plates on the stump, putting Mark's where Fons' was and moving Fons' where Mark's had been.

"Next morning, Mark was up early and washed up at the spring. When he finally walked back into camp he was whittling on a set of teeth. Somebody asked him what he was doing.

" 'Hit ain't funny,' Mark said. 'My teeth shrunk on me last night and I'm tryin' to make 'em fit.'

"Another time, Mark was on a big hunt up on top of the Smokies. There was about fifty or so fellers on the hunt. They was in the Hall cabin and they had got snowbound.

"Mark cooked the meals for three days with one frying pan and a coffee pot and slept on a pile of potatoes. He had a time keeping them fellers fed on what rations they had.

"Somebody asked Mark how cold it was. He went to the door, opened it and went outside for a minute. When he come back in he said he couldn't rightly tell how cold it was because when he hung the thermometer on a nail on the cabin wall outside the mercury dropped so fast it jerked the nail right out of the wall."

Granville chuckled. "Yes, sir," he said. "Mark was quite a feller. And those were the good old days."

Then he was silent for a long time.

"The last big hunt I was on was back in 1946," Granville said. "That was when the TVA took over all my property and I had to move out. But I reserved the right to hunt that fall and I invited all my friends for one last big bear hunt in the Smokies.

"The first day we run sixteen bear and killed three. Reckon there was fifty or seventy-five shots fired that first day of the hunt. Next day we killed two and before the season was over twenty-seven had been killed on Hazel Creek.

"I've still got my bear-huntin' gun," he said. "It's hanging on the wall in there. It's seen its day in my hands, but I can remember. . . ."

He looked off toward the high peaks of the Smokies where the winds of coming autumn were beginning to tiptoe down into the valley.

The sun lay shadows along the street and on the buildings, and the old man leaned back in his rocking chair.

"Yes," he said, "the bear will be runnin' before too long."

The Vanishing Gristmill

Bunches Creek

PERHAPS SOME DAY SOMEBODY WILL GET AROUND TO properly recognizing the role the old water gristmill played during the age of our homespun economy.

Such recognition is long overdue and, unless the historians get busy, future generations never will know the history and romance of the gristmill and the folks who made it a sort of frontier mecca.

About the only monument it ever got was fashioned by a young feller who wooed and won the miller's daughter down by an old water mill on the Hiwassee River and, returning many years later when they both were aged and gray, wrote *When You And I Were Young, Maggie.*

Few of the old time water mills are left, and freshly water-ground corn meal is getting to be as rare as sourwood honey and leather britches beans.

But here on Bunches Creek, in the high reaches of the Great Smokies, is a water mill that has been grinding out corn meal for more than half a century.

Wallace Bradley, an 82-year-old mountain man, built the mill shortly after he established his homestead on the creek back in '98 and set out to make his place provide for all the needs of his family.

He felled trees and sawed boards for the mill house. The mill-stones were cut right on the spot. He channeled water from a small but rapid stream to the wheel in a race made of green boards.

As the water shot over the wheel and turned it, crude cogs of wooden pegs on the other end of the shaft meshed with similar cogs in the upper stone and did the grinding.

"I got plumb tired of seeing my wife pounding corn into meal with mortar and pestle," the old man explained, "so I built a mill. But she wouldn't let me throw that homemade corn pounder away. She's still got it and whenever special company comes she uses it.

"You asked where I got my millstones. Well, I got 'em right here in the yard. One was cut right over there in the branch and the other was cut right there at my mailbox.

"I had a feller who was sort of helping me about the place when I decided to build my mill. He was a number one stonemaster. He'd cut stones all his life, he told me, and he said he would cut me a pair real cheap. I told him all right but asked him where he was going to get the stone.

"Well, he looked at me kind of funny like and said, 'Why you've got the best mill stone here I ever saw,' and began pointin' it out to me.

"He was shore a stonemaster. He cut mill-stones for Aden Carver and Ike Reagan. I reckon he cut 'em for others but I just don't recollect who.

"Eh? What kind of stone does it take? Why, all this you see about the yard here is superprime mill-stone. All of it's fine gray stone—never gets slick. They's just enough hailstones in it.

"Hailstones? Why, that's them little gray flecks you see imbedded in the big stone, sort of like stars they are. It takes little fine hailstones to do a job of cutting."

The old man walked off above the house and pointed with his stick to a big slab of stone buried in the earth with only the surface above ground.

"Now, this here one was a dandy for a millstone," he said, "but I had to build a fire on it one time, so when it come time to cut my millstones I told this stonemaster I was afraid it would crack and we'd better not use it. Reckon we should've used it. Never has cracked. Still, you can't tell what turn a rock will take when you start cuttin' it.

"My bedstone—that's the bottom rock—is a big'un. It'd take two or three men just to turn it over and chip it with mill picks. No, don't reckon you've ever had occasion to know nothin' 'bout a mill pick. I've got several of them around here some place."

He called to his wife, who was sitting on the porch, and asked her to fetch him one. She did. It resembled a miniature coal miner's pick. About eight inches long and an inch wide, thick through the middle and thinning out to a wide sharp point at each end.

"You take one of these mill picks," he said, hefting it, "and chip the face of your stone, cuttin' furrors or ridges in it just like my fingers. Them furrors is what grinds up the corn when it's fed in between the stones. You see, one turns one way so them ridges mashes and grinds the corn into meal.

"I made all my mill picks right here in my own blacksmith shop. Now, it ain't just everybody that can make a mill pick. I reckon one of the best mill pick makers there ever lived was old man Joshua Gibbs. He lived over near Whittier and he was a preacher and a carpenter as well as a blacksmith. Guess you know his son, Hanley, over at Whittier. Well, old man Gibbs could make a millstone pick or a razor. He could sure put a true edge on anything he ground. You know, you have to sharpen a mill pick with a stone."

The old man said he couldn't rightly calculate how many bushels of corn he had ground during his lifetime.

"It's been a lot, I'll tell you. Reckon if I had all the corn meal I've ground I wouldn't have no place to put it and I'd be walkin' in it kneedeep.

"You say you've heard that millers don't like to grind rye or buckwheat? Well, you heard right. And I'll tell you why. You put a run of rye or buckwheat through your mill and it'll ruin the taste of the next corn you grind. Rye or buckwheat is mean to clean out of the mill.

"It takes a good peck of corn to clean the mill after you grind buckwheat. You can't hardly get it all out of there. It goes in and backs up against the log and just keeps a-packin' there on the hub and sometimes there'll be a whole gallon of the stuff in there."

Since he built his mill primarily for his own use, he could do as he pleased. If he wanted to grind buckwheat, he ground buckwheat. The same way with rye.

"I never fussed too much with folks if they happened to bring a turn of buckwheat or rye. Knew they wouldn't have brought it for grinding 'less they needed it ground."

He recalled the story of a boy who once went to a neighbor's mill and had to sit around most of the day waiting his turn. It seems the boy didn't think too much of this mill, which was grinding pretty slow.

After silently regarding the tiny stream of meal dribbling out, the boy looked up at the miller and remarked:

"Reckon I could eat the meal as fast as your mill can grind it. Yep, I'm shore I could."

The miller grunted.

"Well, how long could you eat it?"

"Until I starved to death," replied the boy.

There were not too many gristmills in the mountains back in those days, although there are even fewer today.

But there was one then not too far from folks in every community. Some didn't have far to travel, while others had to travel as much as twenty miles by horse with a turn of corn.

Sometimes it was necessary to stay a day and a night to get the work done. With numbers of folks waiting for their grist, the mill became a social center of the entire region for the male inhabitants.

Some who didn't have corn to be ground showed up to talk politics and religion, swap knives and have some fun in general.

Turns of corn usually were brought on horseback. But some used sleds whose runners were made of sourwood crooks.

If some feller showed up with a turn of corn that was particularly shot through with red grains, someone would usually come up with the stock saying, "A red grain in the grist will stop the mill." For red grains of corn are harder than white ones.

"Red grained corn never seemed to bother my mill none," old man Bradley said. "Them stones of mine could handle anything."

He stood gazing at his mill for a moment.

"It's standin' there, as you can see," he said finally. "Just as good as ever, but I'm goin' to sell it one of these days. I'm gettin' too old and I ain't able to fool with it much any more. Somebody'll come along one of these days wantin' the millstones, any way."

And when they do, another landmark of our homespun economy will disappear into the limbo of forgotten memories.

Other Springs in Other Years

Sylva

THE OLD MAN WALKED THROUGH THE SPRING MORNING telling his grandson of other springs in other years.

There was a spryness in his step that belied his ninety-six years, and he had somehow managed to forget his cane when he left the house.

The cane is a burden for the old man that has been pressed upon him by his daughter and his grandson in their worry for him.

To him it is a symbol of winter rains and the season of snow, and of men who doubt that the sun always comes back again.

Canes and rocking-chairs and shawls all are of a same pattern, each a part of the same symbol, from which the old man shies like a spring colt.

Who, the old man argues, needs a cane when there is sun and spring has come again with soft mists in her hair and a warm wind in her mouth and budding everywhere.

Only the old, the very old, need a cane, and the old man will not admit that he is old.

So, as he walked through the spring morning, he talked of how spring used to come to the mountains and how it was a time of the earth stretching and folks being about the job of planting.

Spring, the old man said, was a time for turning the stock loose to range in the mountains until November when they would be driven in, fat and sleek.

It was a time of clearing the land and a time of plowing.

It was a time of going bare-footed and a time for camp meetings.

It was a time for the peddler with his needles and tin wares to start his rounds.

It was a time for the cobbler to come by and mend shoes.

The whole family, the old man said, worked from sun-up to sun-down.

In clearing new ground, everyone followed the ancient custom of girdling the tree trunks.

This was a quick and easy way to get rid of the shade that otherwise would stunt the crops.

An area of girdled trees was known as a "deadening."

The shrubs and brush were dug out with a heavy grubbing hoe.

These, together with the limbs cut from the felled trees, were piled up by the women and children.

Sometimes, on a windy day, fire was set to an area that was to be used for planting.

And sometimes the fire got out of hand and burned over wide areas, destroying the forest.

There are farmers today who still clear their land with fire.

Spring, the old man said, was a time when it looked like the whole world was on fire.

It was a way to kill off grass that no amount of hoeing would keep from strangling a crop.

The tillage was rude and destructive.

The common plow was a "bull-tongue," hardly more than a sharpened stick with a metal rim.

The harrows were of wood, with locust teeth.

Oxen were used to pull the plow.

After the corn was up, all cultivating was done with the hoe.

For this, the entire family turned out.

The farmer's wife took her place in the field, too.

She helped to plant, hoe corn, gather fodder.

Sometimes, she even walked behind a plow.

A woman's place back then, the old man said, was wherever there were things to be done that meant food for the family.

Corn was the main crop here in the mountains, although some wheat was grown.

But just enough wheat was grown to be used for making the much appreciated biscuits, gravy, and pastries.

Abody, said the old man, wanted to set a table with biscuits and fried chicken and gravy when the preacher came by for Sunday dinner.

Spring was a time, too, when the womenfolks gathered the shoots of Black Gum for tooth brushes.

And the boys made pop-guns and whistles from the elderberry trees along the creek.

The old man remembered how he had made pop-guns and whistles for his grandson when his grandson was only a tad-pole of a boy.

The grandson remembered, too.

Perhaps that was why their steps this spring day had led to the creek bank where the elderberry trees still grow.

And, as on another spring day long ago, the old man fished in his pocket and got out his pocketknife and cut a limb from an elderberry bush and began whittling.

Spring had come again.

The Ballad of Kidder Cole

Cashiers Valley

KIDDER COLE WAS THE BELLE OF THE MOUNTAINS.

A boy in homespun wrote a song about her to soothe a burning heart. It became the most famous banjo ballad in all the land.

He's a retired superior court judge now and Kidder Cole is dead, but the ballad is still remembered and played at square dances when the old-timers gather with fiddle and banjo.

Oh, my sweet little Kidder girl!
You cause my head to spin and whirl,
I am yours, and you are mine
Long as the sun and stars shall shine.

A ballad like "Kidder Cole" never does grow old.

Someday some tunester is going to rediscover it and it will become as popular as it was when Felix E. Alley wrote it sixty-five years ago.

He now lives in Waynesville, basking at eighty-two in the memories of a brilliant career as a lawyer and judge.

But now and then he returns to the valley where he loved and laughed and danced and played his banjo as a boy.

And when he does, the words that chronicle a boyhood romance must run through his mind . . . .

My name is Felix Eugene Alley
My best girl lives in Cashiers Valley;
She's the joy of my soul
And her name is Kidder Cole.

He wrote the ballad about her because he let another mountain youth beat his time. And it took 15 stanzas to soothe his burning heart.

I don't know—it must have been by chance,
'Way last fall when I went to a dance.
I was to dance with Kidder the livelong night
But got my time beat by Charley Wright.

Felix Alley was only sixteen at the time. Kidder Cole was about the same age. They were neighbors. Her father was a merchant and later high sheriff of the county.

It was only natural young Felix's eyes walked after Kidder Cole. She was the beauty of the mountains, and her beauty followed her through the years.

An all-night dance at the home of an Englishman named Grimshaw inspired the ballad. Later a post office was named for him. It was the smallest in the United States until it was closed in 1953.

Young Felix was late in arriving at the dance. And through the doorway he saw, to his bitter disappointment, that Kidder Cole had been claimed by his cousin, Charley Wright.

Charley was bigger than Felix, and he let it be known right away that Kidder had promised him all the dances that night.

"Before the night was over," Judge Alley recalled recently, "I had commenced composing the ballad. While Charley danced away the night with Kidder I reeled off stanza after stanza of the ballad."

If I ever have to have a fight
I hope it will be with Charley Wright;
For he was the ruin of my soul
When he beat my time with Kidder Cole.

Much of the ballad was written after he left the dance and in the months that followed.

When the dance was over I went away
To bide my time till another day,
When I could cause trouble and pain and blight
To sadden the soul of Charley Wright.

Just when he thought his "race was almost run," Kidder went off to South Carolina to school "and left me at home to act the fool."

But she came back the following spring
And oh, how I made my banjo ring;
It helped me get my spirit right,
To beat the time of Charley Wright.

Came the Fourth of July celebration and young Felix figured he would make another try.

Kidder came home the first of June,
And I sang my song and played my tune;
I commenced trying with all my might
To put one over on Charley Wright.

The celebration came and the banjos rang and the fiddles cried. And . . .

When the speaking was over we had a dance
And then and there I found my chance
To make my peace with Kidder Cole
And beat Charley Wright; confound his soul.

Charley came in an hour or so,
But when he saw me with Kidder he turned to go
Back to his home with a saddened soul,
For I'd beat his time with Kidder Cole.

The valley now rang with a new verse, a verse full of boast. . . .

I've always heard the old folks say
That every dog will have his day;
And now all of Charley's joy has passed,
For I've succeeded in beating him at last.

And still young Felix added to his ballad. . . .

Oh, yes, Kidder Cole is sweet;
And it won't be long until we meet
At her home in Cashiers Valley
And she'll change her name to Alley.

Now his ballad was sung, now his tune was ended.
Did he win the belle of the mountains?

"Why, no," said Judge Alley. "Neither Charley Wright nor I won the heart and hand of Kidder Cole, although the ballad indicates I was the lucky one. Youth is quite sure of love."

And although Charley Wright did not win the girl, either, he did win a Carnegie gold medal for bravery several years later. But that is another story.

Frankie Silvers

Kona

CROWNING A GENTLE HILL ABOVE THE PEACEFUL VALLEY is the burying ground where the Silvers have fetched their dead for a hundred years and more.

To the south rises Celo Mountain and far beyond hovers Mount Mitchell. Through the valley flows the Toe River, nursing the land young Jacob Silver staked out for a homestead before he went off to fight in the War of 1812.

At the head of the valley, a stone's throw from the burying ground, stands the two-story house of oak and poplar logs he grooved together and chinked with white clay.

It is probably the oldest inhabited house in all the mountain region. Passed on from father to son in unbroken succession, it has sheltered seven generations of the same family.

Here lived and died its builder at the age of ninety-six; its builder's father, George Silver, who served in the Revolution under Washington; and its builder's son, David, who fought for the Confederacy in the War Between the States.

They are buried in the little graveyard above the house.

Of Jacob's thirteen children, five came to untimely or tragic ends. Two sons died of typhoid fever. One was struck by lightning. Another was thrown from a mule and killed.

And there was Charlie, who was murdered by a jealous wife.

Charlie was one of the first of the Silvers to get a headstone whose markings are still legible.

He lived just across the ridge in Deyton Bend. He was only nineteen when he became the victim in one of the most sensational murders in state history.

On a night muffled by a great snow and blizzard in December

of 1831, Charlie's pretty, blonde wife, Frankie, chopped off his head while he lay on a pallet before the fire.

Before she swung the ax she had eased their sleeping baby from Charlie's arms without waking him.

Frankie dismembered the body and spent the long night feeding it to the flames but the evidence of her crime rose up to trap her and she was hanged at Morganton.

She left behind a legend and the unwanted distinction of being the only woman ever legally hanged in North Carolina.

While she was waiting her date with the hangman, Frankie's kinfolks spirited her out of the Morganton jail and carried her through the streets of the Burke County town in a load of hay.

They had tried to give her a disguise by outfitting her in a man's suit and hat.

Once outside of town, Frankie crawled out of the hay and started tramping along behind the wagon.

But she and her kin were surprised by the sudden approach of a sheriff's posse and she couldn't make it back to her hiding place in the hay.

The sheriff rode up alongside her and spoke the one word, "Frankie."

"My name is Tommy," she replied in the deepest possible voice.

Then her uncle, who was riding the wagon, spoke up.

"Yes, her name is Tommy," he said.

As the sheriff jerked his eyes from the uncle to Frankie, she said hurriedly:

"You want to buy some hay?"

"No. We don't want hay," answered the sheriff. "But we do want you, Frankie."

She was returned to the Burke County jail. And during the last days of her imprisonment she contrived a long, gloomy poem. There are some who say she recited it from the scaffold before her execution on the morning of July 12, 1833.

Be that as it may, a countryside familiar with the dramatic story seized upon the words of the poem and turned it into a ballad.

This is the poem Frankie recited from the gallows:

On one dark and dreary night
I put his body out of sight.
To see his soul and body part
It strikes with terror to my heart.

I took his blooming days away,
Left him no time to God to pray,
And if sins fall on his head
Must I not bear them in his stead?

The jealous thought that first gave strife
To make me take my husband's life.
For days and months I spent my time
Thinking how to commit this crime.

And on a dark and doleful night
I put his body out of sight;
With flames I tried him to consume
But time would not admit it done.

You all see me and on me gaze—
Be careful how you spend your days
And ne'er commit this awful crime,
But try to serve your God in time.

Judge Daniel has my sentence passed
These prison walls I leave at last;
Nothing to cheer my drooping head
Until I'm numbered with the dead.

But O, that dreadful Judge I fear;
Shall I that awful sentence hear?
"Depart, ye cursed, down to Hell,
And forever there to dwell."

I know that frightful ghosts I'll see,
Gnawing their flesh in misery,
And taken and there attended be
For murder in the first degree.

Then shall I meet that mournful face
Whose blood I spilled upon this place,
With flaming eyes to me he'll say,
"Why did you take my life away?"

His feeble hands fell gently down,
His chattering tongue soon lost its sound.
To see his soul and body part
It strikes with terror to my heart.

My mind on solemn subjects rolls
My little child—God bless its soul;
All you that are of Adam's race
Let not my faults this child disgrace.

Farewell, good people, you all now see
What my bad conduct brought on me;
To die of shame and disgrace
Before this world of human race.

Awful, indeed, to think of death,
In perfect health to lose my breath;
Farewell, my friends, I bid adieu,
Vengeance on me must now pursue.

Great God! How shall I be forgiven?
Not fit for earth, not fit for Heaven,
But little time to pray to God
For now I try that awful road.

No man alive knows where they buried Frankie.

But the ashes of Charlie rests here in the burying ground where the Silvers have fetched their dead for a hundred years and more.

Post Office is Link to Past

Flat Rock

THERE'S HARDLY A MAN ALIVE WHO REMEMBERS THE sound of the stage driver's bugle announcing the arrival of the post from Charleston.

The Buncombe Turnpike is only a hazy memory, and no man is still alive who witnessed the opening of the first post office here 126 years ago.

The stagecoach has come and gone. So has the old turnpike and its toll gates. Only the post office remains as a link to the past. And it may go if the Federal government has its way.

The U. S. Post Office Department has announced it "contemplates" closing the office here, and Flat Rock patrons are determined it will not happen.

The post office dates back almost to the beginning of the town.

Flat Rock was born out of the first real estate boom in Western North Carolina.

It is the oldest summer resort in the mountains.

Residents of the South Carolina and Georgia lowlands discovered it back in 1812 as a refuge from the burning heat and the mosquitoes.

By 1820 the stream of traffic was so heavy through Saluda Gap that North and South Carolina entered a joint venture and issued state bonds to build the Buncombe Turnpike.

Four years later the turnpike was completed, and in 1829 the Flat Rock post office was established to handle the ever-increasing volume of mail.

With Charles Baring of Charleston founding the community, some of the most distinguished men in the history of South Carolina followed and built homes.

The names roll with the history of the Palmetto State—Rutledge, Lowndes, Elliott, Pickney, Middleton, Memminger.

From Savannah came the Molyneux and the de Choiseuils, one a British consul, the other a French diplomat.

Here in 1834-36 the summer residents from Charleston and Savannah built the church of St. John's-In-The-Wilderness, one of the oldest Episcopal sanctuaries in the state.

The home of Judge Mitchell King was one of the first built. It went up in 1829, the year the post office was established. Judge King, incidentally, donated the land upon which Hendersonville stands.

The history of the Flat Rock post office is almost the history of the U. S. postal service.

For it has witnessed the revolutionary changes in the handling and transport of mail.

In the early days, ten to twelve days were required to carry the post from Charleston to Flat Rock by stagecoach.

It was carried in a leather mail pouch. There were no stamps. The first stamps were not issued until 1847. The penny post card made its debut in 1893.

Until 1851 post rates were a premium, and then they were reduced. Letters were charged by distance. The distance limits were removed in 1861 and first class letter postage was dropped to three cents in 1863.

The post office then—just as it is now in most small towns—was a meeting place for news and gossip and jokes.

Folks found the postmaster a genial man, and the standard question poked at him in those days was:

"What's your price for three-cent stamps today?"

He would grin, then reply:

"Same as they were yesterday. Ten for thirty cents."

No one remembers what the first post office was like here or where it was situated. It could have been in the old Farmer Hotel. But more than likely it was in one of the stores with the storekeeper the postmaster.

There was a keen rivalry between the postmaster and the stagecoach driver. Each was an important man. Each had his fingers on the pulse of the people. And each tried to outdo the other in spreading the news.

The stagecoach driver perhaps got the better of the acclaim.

He was a hero to all the boys and girls.

He had a long whip and a long horn. He was expert with both

He was known by everyone. Both old and young. And the tales of his adventures on the road were poured over and told over and over from one trip to the next.

He was the radio and newspaper of his time.

He collected news at every stop, broadcast it at the next.

He was a familiar figure on the Buncombe Turnpike until almost the turn of the century.

The Spartanburg to Asheville Railroad put him out of business.

And now the post office he helped to make a part of Flat Rock is threatened with the same fate.

[Editor's note: The publication of this story resulted in a flood of protests to the U. S. post office department and the decision to close the Flat Rock post office was reversed.]

The Apostle of Grandfather Mountain

Linville

THEY CALL HIM THE APOSTLE OF GRANDFATHER MOUNTAIN.

His real name is Joe Lee Hartley.

He is a thin, wiry mountaineer of fine countenance who belies his 84 years.

His temple is the great out-of-doors here among the towering peaks of the Blue Ridge where he worships with song and prayer.

He is an authority on Shakespeare and the Bible, and quotes from both with equal ease.

He is the founder and moderator of the now famous "Singing on the Mountain," an annual old-time singing convention started back in 1925 and held each year since on the fourth Sunday in June.

It is an all-day affair, with dinner on the ground.

Hill folks from half a dozen states in the Southern Appalachians gather by the thousands here on a rolling meadow at the foot of ancient Grandfather Mountain to sing hymn tunes long cherished in the mountain church.

It began as a reunion of the Hartley clan but in the years since it has grown into a public affair, and more than 35,000 persons are expected to attend this year.

There is nothing like it in all the land.

It is more than just a singing on the mountain.

Highlanders who have drifted off to the cities come back to mingle with aunts, uncles and cousins and to open their ears to tunes they heard long ago.

They all gather to sing with joy and sorrow, with pride and pleasure, of the scene about them, matching their skill with that of old or young who boast of book learning.

The festival draws scores of singing classes with their proud singing masters who still survive in the mountains and whose badge is the tuning-fork that is used to "pitch" the tune.

Soloists, duets, trios, quartets and choruses sing their favorite hymns.

Many of them sing in a solemn chant of the sixth century to which mountain folks for generations adopted the words of their traditional hymns.

There will be sermons, too.

Mountain preachers will wade into the bootleggers and stomp on them with both feet.

There will be prayers for the people of the world.

And Joe Lee Hartley will be praying for the fair weather that has blessed the day of singing each year since it started.

Both Joe Lee and the singing gathering demonstrate the essential durability of the hill folks.

The old man once figured he was destined to live 200 years but after worrying with a set of store-bought teeth a while back he said he guessed a hundred would about be his limit.

As the warden of Grandfather Mountain, Joe Lee has spent a lifetime on its sides and peaks and figures he has walked 119,592 miles.

"I began walking when I was six years old," he explained. "I walked an average of one mile a day to an old log schoolhouse at Cool Springs in Watauga County."

He came to Linville when he was twenty and went to work with the Linville Development Corporation as a water boy for sixty-five cents a day.

In 1906 he was appointed state fire warden and roamed from Blowing Rock to Linville Falls, averaging walking thirty miles a day.

But he continued to work for the Linville Development Corporation which was started by Hugh MacRae, whose grandson, Hugh Morton, now owns Grandfather Mountain and employs Joe Lee.

Grandfather Mountain is Joe Lee's pride and joy, and he considers it the greatest wonder of the world.

"The Grandfather," Joe Lee says, "stands up as a monument to God's glory."

Besides being a champion walker of the hills and a singer, Joe Lee Hartley is a poet.

Not long ago he composed a poem "Morning On The Grandfather Mountain."

Morning on the Mountain
And the wind is blowing free
Then it is ours just for the breathing.
No more stuffy cities where we have to pay to breathe
Where the helpless creatures move and throng and strive to breathe.

Morning on the Mountain
And the air is like the wine,
And it seems that you see all creation
No house to stop my vision—
Except miles away, on this glorious day of May.

Lonesome—not a minute, while we have these mountains here
That were put here just to please
With their blush, frown and cheer
They are waiting when the summer sun gets sizzling hot.
We just go camping on them with a pan and coffee-pot.

Morning on the Mountain
Have you ever seen the moonlight
Turn the Balsams to a silvery flame
And that Rhododendron thicket yonder—
Well it smells just awful sweet
When the Honey Bee has been shaking it
For its smell is hard to beat.

Lonesome—well I guess not
I have been lonesome in the towns
Yes the wind is blowing free
So just come up into God's beautiful country—
Get a breath and see.

Yes, they call Joe Lee Hartley the Apostle of Grandfather Mountain.

The First Gold Dollars

Rutherfordton

IF YOU'VE GOT A POCKETFUL OF BECHTLER GOLD DOLLARS stashed away you can swap them for a couple yachts and the life of Riley.

Minted here when the county was the gold-mining center of the Nation, they are bringing a fancy price from collectors who apparently print their own folding money.

In the numismatic market a genuine Bechtler gold dollar will get you a hundred or more Washington prints on the only paper of its kind autographed by the first Republican woman treasurer of the United States.

De Soto missed this spot by some seventy miles when he came seeking a fabulous "golden city" in the Carolina highlands back in 1540, but Christopher Bechtler had no trouble finding it 290 years later.

By then, they had been turning up more gold than any other spot in the United States for forty years and news of the gold-mining industry here had even reached across the Atlantic into the home of Bechtler in the Grand Duchy of Baden.

A skilled metallurgist by profession, Christopher Bechtler arrived here in 1830 and proceeded to make himself a million dollars.

He was the first man in the United States to coin gold dollars.

He had the only privately-operated mint in the country.

When Bechtler arrived in Rutherford County with his two sons and a nephew, he discovered that the only medium of exchange was gold dust.

State currency at the time was rare and the nearest government mint was at Philadelphia.

So Bechtler sought and obtained government sanction to coin $1, $2.50 and $5 pieces from native gold.

He also set himself up in the jewelry business.

The *Carolina Spectator and Western Adviser* of August 27, 1831 carried a Bechtler advertisement soliciting the gold coinage business of the miners of South Carolina and Georgia and concluded:

"He has on hand a handsome assortment of jewelry, watches, etc. Any particular kind of jewelry will be executed to order in neatest and most skillful manner."

Bechtler also was a gunsmith and invented a device for firing a rifle at the rate of eight shots a minute.

He even did some gold prospecting on land he purchased some six miles from here on the Marion highway and where he built his home.

But his primary interest was in minting gold coins, and from 1831 to 1940 he coined $2,241,850.50. During that period a total of $3,625,840 in gold passed through his hands. Of this amount, a little more than $2,000,000 was coined for the United States mint.

Bechtler coins were of various sizes and weights, but he minted only three denominations.

Since all the gold that came his way was not the same there was a wide variety in the size and weight of his coins. And Bechtler used the exact amount of gold to make the coins assay to their gold standard.

Because some gold contained more foreign matter it weighed more, but everyone of Bechtler's coins had the amount of pure gold required by the government.

There was a difference in the color of gold, too.

The gold mined in the mountains of North Carolina and in South Carolina was of a dull color. The gold that came from the Georgia and central North Carolina mines was a bright yellow.

The press used by Bechtler to mint his coins is on display in the Museum of the American Numismatic Society in New York.

Some of the dies he used are in the State Hall of History at Raleigh. Others are owned by South Carolina and Georgia descendants of Bechtler.

Many of the Bechtler coins were re-coined when the Charlotte mint was established in 1837.

Rutherford's gold fever reached its height in 1830 but subsided in the greater excitement of the California rush of Forty-Nine.

The Bechtler family consisted of Christopher, two sons, Augustus and Charles, and a nephew, Christopher, II.

Three years after coming to Rutherfordton, the elder Christopher and Augustus became naturalized citizens of the United States.

At the death of the elder Bechtler, Augustus continued to coin gold and make jewelry, and when he died a few years later young Christopher carried on the work.

But because of a lack of interest, he soon gave it up and moved to Spartanburg, South Carolina.

The bodies of the elder Christopher and his son Charles, who committed suicide, were buried near the old home place which was destroyed by fire in 1842, but were later moved to a Northern state and re-interred.

Sir Alexander's Swindle

Franklin

TWO CENTURIES AGO, A SCOTTISH BARONET WITH A WILD desire for power proposed the creation of a national homeland for the Jews here in the mountains.

The plan called for settling 300,000 Jewish families within the domain of the Cherokee Indians, with himself as leader and chief financier.

In the scheme of things, he figured himself as the Messiah destined to lead the Jews into a new Canaan.

The visionary was Sir Alexander Cuming, speculator, confidence man and defaulter, who had a gift of brag the Indians liked and as a bluffer was a sheer genius.

Sir Alexander may have pictured himself as a kind of John Law, able to float a "bubble" of specualtion here in Carolina as Law had done in Louisiana.

He dreamed up the Zionist scheme after he had come into these mountains and talked the Cherokee into acknowledging King George's sovereignty over them.

But he kept the plan to himself for a dozen years before he attempted to peddle it in the money houses of London.

He used it as a last resort to win fame and fortune and power, a trinity that had forever eluded him but which had driven him into one wild scheme after another.

To meet the expenses of this colonization plan for the Jews, Sir Alexander offered to raise a subscription for a half million pounds sterling, on which capital provisional banks would be established in the New World.

Some of the most learned and most wealthy Jews of London gave ear to his proposition, and for a time he thought his dream would come true.

But before he could latch on to the needed capital, word of his earlier swindles and bursted bubbles got around and folks began avoiding him as if he had the plague.

He soon fell into debt, and was imprisoned.

He died penniless and unrewarded, a poor brother of the Charterhouse.

Yet, there had been a time when both fame and fortune touched him briefly, and chances are if one of his land speculation deals in Carolina had not blown up he would have been able to create a home for the Jews in the mountains of Western North Carolina.

For Sir Alexander pulled off one of the biggest coups in early frontier diplomacy right here in what is now Franklin but which in 1730 was the Indian town of Nequassee.

It happened at a time when England and France were jockeying for territorial and commercial supremecy in the New World.

Sir Alexander, with no capital but a bold front, had come to Charlestown in 1730 and proceeded to impress himself upon the colonists as a man of great estate who had come to engage in a vast promotional enterprise which would do wonderful things for them.

He first proceeded to borrow money on short-term notes which he paid promptly and established his credit. Then he plunged.

He erected a loan office and signed great quantities of his notes and emitted them upon loan at ten per cent interest, the borrowers mortgaging their estates to him for security.

While this was going on, Sir Alexander took it upon himself to make a journey into the Cherokee country for "scientific exploration."

It was at a time when the English were afraid the Indians were about to ally themselves with the French.

With no authority whatsoever, Sir Alexander proceeded to do what the frontier diplomats had been unable to do.

While experienced frontiersmen held their breath, he easily obtained from the Cherokee, "on bended knee," their apparent submission to King George.

At the village of Keowee, where three hundred Indians had gathered in the townhouse, Sir Alexander produced a keg of rum and abruptly called upon the chiefs to drink the king's health on bended knee, and thus acknowledge King George's sovereignty over them.

They did it without hesitation, and thereupon Sir Alexander got his idea for a bigger scheme.

He traveled on here to Nequassee, capital of the Cherokees, and persuaded the head man to send for all the chiefs of the region for a "big talk."

When they arrived a few days later, he proceeded to bind them to the English, and suggested that seven chiefs be selected to accompany him back to England and there be presented to King George.

Highly elated with his success, and sure the king would reward him well, Sir Alexander hurried back to Charlestown with the seven chiefs.

There he bragged of his coup, outfitted his red charges in knee-length coats with lace at the cuffs, tight knee breeches, white stockings, and pumps with silver buckles, and set sail for England.

He was hardly out of the harbor when the folks of Charlestown discovered they had been bilked by Sir Alexander, that his treasure house was empty. They had nothing but scraps of paper to show for some fifteen hundred pounds sterling he had taken from them.

Sir Alexander and his Cherokee charges arrived at Dover the first week in June of 1730 and 12 days later the chiefs were presented to King George in London.

Sir Alexander was not there for the ceremony. Word of his swindle had reached London and he had been told it would be a good idea to stay away from Buckingham Palace.

During the next two months the Cherokee were the toast of London. Crowds followed them wherever they went. They were wined and dined, taken to the theatre and treated as visiting royalty.

During this time a treaty had been drawn up for their signatures—a mark since they could not write—and they were called to the palace in Whitehall.

There in an elaborate ceremony they made their marks on the paper that bound them to the English.

The instrument—in effect a bill of sale—was prepared for the Lords of Trade. It guaranteed to endure "while the rivers continue to run, the mountains to stand, or the sun to shine."

The Cherokee bound themselves to have no trade or alliance with any other nation, specifically the French. The treaty stipulated that none but the English would be permitted to build forts and cabins or plant corn in Cherokee country.

In return for their acceptance of the treaty the Cherokee chiefs received the usual glittering promises of love and eternal friendship, together with a substantial quantity of guns, ammunition, powder, gun flints, hatchets, and red paint.

At one point in the ceremony, one of the chiefs named Oukah Ulah politely and indirectly referred to the mysterious absence of Sir Alexander.

"We have looked round for the person that was in our country," he said. "He is not here, however we must say, he talked uprightly to us, and we shall never forget him."

The Cherokee chiefs sailed for home without again seeing Sir Alexander who somehow managed to escape any penalty for his swindle.

Yet he continued to annoy the king and the Board of Trade with his wild schemes, even going so far as to nominate himself for the governorship of Carolina.

He claimed he was the proper man for the job, in fact the only man capable of managing the Indians.

But this was all to no avail, and he was heard from little until he came up with his idea for creating a homeland for the Jews.

Readin', 'Ritin', 'Rithmetic

Sylva

GONE IS THE LITTLE RED SCHOOLHOUSE AND, WITH IT, McGuffey's Reader and Dr. Noah Webster's famous "blue back" speller.

But there are those who remember.

My mother remembers, and so does my grandfather.

My grandfather remembers many things, wonderful things.

And well he should.

He is 96, and his mind is as clear as a school bell on a frosty morning.

His wit is still as sharp and just as mischievous as it was in those days long ago when it got him into trouble, as it has occasion to do now.

When he talks of "the master" there is mischievous laughter in his faded blue eyes, which are still sharp enough to spot a dropped pin on a carpet more quickly than his grandson who has 20-20 vision.

And the chuckle that rises out of his yet strong throat is contagious when he spins a story.

His was a school of manners and strict discipline, he would have you know, ruled by a heavy hand with a heavy rod.

It was a school where the boys, upon entering the room, had to take off their hats and bow and the girls had to curtsy.

School hours were long—from "an hour by sun" in the morning to "an hour by sun" in the evening.

But they were of only a few months duration.

They began after the fall crops were in and let out when it was time for plowing.

The pupils brought their lunches, and during the "dinner spell" they gathered in groups on the rough, hard benches in bad weather and on logs in the forest in pleasant seasons.

They had no paper, so they used slates and slate pencils.

And there seems to have been an affinity between the red-felt-bound, wood-frame slates and their juvenile owners.

My grandfather says a slate would last two or three generations if it survived the heads it crowned, which seems to have been a harmless pastime in the moments when it was not being filled with words and crude pictures.

The schools were one-room, and drinking water came from a well or a spring.

The school over in Macon County that my grandfather attended had a well, and it was the object of much devilment.

Someone—he chuckles deep when he recalls this—was always jabbing a hole in the side of the well-bucket and then leaving it to spray everybody else.

Sometimes the bucket "accidentally" slipped from the rope and went flying to the bottom of the well.

When this happened it took most of the school day for two of the larger boys to go to a distant well or spring to fetch water for the other children.

The one-room building was heated with a cast-iron stove which teetered uncertainly on brickbats in the middle of the floor.

They, too, were objects of temptation.

Coltish boys—again the old man laughs when he tells about it and there's that mischievous twinkle in his blue eyes—could not refrain from giving them sly kicks.

This would result in the joints of pipe come sprawling onto the floor and break up school for an hour or two while the stove and pipe were put back into place and the soot swept out.

"It's a wonder we didn't burn down the schoolhouse," he recalls, "but the worst that ever happened was a room full of soot and smoke."

My grandfather never learned much about geography in school except that g-e-o-g-r-a-p-h-y meant "grandpap et old gray rats at Paul's house yesterday."

But now some eighty years later he can put his finger on Formosa and tell you that his young friend Bill Miller of Waynesville, who not too long ago used to trade tobacco with him and argue about the bite of a good briar, is a newspaperman there.

And he knows, too, that the *Queen Mary* berths on the Hudson side of Manhattan and that the United Nations is housed over on the East River.

A preacher friend of his a couple years ago happened to mention in a sermon something about the United Nations being on the Hudson River.

The old man called him on it when church broke up, and the minister who happened to have a doctor of philosophy degree got a big bang over being corrected.

After a trip around Manhattan by boat once, my grandfather reckoned that he had seen about a third of New York City.

The geography he studied made known the laconic fact that "an iceberg is a large mass of ice floating in the sea" which has always made him wonder what those ice jams on the river in his boyhood could be called.

The radio and television have taught him many things 80 years after he went to school.

He will argue finance and taxes with you, but he still can't understand why a pound of blackeyed peas costs four times more than when he was a boy.

Many a modern day boy has nursed a secret desire to burn down the schoolhouse, and a few have tried.

But in the old man's youth things were different.

Once he joined in "a chopping" and "a raising."

"What's that? Why, son," he explains patiently, "that meant we boys had to heft an axe and help put up the school."

There's Nothing Like Cherry Bounce

Cherry Mountain

OLD MAN OWENS MADE HIMSELF A NAME FROM THE CHERRY trees that troop across this mountain.

When his crops failed back in 1845 they put him into a business his ancestors had practiced in the peat bogs and green hills of Ireland.

He became the master distiller of the Carolina highlands.

And there's never been a more potent concoction than his Cherry Bounce.

It was a mixture of corn likker, honey and cherry juice.

One good slug before breakfast and a man would spit in a wild-cat's eye.

For more than half a century he made corn likker and brandy and picked his cherries.

And for more than fifty years he fought the government, refusing to pay tax on the whiskey and brandy he made and sold.

He was a character never to be forgotten.

He was a leprechaun of a man, round and red of face. He wore a shiny stove-pipe hat. He wore no tie to hide his collar button. Homemade galluses hitched up his baggy pants, and his coat and vest lung loose. He talked in a high, cackling voice.

His home here in the Rutherford County hills was known far and wide.

And come June when his cherries were ripe there was a celebration.

Folks came from all-over. They came from Tennessee and Georgia and South Carolina. They came by foot, by horse and mule-back, in wagons and carriages.

On these occasions, Amos Owens provided the food and the

whiskey and the Cherry Bounce. And there was always a fiddle and there was dancing.

If some of his guests got too much Cherry Bounce there was always the cellar where they could sleep off the effects and start all over again.

But he was always having trouble with the government agents, which mountaineers referred to as "red-legged grasshoppers," a phrase coined by Zeb Vance.

These agents were forever after old man Owens about the tax due them on the whiskey and brandy he manufactured.

In those days it was legal to make whiskey in North Carolina but only if a tax was paid on each gallon of spirits.

This old man Owens refused to do.

He argued that the land was his, the corn and the cherries. The still was his, too. Why in the name of justice, he would shout, should he split his profits with the government.

But it was all to no avail.

Each term of court that was held, his name was always called. And he was always there to answer the charges. Most of his trials were held in Asheville, Charlotte, Rutherfordton or Marion.

When he came in for his trial he would come in his wagon, and it would be loaded down with potatoes and his famous beverage —Cherry Bounce. The potatoes were camouflage for the Cherry Bounce.

Of all the times he was called into court, he only had to serve three prison terms, but he had nine distilling outfits destroyed by the government agents.

Yet, he continued to make whiskey, right up to the time of his death.

When he managed to evade a prison sentence he would make a bee line from the courthouse to his wagon where he proceeded to sell "twenty bushels and forty gallons of taters."

The 'tater market was always bullish when old man Owens hit town.

Judge Dick was usually the presiding judge at the old man's trials and he tried to persuade the old blockader to give up distilling.

"Uncle Amos," Judge Dick said on one occasion, "I want to tell you something. You've given this court lots of trouble."

Never at a loss for words, the old man said:

"And, Jedge, I want to tell you sump'n. This here court's give me lots of trouble."

When old man Davis came up at another term of court charged with manufacturing and selling Cherry Bounce without paying the tax, the judge said he was forced to send him away to prison.

Judge Dick went on to say:

"And I have never manufactured, sold or drunk whiskey."

Old man Owens cocked an eye at the judge.

"Jedge," he said, "you've missed a durn lots of fun if you hain't never made, sold nor drunk no likker. Jedge, do you know what the guv'nor of North Carolina said to the guv'nor of South Carolina? Waal, Jedge, them's my sentiments."

The years sped by and he became a fixture in the court of Judge Dick.

When he had reached his seventies he was sent away to prison for a short term.

But when he came out this time he was a changed man.

He joined the church and stopped making Cherry Bounce.

A few years later he died, well over eighty.

But his Cherry Bounce is still remembered.

And the cherry trees still grow here on his mountains.

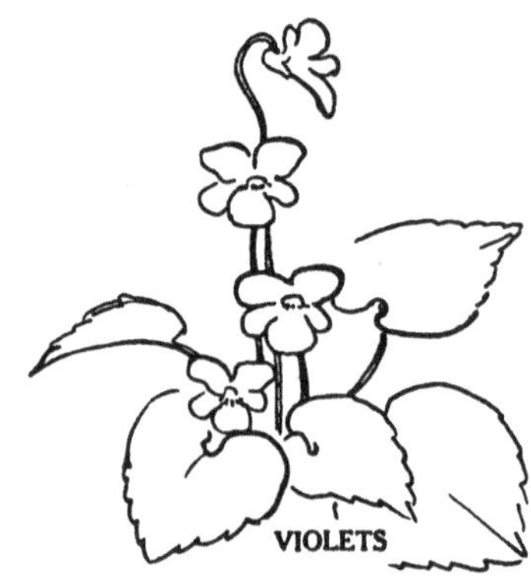

Tom Wolfe's Month

Altamont

THIS WAS HIS MONTH, AND NOW—OCTOBER HAS COME again, bringing with it a golden pattern of harvest time.

He was a child of October and October was when he came home again, back to the lost hills of Old Catawba, with the smell of fallen leaves and wood smoke in the air.

He was a giant of a man and he walked tall upon the earth, and adjectives walked through his mind like bright threads on a loom.

A million words and more flowed from his pen and Altamont became a synonym for Asheville, Old Catawba for North Carolina, and October—October came to mean a time of hope and joy and sorrow, life at full tide.

The Altamont of his *Look Homeward, Angel* was the town where he was born and not this village in the Avery County hills where October is painting the landscape with brilliant hues of blazing colors and the first frosts are beginning to walk down from the high peaks.

October was his month and he wrote of it and spoke of it in words of prose and poetry, and although he traveled far and wide, no land could match the October of his hills.

On a day like this, he would say, on a day like this, when the wind stirs and scuffs the leaves . . . October has come again, bringing with it huge prophecies of death and life.

October in the hills of home, he said, October in the hills of home is the promise that all that has been upon the earth will return again, and will abide forever.

And this was the song he sang:

"*October is the richest of the seasons . . .*

"*. . . the fields are cut, the granaries are full, the bins are loaded to the* *brim with fatness, and from the cider-press the rich brown oozings run. . . .*

"*The corn is shocked . . . the barn is sweet with hay and leather, wood and apples . . . the late pears are mellow on a sunny shelf . . . the pantry shelves are loaded. . . .*

"*October is the richest of the seasons. . . .*

"*. . . the chinkapins are falling . . . the sun flames red and bloody as it sets . . . there are shrewd whistles to the dogs, and frost and silence. . .*"

Yes, this was his month, and October has come again.

From the Blue Ridge to the Great Smokies, October is unfurling its colors across the hills of Old Catawba.

And in the valleys and on the hillsides, mountain farm folks are busy. They are busy, too, in the barns and in the kitchens.

Spring planting has come to fruit, the gamble of summer passed.

Soon the trucks of tobacco will be on their way to market and once again the fluid, garbled tones of the auctioneer will spell out the golden return.

October means many things to many people. It is money on the farm . . . football time . . . county fair time . . . canning time.

October is hound music ringing from the hills . . . it is the opening door on the hunting season . . . it is the possum in the tree . . . the dropping of persimmons.

October means the opening of the bear season . . . a time to stalk the big blacks and spin tall yarns. It is a time when man can choose to sit and look and dream or climb and hunt and kill.

October is square-dancing, bean-stringings, corn-shuckings.

It is fires winking in the sharp nights from the molasses boilers . . . it is cider and apple butter, dried beans and dried peppers . . . it is pumpkins and hot pies.

October is a time when a man calculates how many pounds of pork his hogs will bring. It is a time when he watches the turning leaves and examines the thickness of the corn shuck to determine what kind of winter it is going to be.

October is man's golden month, a time when the last of his harvest is in and he can look forward to days of loafing and nights by the fire. And, because this has been a good harvest, he can buy that washing machine he promised his wife, he can trade in his old car, he can buy a new suit and a dress for his wife and clothes for his children.

Yes, October has come again.

And the giant of a man who painted October in words that matched the colors that run through the hills would find that his month is still a month of hope and joy.

The Spool-Thread Banjo

Whiteside Cove

THERE ARE SOME WHO MAY REMEMBER THE OLD J. & P. Coat's Cotton Spool advertisements.

They pictured a barefoot boy playing a banjo beside a mountain stream.

For some thirty years they were a part of the American scene—and then they disappeared.

It is more than likely that not more than one person in half a million know the story of that particular advertisement.

You see, the boy really lived, and he did play a banjo.

He lived right here in Whiteside Cove.

Back about 1882, when the boy was eight or nine years old, one of his brothers made him a banjo.

It was unique as banjos go. The head was made from a cheese hoop over which was stretched a tanned ground-hog skin. The neck was fashioned from a piece of wood with a pocketknife.

The banjo strings were made of J. & P. Coat's Cotton Spool by twisting strands of thread into the properly varying sizes and then waxing them with homemade beeswax.

It was the first banjo the little boy had ever seen.

When the banjo was finished, the boy soon learned to play on it, not only hymns, but all the old mountain melodies.

It was his pride and joy.

And because his health was none too good, he had plenty of time to play his banjo and make up tunes out of his head.

Yet, living on a farm, he had certain chores to do that were not too strenuous, such as going to mill, driving up the cows to be milked, and going to a neighbor's to borrow a chunk of fire when their own went out.

Matches were scarce and costly in those days. The boy's family usually bought one box a year. They came in round wooden boxes and there were a hundred matches in a box. They cost fifty cents a box.

Not too long after the little boy got his banjo there came a heavy rain that sent all the creeks in the cove out of banks and flooded the land.

It happened that the day the heavy deluge struck that a man by name of Childs and his sister, both of New York, stopped at the boy's house and became waterbound for several days.

One day Childs saw the boy's crude banjo and asked what it was. The boy told him it was a banjo and explained that it was the only banjo he had ever seen.

"Play it for me, son," the man said. "Play me some of the old tunes. Just play me anything."

"I've got a broken string," the boy explained, "but I'll be glad to play something for you as soon as I make another one. It won't take long."

The boy then asked his mother for some thread from her sewing basket, and then from a spool of J. & P. Cotton Spool he made and waxed a string.

They sat before the fire and the boy played all the tunes that he knew.

When the boy had finished, Childs asked to see the thread.

"Well, what do you know," he said. "I own the majority of the stock in the company that makes that thread. I knew it was good for many things, but I didn't know until now that it was good for making banjo strings.

"When I return to New York," he told the boy, "I will send you the best set of banjo strings I can find in the city."

A couple days later, with the flood over, Childs and his sister rode out of the cove on their horses and headed back to New York.

Weeks passed, and then one day a letter came for the boy.

It was from Childs and it told the boy if he would inquire at Walhalla, S. C., some thirty miles to the south and the nearest freight office, he would find a package.

The boy found a neighbor who was making the trip and asked him to pick up the package.

When the boy got the package and opened it, he found not only many sets of strings but a very expensive banjo. The price tag was still on it—fifty-six dollars. Which was a heap of money back in those days.

At that time the trademark for the thread, which was displayed on store fronts, trees and other public places, showed a picture of a barefoot boy standing beside a stream, fishing with a line made from the thread.

Printed on the sign were the words:

"J. & P. Coat's Cotton Spool Is Strong."

A few months later, the boy received another letter from Childs.

It told the boy that he had induced his board of directors to change the picture on their advertisement.

And soon thereafter, posted on store fronts and other places was the same advertisement as before, except it was a picture of a barefoot boy playing a banjo with strings made of J. & P. Coat's Spool Cotton.

The boy treasured his new banjo—the finest in all the mountains.

In fact, he was the only person in the hills with a storebought banjo and he became quite an artist.

He made music for the mountain dances here in the cove and up at Cashiers, went into adjoining counties, and even into Georgia and South Carolina.

Years later the boy swapped his banjo for two books, a small volume of general history and a book of speeches—political, legal, educational and religious.

That's how he started getting his education.

In time he got another banjo, and when he went off to school at Cullowhee he carried his banjo with him and played it and sang the songs he had made up.

One was a ballad about a girl in his own cove. It became one of the most famous banjo ballads in all the land. You perhaps have heard it.

In time, the boy went on to become one of the most distinguished men in all the mountains.

He became a lawyer, then a judge.

He no longer plays the banjo, but he remembers how it was when he did.

He lives at Waynesville now.

His name? Judge Felix E. Alley.

The ballad he wrote? *Kidder Cole.*

He is retired now, but he likes to sit and prowl through his memories.

And sometimes he wonders what ever happened to the J. & P. Coat's Spool Cotton.

It's been a long, long time since the landscape flaunted the picture of a barefoot boy with a banjo beside a mountain stream.

Minstrel of the Appalachians

South Turkey Creek

SOME FOLKS ARE BEGINNING TO DOUBT THAT ELIZABETH the Virgin Queen of Merry Old England is dead.

Responsible for this wavering is a solemn looking man of 74 who, far from being solemn, likes nothing better than to spend a night singing, making music and dancing.

They call him the Minstrel of the Appalachians, a mountain-born troubadour who is keeping Queen Elizabeth alive here in the hills where he discovered a forgotten England.

His real name is Bascom Lamar Lunsford, and there's not a man in all the land that can match his stock of tunes that were sung on the village greens in Shakespeare's time.

He is the pappy of the Mountain Dance and Folk Festival which opens in Asheville "along about sundown" next Thursday.

This will be the 35th year for the big shivaree of the hills, which really is the biggest show of its kind in the nation, albeit similar types are now held in many sections of the country.

Actually, the festival is a roses-for-the-living monument to the great work Lunsford has done in preserving the wild, sweet, lonely tunes your great-great-great-great-grandpappy might have played at the court of Queen Elizabeth.

And the minstrel man himself will be right there to see that only the old tunes and lyrics are played and sung.

Even at 74, Lunsford can do a mean shuffle, and don't go laying any money that he won't be still on his feet when everybody else is catching their breath and sitting one out.

He will dance all night, calling the sets himself, as long as anybody will play mountain music, real mountain music, like *Sourwood Mountain.*

Besides being a dancing man, he is a ballad-singing man, a fiddle-playing man and a banjo-picking man.

Born in Madison County, he was raised between Rabbit Ham and Sandymush, which, incidentally, came by its name when some folks camping in the area happened to kick some sand in the mush they were cooking.

As a boy, his mother encouraged him to fashion fiddles out of gourds, and his schoolteacher father would sing the old ballads to him.

For some fifteen years he moved about the hills, singing and playing and dancing. He stowed away tunes in his memory.

Then he became an auctioneer, later taught at Rutherford College, then turned to law, dabbled a bit in politics, edited a country paper, and for a short time during World War I was a Department of Justice Agent in New York.

Following the war he confined his efforts to law practice and running his 140-acre farm here on South Turkey Creek where he built a house with a huge living room large enough for square dancing.

Lunsford didn't do too much with his law practice; he was forever out roaming the hills searching for the old songs, collecting them and remembering them.

He was afraid as the old folks passed on they would take with them to their graves all memory of the tunes and lyrics which once the mountain people had sung with such joy.

So he spent more and more time traveling through the hills, stopping at one-room cabins with his fiddle or banjo, playing and singing, and worrying folks for the ballads and tunes they could remember.

Sometimes he would mention old Sir Thomas Lunsford, the first of the Lunsford line in America who had spent some time around Buckingham Palace.

He would remind the folks of the hills that maybe some of their folks hung around the court a bit, too.

And he would tell them how their square dance tunes came straight from the jigs and reels and hornpipes of England, Ireland and Scotland.

It was his way of trying to awaken the pride of his own people in their traditional music.

He did a good job of it.

Somewhere along the way he set out to make himself a one-man repository of the old tunes.

And he did well in that, too.

Lunsford has gathered more than 3,000 songs, ballads, fiddle tunes and dance calls, the largest known collection in the country, and he's still collecting.

He has recorded some 500 for the Library of Congress.

Lunsford is a folklore scholar, too. He has lectured at Columbia University and throughout the country.

None has labored more successfuly to rediscover and put back into circulation the great wealth of music buried here in the hills.

He also has had great influence in keeping the mountain dance authentic.

He's got a great helper in this field in Sam Queen of Maggie, dancin'est man in all the land, who set 'em on their ear at New York's Waldorf-Astoria with his clogging.

Back in 1939, Sam, with his Soco Gap dance team, and Lunsford gave a command performance at the White House during the visit of King George and Queen Elizabeth.

Sam led his dancers into the figure Walking The King's Highway while Lunsford leaned against the gold piano and picked his banjo.

The king smiled and the queen patted her foot.

It was a great day for both Sam and Lunsford, perhaps even greater for the minstrel man, who in that brief moment was doubly paid for all the years of wandering the hills to keep the tunes and lyrics of Elizabeth the Virgin Queen alive.

If you should come this way looking for Lunsford, just take the bridge over South Turkey Creek and follow your ears.

Could be you would hear the ballad-singing man singing *Gypso Davy*, a Scotch legend about a banished gypsy king, Johnny Faa, who took the wife of one of the lairds with him when he fled.

So late in the night when the landlord came
Inquirin' fur his lady,
The answer was quickly replied
"She has gone with Gypso Davy."

Or he might be singing the ancient ballad *Fair Margaret and Sweet William.*

Back some twenty-five years ago, Lunsford published *Thirty and One Folk Songs From the Southern Appalachians*, representative examples of a great store of folk-literature and, while traditional in many instances, may be ranked as true types of the American folk-song.

"*Little Margaret*, which may be heard at Roaring Fork, in the shadow of the Great Smokies," Lunsford explained, "is *Fair Margaret and Sweet William*, handed down by oral tradition.

"Other numbers which show the influence of a former period are *Johnson Boys*, which bears a strong resemblance to *Go Way, Go Way*. *Black Jack Davie* may be traced to *Gypsie Laddie*. *I'm Going Back To Georgia* and *Old Smoky* derived no doubt from *The Wagoner Lad*."

Yes, when you talk to the Minstrel of the Appalachians and hear him play and sing the old ballads, you begin to doubt that Elizabeth the Virgin Queen is dead.

The Old-Time Drummer

Murphy

YOU NEVER SEE HIM ANY MORE, BUT TIME WAS WHEN HE traveled the wilderness, peddling his wares and carrying spicy conviviality to the mountain hamlets.

The only monument he ever got was a hostelry bearing his name, but it, too, has faded into the limbo of forgotten memories.

Liquor and fancy off-color stories were his stocks in trade, and for half a century he was the purveyor of all the lively yarns afloat in America.

Everybody knew him.

He was the drummer, a commercial salesman whose name got fancied up with the advent of the horseless carriage, the mail-order catalogue, and the advertising boys.

They turned him into a sales representative and toned him down.

And when they did, the old-time drummer disappeared from the American scene.

He went the way of the country store and the Populist Party.

But he is not forgotten.

Folks still remember him and his ways.

Up until the late twenties, he was as much a part of life in the mountains as cornbread and molasses.

This was one of his favorite spots.

He stayed here at the Dickey House, which was better known as the Drummers Home.

It was a sort of rendezvous for the drummers of the Murphy Branch, the run from here to Asheville.

Before the railroad came this way at the turn of the century, the drummer made his rounds by horse and buggy, taking months to visit his customers who were scattered far and wide.

The old-time drummer never got in a hurry.

And wherever he stopped, he was as welcome as Christmas and as lively as the Fourth of July.

In the early days, he carried his wares with him and sold from the trunks he carried.

The dry-goods salesman's trunks were filled with bolts of goods and shoes.

But the hardware salesman brought only new patterns and designs of goods, for he sold the same implements that had been standard stock for generations.

The medicine drummers were the dandies of the road, the high-pressure salesmen, slick talkers and flashily dressed, spouting the virtues of Lydia Pinkham and Peruna.

Selling was not the drummer's sole task.

In many instances he helped to establish stores and gave advice on general business procedure.

To the store folks, and the hangers-on, the drummer was a sort of plumed knight, a man of the world who had traveled and seen many things.

He was the newspaper and the radio of his day, a traveling commentator.

He would spend hours around the pot-bellied stove giving the latest news from other sections of the mountains where he had visited.

It was a subtle approach to making his pitch for an order.

The drummer had to be a master storyteller, a keen judge of a man, a walking encyclopedia.

After salesmen traveled through the territory for several years they built up a trade which was theirs for the trouble of writing orders.

Drummers such as the beloved and well-remembered Wallace Blackwell of Waynesville covered the same territory year after year, right up to the time they retired or died.

Companies didn't switch their salesmen, for they learned that the more a man traveled the same route the better their products were appreciated and easier to sell.

But it made it tough on the drummer. He had to keep up with the jokes and the stories, else a merchant would accuse him of telling the same ones twice.

The drummer knew all the storekeepers from Asheville to Murphy. He knew every crossroads store, no matter where it was located, or how difficult the travel was to reach it.

He knew who to trust for a year to pay a bill and whom not to risk even ten days.

Faithful drummers made a sentimental appeal to both the storekeepers and their daughters, wooing them both.

It was a trick of the trade to bring along a present for the storekeeper's daughter, something straight out of New York or some other far place.

Some of the drummers carried "good will" samples which they gave away.

They gave away calendars, almanacs and tin pie plates.

Then there were samples, such as needles, medicines, soda and baking powder.

Sometimes a merchant would over-buy on a product that had been over-sold to him, and, when he did, the drummer had a hard time making another sale to this particular customer unless he had a good excuse.

A change in styles, particularly in womens' wear, could wreck a drummer's reputation and saddle a merchant with out-dated goods.

Once, David M. Hall, a prominent merchant in Sylva, stocked rather heavily on ladies' spike-toed, high-button shoes. Slippers hit the market before he could move his stock.

But he had one faithful customer who refused to go along with the styles.

She continued to wear the high-button, or high-laced shoes, for a good dozen years after they went out of style, and Hall finally got rid of the last pair.

This faithful customer of his bought up the last two pair along about 1930, and nobody ever did know what she did for high-laced shoes after that.

No, you don't see the old-time drummer any more, but there are folks who remember him, this traveling man of the derby and the two-horse buggy who was an institution.

An Old-Timer . . .

Sylva

AN OLD-TIMER IS ONE WHO REMEMBERS—

When the surrey with the fringe on top was the Cadillac of its day and not a popular song.

when it was almost a scandal if a lady showed an ankle in getting in or out of a carriage.

when bustles were fashioned of flexible wire and not of pelon and nylon.

when box suppers were events and not pickups at the corner delicatessen.

when the whole town turned out to meet the evening train.

when medicine shows came to town as regular as the first frost.

when one of today's popular soft drinks was advertised as a brain tonic and intellectual soda fountain beverage.

when babies, regardless of sex, were decked out in a swirl of ribbons and rosettes.

when high button shoes were all the rage.

when grandmothers smoked corn cob pipes.

An old-timer is one who remembers—

when a pocketknife was called an apple-peeler.

when a young feller wondered if the light of his eye could milk, knit garters, make apple butter or dance a reel after midnight.

when a paper bag was called a poke.

when branch water was fit to drink.

when the social calendar swirled around corn-shuckin's, sewing bees, quiltin' frolics, bean stringin's, apple butter stirrin's, and molasses pulls.

when soft soap was made at home by cooking lye water, drained from an ash hopper, with grease from cracklin's.

when grandmothers had curtains to their bonnets.

when buckwheat cakes were a luxury and millers cussed when a turn of buck wheat was brought to the mill for grinding into flour.

when a mountain man's economic status could be calculated by the number of hound dogs about his cabin—the more the poorer.

when coffee came in beans and a man parched and ground his own.

when gritted bread was a mouth-watering summertime treat.

when corn bread was baked in ashes.

when peartening juice fresh from the still was called baldface whiskey.

An old-timer is one who remembers—

when second-hand wares were called calamities.

when a timberman who peeled bark from logs was known as a bark spudder.

when buggy whips, saddles and harness hung in prominence in the local hardware store.

when dosing with ginger tea and boneset and sage was a popular home remedy for colds and coughs.

when asafetida was worn on a string around the neck.

when mothers took their baskets of eggs to the store in place of spending money.

when the country store was America's greatest forum for free expression and discussion.

when a hitching post or tie rail was in front of every store, emporium or other commercial establishment in town.

when a lawyer drew a will for a dollar or a deed for seventy-five cents.

when a country newspaper publisher received his pay for subscriptions in everything except money.

when a preacher whose sermon lasted only an hour was considered to have done no more than skim the cream of his text.

when guessing the weight of animals was one of the popular contests of the county fair.

An old-timer is one who remembers—

when anvil shooting was a part of every Christmas affair.

when *Blood Hound*, *Good and Tough*, *Free Silver*, *Legal Tender* and *Cornbread* were popular names of plug tobacco.

when the Admiral Dewey Health Corset hit the market and caught the eye of waist conscious maidens.

when fascinators were worn by both men and women.

when the technique of buying underclothes for a woman resembled that of buying liquor in prohibition days.

when preachers bemeaned slit skirts.

when men wore paper collars.

when infections were combated with turpentine and pine resin.

when the traveling shoe cobbler came around twice a year.

when it was a custom to pound the newly arrived preacher or newly weds.

when bear's oil, beeswax and ginseng were used to pay for services or goods.

when youngsters used a hornbook to learn their letters.

when slates were used instead of paper tablets.

when the mail was carried by horseback or hack.

when long sweetening was honey and short sweetening was maple sugar.

when the washing machine was an iron pot and a scrubbing board.

when borrowing was universal.

when the washbowl and the pitcher sat on the back porch.

An old-timer is one who remembers when a man had time for whittling.

He is one who remembers when.

The Corn Shuckin'

Webster

AUNT EDE USED TO SAY WHEN YOUNG FOLKS GATHERED for a corn-shuckin' there was a heap more courting and frolicking done than work.

She would grumble that the annual corn-shuckin's here at the Hall place were fun for everybody except her, since she had to do all the baking and cooking for the soiree.

Aunt Ede weighed two hundred and twenty pounds and was as black as midnight. She smoked a corn-cob pipe and lived to be almost a hundred. She was born a slave but spun out her years in freedom as an institution in the Hall household.

She always made a big fuss and to-do when Mrs. Hannah Hall planned a corn-shuckin' or a molasses pullin' for the young folks in the community, but folks agreed that when the occasion arrived Aunt Ede seemed to sort of take on new life.

The young folks made over her at such times, and, before the night was out, Aunt Ede would be serving up roasted sweet potatoes out of the fireplace, dusting off the ashes with a turkey wing.

This was a sort of ritual with her that spoke more eloquently than words and sent everybody home with a longing for the next corn-shuckin' at the Halls.

As practiced by the Halls and elsewhere in the mountains, a corn-shuckin' was a gala affair, a social occasion attended by young folks for miles around.

When the year's harvesting was done, and the frosts were beginning to tip-toe down from the hills, the word would go out that a corn-shuckin' was to be held on a certain night.

This was a signal for a big time.

Now just sitting down to a big pile of corn and shucking it out is work. That is, if a feller had to do it alone. But when it meant seeing your best girl, that was different. That's when work went out and play came in.

Nobody knows who first thought up a corn-huskin' on a boy-girl basis, but he was a smart man. He was wise enough to know that if he wanted a crowd big enough to do the job he would have to have some other attraction than merely a group of countrymen sitting around a pile of corn and working away until midnight.

So, the corn-shuckin' became a social event.

When the night arrived for the corn-shuckin', the young folks marched right out to the big pile of corn, generally piled up near the barn, so it could easily be gotten into the corn crib.

A boy and a girl would pair off and then everybody would group themselves in a circle around the mountain of corn. Sitting there, they would start shucking to beat the band.

As the shucks began flying, conversation would rise and fall. Sometimes a girl's laugh would lift above the murmuring, as she teased the boy by her side, or tried to disentangle her hand from his among the mottled unshucked ears.

Usually, somebody brought along a fiddle. The fiddle would cry and the shuckin' couples would sing. Mostly the songs were the old time ballads. And sooner or later somebody would break out with:

Oh, I'm gwin' to the shuckin',
I'm gwin' to the shuckin' of the corn.

In the early days of the corn-shuckin', before it became a strictly social affair for the young folks, the host would bury a jug of corn whiskey in the center of the pile of corn.

This created some tall competition among the men-folks, each working at top speed to be the first to reach the jug and get the first go at the peartenin' juice before passing it on to the others.

As a reward for reaching the jug first, the lucky fellow could tilt the jug until his Adam's Apple bobbed three times. The other fellers only got one bob and, when it had passed the circle, if any was left, the finder got another go at it.

But as one early-day corn-shucker set down in his memoirs, he learned as a boy at a corn-huskin' that competition is the mother of cheating, falsehood, and broils.

"When a man turns up a jug," he wrote, "it's next to the impossible to prevent a second bobbin' of the Adam's Apple, even if one feller's got his hand on the jug and another feller has got his hands around the partaker's throat."

Actually, nobody ever got around to figuring how to penalize the fellow who sneaked an extra swallow, so that's where the broils got into the act.

A fellow limited to one swallow who took two usually got a poke in the nose from the finder of the jug, which was seldom, since everybody expected a man to hold onto the jug until it was grabbed by the next fellow.

Sometimes, when a fellow let his Adam's Apple out of gear, the others would pick him up and toss him into the corn crib and shower him with a barrage of shucked corn.

But there was one custom that prevails even until today, albeit corn-shuckin's are about a thing of the past.

And that's where the courting and the frolicking took over from the boys with the jug.

When the corn-shuckin' became a real social affair, somebody thought up the idea of the red ear of corn as a hilarious contrivance for promoting an opportunity for a kiss.

Thus, the red ear of corn became a substitute for the jug of peartenin' juice.

When a young fellow found a red ear of corn he got to kiss the girl of his choice publicly.

When my mother was a girl she threw a conniption fit, so she says, when a young fellow latched on to a red ear of corn and then proceeded to give her a buss before everybody.

It was her first corn-shuckin', and it was right here at the Halls, Young David, the son of her hostess, singled her out when he come up with an ear of red corn.

"He kissed me right there before everybody," my mother laughingly recalled, "and I bursted out crying and ran to Mrs. Hall. I thought I was ruined. It was the first time I had ever been kissed by a boy. Mrs. Hall told me she would whip David, but Aunt Ede just grunted and told me to go on back, maybe he would find another red ear."

When the preacher's daughter got bussed, my mother felt better.

"You know," she said, "nobody found another red ear all night."

As Aunt Ede used to say when young folks gathered for a corn-shuckin' there was a heap more courting and frolicking done than work.

King of the Sorghum Makers

Barker's Creek

HE'S THE UNCROWNED KING OF THE MOUNTAIN SORGHUM boilers, a molasses-makin' man from a molasses-makin' clan.

Folks here in the hills call him the "masterest sorghum boiler" in all the land.

His name is Rufus Brevard Monteith.

There is the look of autumn in his eyes and his weathered face is as homely as a plowed field ready for sorgo planting.

At 73, he plies a craft that really got its start 4,000 years ago when the Pharaohs began cultivating sorghum which, incidentally, is a grass and not a cane.

He grew up in the cornbread-and-molasses era and turned to making sorghum syrup because it was a thing the Monteiths had been doing best since the first of the clan hacked out a homestead in the hills.

His grandmother was making long sweetenin'—that's what mountain folks call molasses—when the Yankee blockade chased sugar right off the kitchen table back in the 'Sixties.

She had the golden touch and she passed it on to her son and her grandson who has been making molasses the old-timy way for fifty-five years.

Hill folks who can taste molasses and tell you right off the bat the man who made it say there's a certain something about Monteith syrup that distinguishes it from any other that has ever been made.

"Why," says my grandfather who is ninety-six and who made many a gallon, "you can might nigh tell Monteith molasses just by lookin' at 'em. When you pour 'em out on your plate they pour like no others. And when you taste' em, you know for sure."

Folks have been beating a path to the Monteith sorghum mill

for years, carrying a jug and a hope they can wheedle the old out of a bit.

For Rufus makes molasses only for his own table and for a few of his friends who put in their orders along about the time he plants his sorghum.

"It's got so I can hardly keep enough back for my own family," he said. "Reckon I could sell every drop I make, if I had a turn to. I've been makin' for weeks now and haven't got around to makin' any for myself. What I've been makin' has been for folks hereabouts who grow the cane and bring it for me to grind and boil."

Until five years ago he had his sorghum mill down in Swain County, where he was born, but then he moved into the Barker's Creek community and set up his mill beside the Tuckaseigee River and right on the lip of U.S. 441.

"Before I come here," he said, all the time stirring the green juice in the big open vat, "I run a custom mill in Swain. That is, I made molasses for everybody. Folks brought their cane in from all over. Some come from as much as thirty miles away.

"Reckon I've made enough molasses in fifty-five years to fill that river to over-flowin'. Time was when I made on an average of a thousand gallons a year and that's a lot of molasses to sop up with hot corn pone or hot biscuits. I'm a corn pone man myself.

"Most I ever made in one year, I reckon, was when I was running the custom mill. Made 1,420 gallons and never got to shut the mill down until the 22nd of December. I was so whupped I never wanted to see another drop of molasses."

Now he averages only about six hundred gallons a year.

"A feller should hold down to about that," he said. "That takes about three or four weeks and don't break a man's back."

There was a smell of frost in the late afternoon air. The sky was overcast.

"If you don't get your cane cut in the fields before frost," he said, "you've lost your crop. Already had three frosts this year but my cane was already cut and under cover.

"Frost will ruin cane if it hits it, even after it's matured and ready for the mill and the boiler. The frost gets into the blade and runs into the stalk. That causes the juice to turn sour.

"Some folks have still got cane standin' in the field. They might as well forget about it. I shore don't want none of it coming to my mill."

There's really a subtle art to making molasses, a technique that a man can't learn in a day or a year or ten years.

"A man's got to have a feelin' about molasses," Monteith said. "If you make it too thin, it'll clobber and sour, just like milk. If you make it too thick it's too hard to handle and gets gummy but it don't hurt the taste none. There ain't no set rule to makin' molasses. A clock don't do no good to go by. You just get a feelin' when it's ready, and there you are."

Until a few years ago, sorghum makers were getting about as scarce as Civil War veterans, which meant that it was heading fast into the limbo of lost arts.

But since Monteith moved his sorghum mill to the banks of the Tuckaseigee there's been a sudden revival of sorghum making.

"Seems like folks are growin' more sorghum now," he said. "Don't know the reason, unless it's maybe because they know I'm right here on the road where it's easy to haul to."

Be that as it may, however, sorghum making for a hundred years has been sort of an autumn festival among mountain folks.

Like corn-shuckin's and bean-stringin's, sorghum making answered a social need as well as an economic need. For mountain folks always have used their seasonal tasks as an excuse for having a bit of fun while they worked.

For years after the Civil War, coffee and all other substance were sweetened by sorghum. What little white sugar there was when things became plentiful was saved for special occasions when guests were present.

Molasses have a pleasing taste which is not duplicated in any other sweet. It is a sweet taste which suggests a malty flavor.

Sorghum seeds are small and brownish, sometimes red. Instead of growing on the cob in a shuck like corn, they grow on top in a tassel made up of the little seeds.

Once the sorghum is planted it grows like corn and requires about the same care. Too much rain near the end of the growing season reduces the yield of syrup.

After the sorghum has matured, the stalks are stripped of their blades while still standing and then cut and carried to the mill.

The sorghum is gathered in huge bundles and its juice is extracted in a ring-around mill. The mill has a crusher and the stalks are jammed in. One man feeds them in on one side and another grabs them on the other, gives them a twist and hands them back to the first worker to go through the crusher again.

A mule or a horse is hitched to a pole and walks round and round, furnishing the power for the grinder, which is composed of two cogged wheels between which is fed the sorghum stalks.

The juice is then cooked in a huge trough under a shed. The trough is separated into compartments about six inches apart with alternating openins.

"The juice," Monteith explained, "is poured in one end and as it cooks it moves from one compartment to another of its own will, winding in and out like a snake, until it comes to the end where it is drained into a barrel.

"You have to keep skimmin' it while it works in the front half of the boiler. The skimmin's are green and as the juice works toward the end a white foam gathers. This is got be taken off, too.

"We save the white foam. That's what you use in candy-pullin's. It makes the finest candy in the work.

"Now some folks save the green skimmin's. Some folks guzzle 'em. They'll make you drunk. I ain't a drinkin' man myself, but them that do has told me that corn whiskey is sweet compared to sorghum skimmin's.

"Folks have been known to make sorghum whiskey out of 'em, too. I remember one time back in Swain a feller come to me with some cane and wanted me to grind it for him. He brought along two big barrels to hold the skimmin's. Well, I never asked no questions but I had a right good notion what he was gonna do with them skimmin's. He had a reputation as a blockader, that I knew. So I ground up his cane and made his syrup, but he seemed more interested in the skimmin's. Stayed right there the whole time and saw to it that none of them skimmin's was thrown away. I made 240 gallons of molasses for him and filled both his barrels with skimmin's. He loaded 'em on a wagon and hauled 'em off. Never did know what he done with 'em, but I've got a notion and I reckon it's a right one."

Monteith said in the past few years several new kinds of sorghum seed has come on the market.

"Some of it's pretty good," he said, "and some ain't as good as the old-timey kind. Now, I make my molasses out of a cane I call honey-drip. It won't go to sugar. Some folks use one that's called sugar-drip, but it won't keep too long and will get right grainy.

"I've been trying one called red-fox tail and it's might nigh as good as honey-drip."

Monteith kept stirring the green juice, keeping the skim off, and talking at the same time, while nearby his son fed the sorghum stalks into the mill and the horse went round and round.

"I reckon I've got a few more years of molasses-makin' in me," he said, "but I've been training my two boys and my granddaughter how to make sorghum and I reckon they'll carry on when I'm gone.

"Somebody's got to keep on makin' molasses, else coming generations won't never know what real old-timey mountain molasses and corn pone is like."

He looked into the gray sky.

"Frost is a comin' tonight," he said, "but we've got our cane covered and give us about a week more and I'll have all my molasses-makin' done for this year."

He went on stirring the green juice, this weathered little mountain man they call the "masterest sorghum boiler" in all the land.

Quiltin' Woman

Bunches Creek

YOU WOULD RECOGNIZE HER IF YOU SAW HER.

She is the spinner standing at the high wheel, the thread of the years in her hands.

She is the pioneer heroine of the hearth and the quilting bars.

She is the homesteader's woman who followed him into the wilderness and gave him her heart and hands and children.

Her name is Eliza Jane Bradley.

She is eighty-three, but she is young at heart, and her hands are strong and able and willing.

The years have bleached her hair and etched her face with tiny wrinkles.

There's a twinkle in her dark eyes and a lilt in her voice.

She lives here in the high reaches of the Smokies where the frosts walk early and spring comes late.

Her husband was splitting rails and she was in the kitchen sorting out a basket of freshly picked gourds for drying when I came to the house.

The day was gray, fog hung about the peaks and there was a chill in the air, so we sat before the fire in the front room and talked of old things and old ways.

"We come in here from across the mountain in 'Ninety-Eight when there was hardly a foot path," she recalled. "We had to carry the children—there was three of them then—on our backs.

"There was nothing here but wilderness. We camped out while we cleared the land and raised our house. My husband built everything on the place, even the furniture. Built a mill. It's still standing. I helped him. Helped him build and set out the orchards and plant the hillsides.

"We were both young then. I was 25 and my husband about the same age. We'd been married about eight or nine years then. That picture up there on the wall was taken when we got married. I was sixteen."

A big, heavily framed picture hung above the mantel where the clock ticked away time. Surrounding it were pictures of George Washington, Woodrow Wilson, and Franklin D. Roosevelt.

"We accumulated pretty fast—children and stock. Had twelve children in all, but some of them didn't live to get grown.

"I never was afraid of work. I've done a little bit of everything. That's the only way folks can get along and make something. You've got to plow and hoe and plant and sow and reap.

"Many's the night I've spent carding and spinning. I've still got my spinning wheel and I still spin. We had our own sheep and got our own wool. Kept sheep up until about ten years ago, but I got tired of following 'em around over the mountains, so we sold 'em. But I had enough wool sheared off to last me. I've got more'n I'll ever use."

She got out of her chair and moved over to a closet. She opened the door and pointed to a big basket of wool.

"It's just like it was sheared off the sheeps' backs," she explained. "Don't wash it until I get ready to use it. That way it keeps."

Then she opened a chest standing at the foot of the big bed and began to pull out one quilt after another.

"I reckon I'm the quiltin'est woman in all the land," she said. "Guess I've made nigh on to a thousand quilts in my time. Don't quilt as many as I used to. Only do about twelve or fourteen a year now. Been making quilts since I was five.

"I remember when I was five my mother let me piece in the little pieces. I caught on real fast and kept right on making 'em. Now, this one's called a string quilt. It's made by piecing strings on pieces of paper. Sometimes you tear away the paper after the quilt is made. And sometimes you let the paper stay on. Used to leave the paper on back when we had powerful cold winters. The paper made 'em warmer.

"This one I call *Trip Around the World.* See how the layers of piece-goods run all the way around the quilt. And that one is called *Bleeding Heart,* and that's the one I call the *Flag Quilt*—see the stars and stripes."

Mrs. Bradley said she wasn't one for quilting bees and quilting frolics.

"I believed in doing my own quilting, then I could claim it all for my own," she explained. "I had my own way of piecing 'em and I had my own stitches."

She folded the quilts and put them away, then took her chair again by the fire.

"Used to do some huntin' myself, too," she said, a slow grin spreading over her face. "I've shot about everything 'cept bear. I killed squirrel and pheasant and rabbit, lots of 'em.

"I've still got my rifle and I still hunt sometimes. But it's just now and then. I'm gettin' too old and my eyes ain't as good as they used to be. I couldn't hit nothin' now without practicin' up a little.

"Last year I went out to hunt me a mess of squirrel. I was down there near the creek. I spotted some of 'em a-playin' in the trees and I fired away but I couldn't hit 'em. Missed 'em as clean as you please."

Her husband interrupted.

"She killed a fox not too long ago, though," he said. "I was settin' down at the creek and heard her fire her rifle and then I heard the dogs a-barkin'. Well, I hurried up there above the house, and she'd killed as purty a red fox as you ever saw. Shot him right through the head."

She poked at the fire a moment.

"Not many foxes now," she said. "But when we first come in here there was a heap of 'em. They would get our geese and ducks and everything."

All the children are gone now, and just the two of them live here. But they go about keeping house about the same as they always have.

"I still make ground meal in the old-fashioned way," she said. "I make it by pounding it with a heavy pestle in a wooden block, Indian fashion. My block's made of white oak. My husband made me one once out of buckeye but it peeled and the peel got in the meal. It was no good. I had him to make me one out of oak.

"We raise just about everything we eat. Come let me show you my cellar."

She led us outside and under the house. There in orderly rows of shelves lining the sides of an earthen cellar were cans of bunch beans, grapes, pork, wild greens, red and yellow peppers, okra, dried milk, krauted mustard, cucumber pickles, apple sauce and apple butter, plums, peaches, cherries, salad peas, rhubarb butter, tomatoes, carrots and kraut juice.

"Kraut juice," she said, "is the best cough remedy there ever was."

From the cellar, she led the way to the kitchen.

Hanging behind a wood-burning stove were strings of dried beans. On the floor was a big basket of gourds, which she had washed and had sorted out for drying.

"Now look," she said, pointing across the room, "I've got an electric stove, too. And over there in that room I've got a washing machine. But I still keep my wood stove just in case the power goes off."

Above the kitchen table with its white cloth hung a sampler on the wall which proclaimed:

But every house
Where love abides
And friendship is a guest
Is surely home and
Home sweet home
For there the heart can rest.

She brushed back a strand of hair out of her eyes and smiled.

"It's been a good home," she said. "We've been blessed with children and with plenty, and now there's only the two of us here. But our children come back to visit us, and that is good."

The Pioneer Iron-Makers

Forge Mountain

THIS MOUNTAIN STANDS AS A FORGOTTEN MONUMENT TO the pioneer ironmakers of the southern Appalachians.

It is a reminder of gaunt days when rugged men gave their brawn and brains to a tough struggle for primitive survival along the nation's frontier.

For here above Mills River in Henderson County was one of the region's first ironworks from which flowed the precious metal that furnished horseshoes, plowshares and pruninghooks for those who first tilled the savannahs of the French Broad and the Swannanoa.

Two others hammered out great loops and bars of iron on Hominy and Reems creeks in Buncombe County under the crest of Charles Lane whose son forsook his native heath to become the territorial governor of Oregon.

All three were established shortly after 1788 when the state offered lands unfit for cultivation as a bounty to anyone who would build and operate an ironworks.

Land grants also were issued to Messer Fain in Cherokee County where bloomery forges blossomed along Hanging Dog, Owl and Persimmon creeks.

Until these forges started, little iron had been manufactured west of the Blue Ridge, although there was a critical need for it on the frontier.

Between the end of the American Revolution and the beginning of the state's bounty system, settlers brought in iron from east of the mountains but the price was so dear its use was prohibitive.

This was all changed with the local manufacture of iron, and ordinary blacksmiths soon began turning out axes, hatchets, drawingknives, chisels, augurs, horseshoes, horseshoe nails, bolts, nuts and even pocketknives.

For the next half century, the mining of iron ore and the making of iron was a prosperous business in the mountains but it was destined to be short-lived.

Development of the industry in Pennsylvania and Alabama, and the opening of the great ore deposits of the Lake Superior region, marked the end of the ironmaker in North Carolina.

The Cranberry mine in Avery County held out until 1938 when it closed after yielding two million tons of magnetite ore. The Cranberry forge was built in 1843.

Now there are only names in old documents and a mountain to show that the ironmakers practiced an art here that caught the fancy of Egyptians four thousand years before the birth of Christ.

During the early part of the 19th century, Cherokee County probably had more forges than any other county in the state.

These included the Lovingood Bloomery Force on Hanging Dog, two miles above Fain's Forge; the Lower Hanging Dog Bloomery Forge, five miles northwest of Murphy; the Killian Bloomery Forge; Shoal Creek Bloomery Forge; Persimmon Creek Forge, and Owl Creek Forge.

The manufacture of iron in the old time forges was crude and difficult.

When the ore was in lumps or mixed with dirt it was crushed by "stompers." These were of hardwood beams raised and dropped by a cogged horizontal revolving shaft.

When the ore was fine enough it was washed in troughs to separate it from as much foreign matter as possible.

It was then ready for the furnace.

The furnace had a rock base six feet by six and was two-and-a-half feet high. On three sides of this base, walls of rock were erected, leaving one side open.

A nest was left in the bottom of the base or hearth. Through the middle ran a two-inch blast pipe. Air was injected into the pipe by a stream of water passing through wooden tubes. A small fire of chips was started in the nest above the mouth of the blast pipe.

Several bushels of charcoal were placed over the fire and blown into a white heat. A layer of ore was spread on the charcoal and as it was heated another layer of charcoal was placed above, and on it still another layer or ore.

This was gradually melted, the molten ore settling into the nest and the silica remaining on top.

Into the mass of melted iron was thrust an iron bar which was used as a handle for turning the ore that stuck to it after it had been withdrawn and placed on an anvil to be hammered.

The melted ore that was drawn out was called a loop.

The hammer and the anvil weighed about seven hundred and fifty pounds each. The two were interchangeable.

The anvil was placed on white oak beams, about the size of railroad crossties, which spanned a pit dug in the ground in order to give spring to the blow made by the hammer.

A strong beam ran through the eye of the hammer, the other end working on a pivot or hinge. Near this hinged end was a revolving shaft shod with four large iron cogs.

These cogs lifted the hammer rapidly, while above the handle a wooden "bray" overcame the upward thrust, and gravity drove the hammer down upon the heated mass on the anvil.

Old reports said such blows were rapid and heavy and, under favorable conditions, could be heard at least ten miles.

When all foreign matter had been hammered out of the loop, it was divided into two or more loops of twenty-five or thirty pounds each.

A short iron bar, to serve as handles, was welded to each piece, and they again were placed in the furnace, reheated and then hammered into bars from nine to twelve feet in length.

Sometimes they were divided into smaller pieces for wagon tires, hoebars, ax-bars, plowshares, plowmolds, harrowteeth bars, and horseshoes.

There was an extra charge for "handage" in the case of wagon tires because they had to be hammered out much thinner than the other pieces.

When each bar or smaller piece was finished, cold water was poured over it to give it a hard, smooth finish.

The ends of the iron bars were went like the runners of a sled or skiis. This was so they could be bound together by iron bands and dragged over the rough trails by a single ox.

In this crude fashion, many tons of iron found their way from Forge Mountain to the homes of settlers where wagons could not travel.

Yes, those were gaunt days when rugged men gave their brawn and brains to a tough struggle for primitive survival along the frontier.

And this mountain stands as a forgotten monument to the pioneer ironmakers.

Road of Shattered Illusions

Lower Savannah

THE ROAD BACK TO CHILDHOOD IS A ROAD OF SHATTERED illusions.

For things remembered are no longer the same.

Time has blurred the old familiar landmarks and the years have whittled away the bigness of things.

Only those who return to the remembered scenes of their childhood become aware of what a change the years can make.

I discovered this today when I came back to a place I knew as a child.

And, in a way, I am sorry I came back, for nothing is the same as I had remembered it.

For years I had lived with the memories of the old homeplace where my father had lived as a boy and where my grandfather died here in the hills above Dillsboro.

Somehow I had come to believe that of all things and all places this spot could never change, yet I found one excuse after another to stay away.

Now I know why.

Nothing is the same. Nothing is the way I remembered it.

The springhouse, shaded by a gnarled old oak, is gone.

So are the crocks of milk that stood cooling in the trough of water, bleached cheesecloth tied about their necks.

The peach trees have withered and died and the apple trees have been cut down.

The grape arbor is gone, too.

The old mule is dead, the barn torn down, and the sled for hauling wood has disappeared.

The cider-mill and the ash-hopper are only memories.

The big iron pot in which my grandmother boiled her clothes

is cracked, the handle broken, and lies rusting in the little branch that runs through the backyard.

The hills of pine have been leveled.

A highway slices through the back acres and the old horse-and-buggy road through the front is only a scar on the landscape.

Only the house and the big chestnut oak whose great limbs hang above the roof remain to give the place any semblance of what it once was.

But the house has changed, too. The oak shingles hewn by my grandfather have been replaced with a metal roof. And the house is beginning to sag.

Gone from the big front room is the spinning wheel, where, no-one remembers. The quilting bars have disappeared, too.

But the old clock still ticks away time on the scarred mantel above the fireplace on which my grandmother cooked, even though she had a woodstove in the kitchen.

There's a little box on the mantel, too, and in it is a Minnie ball, one my grandfather carried back in his leg from Chickamauga and finally got around to cutting out himself with his pocketknife one spring when he was plowing.

The big bed on which my grandfather died is still there in the front room, fast by the fireplace. And over it is spread one of my grandmother's coverlets.

There's a certain smell that seems to cling all around. Don't ask what kind. The smell of old homes, old furniture, old bodies, old dreams.

And sometimes there is a creaking of old timbers, and when you walk back to the kitchen the boards in the floor protest.

I looked for the wooden bucket and the gourd that used to sit on a table by the kitchen door.

And then I went through the door and out to the well, which is still used. But the old wooden handle has been replaced by one of iron, and the rope was new and the bucket was aluminum.

I looked off toward where the barn used to stand, and to the pastures beyond which have been cut up and sold off and flaunt new white bungalows.

The cows and the sheep and the goats are gone.

The chickens don't scratch in the dirt about the house.

There's only a slight depression in the earth where the barn stood, and I remembered the last time I had stood there.

Neighbors with saw and hammer had been there then, making a coffin of pine for my grandfather. And I remember how they talked in hushed tones, their hammers ringing in the September afternoon.

And I remember when we had gone to the cemetery and then come back how my mother had said to my father that it wouldn't be the same any more.

But then, I was only a child of six and couldn't believe that my grandfather's going away would change the world I knew.

I didn't know that the visits thereafter would be few and far between and then finally stop.

I didn't realize there would be no more cider or johnny-cakes cooked on the hearth.

But I know now.

Just as I know that the old oak in the front yard isn't half as big as I remembered it.

Or that my grandfather's land didn't stretch to the end of my eye-reach.

Nothing is the same as I remembered it when I was a child.

But I have my memories, and in time they will wipe away this visit that shattered my childhood illusions.

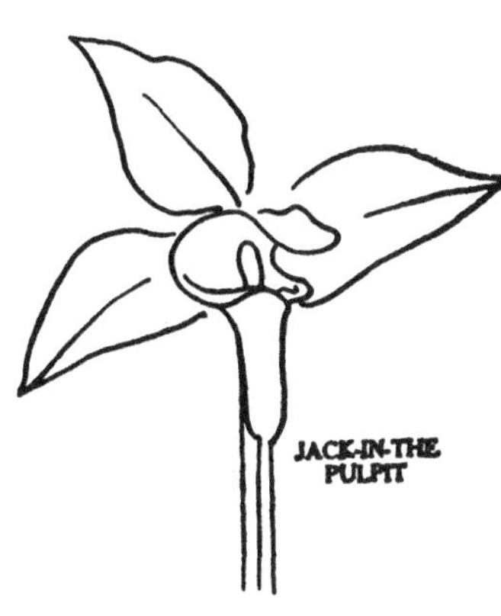

The Fiddlin' Ballad-Woman

Love Field

SAMANTHA BUMGARNER, THE FIDDLIN' BALLAD-WOMAN OF the Carolina hills, fussed with the miseries of age and waited achingly for spring to warm the lameness in her gnarled fingers.

It was a cold, gray afternoon with the clouds hanging low over the valley south of Sylva and there was the smell of snow in the air. But in the little white bungalow perched on the slope of a hill above a running brook there was a warmth that did not come from the coal-burning stove.

There was a wistfulness about the gray-haired ballad-woman as she sat tall and straight in her rocking chair and talked, peopling the room with memories of her wanderings and the songs she has made up out of her head.

At her feet stood a box crammed with yellowed newspaper clippings and tattered pages from a ruled tablet covered with pencil scrawls. They told of the strange and tragic happenings here in the mountains, of murder and death and lost love, the unusual and sinful doings that had gone to form the woof and warp of her songs.

For more than sixty years she has been chronicling such happenings and going-ons, weaving them into ballads and making up tunes to suit them.

She is the last of the old-time balladers, and the cry of her fiddle and the twang of her banjo are known wherever music-makin' folks gather.

Her fame has spread far and wide.

She has wandered up and down the country and across the land—to New York and Washington, New Orleans and St. Louis, Chicago and Kansas City. Even into Old Mexico.

She has fiddled for a king and his queen.

Long before radio discovered mountain music, she was a recording star for Columbia Records with such tangy tunes as "Shout, Lou," "Wild Bill Jones," and "Big-Eyed Rabbit."

She also made recordings for a record firm in Liverpool, England.

In the early Thirties she could be heard nightly from Del Rio, Texas, where she had her own show, one of the first of its kind, over the then most powerful radio station on the North American continent, Dr. John Brinkley's exiled station whose transmitter was in Mexico.

For years she has been a familiar figure at the Asheville Folk Festival.

Samantha began playing a banjo and making up tunes out of her head when she was fifteen. How long ago was that?

"I ain't a-tellin'," she laughed. "Now if you want to guess my age and you hit it right, I'll tell you. But if you don't, then you'll just have to keep on a-wonderin'."

She came by her fiddle and banjo playing naturally.

Her father, Has Biddix, who died in 1930 at the age of 78, was "a fiddle-playin' man from away back," who could make his sour-wood fiddle "croon like a lovin' woman."

"He wouldn't let me touch his fiddle," Samantha recalled, "but when he wasn't at home I would sneak it out and play. Finally, he bought me a banjo and I used to go with him and play around over the country."

When she got married, her husband, Carse Bumgarner, gave her the first fiddle she ever owned. It wasn't long after that when their home burned and she lost both her fiddle and her banjo.

"I got another banjo," she said. "But it was a cheap one. I called it a ten-cent banjo. We was in Canton and they was having a fiddler's convention. Somebody entered me in the banjo contest. First contest I was ever in, and I was nervous.

"I knew I couldn't hit a string. Besides I had that old ten-cent banjo. And here I looked up and saw all these fine banjos coming in from Asheville. I wanted to leave but they wouldn't let me.

"I tell you, I was so nervous I didn't know I was hitting the strings. But I won the contest. And I've been winnin' 'em ever since."

Her head is full of ballads and folk songs.

"I reckon," she said, "I could play from now on and never play the same tune twice."

Her favorite ballad?

"*The Last Gold Dollar*," she said. "I wrote it, you know. Got the idea when the government took up all the gold."

How does it go?

"Can't tell you unless I play it," she said.

She eyed her banjo over in the corner. Then she looked at her gnarled fingers, swollen with arthritis. Finally, she got up and got her banjo and began tuning it up.

Her fingers plucked at the strings. She threw her head back and began singing:

Love me, babe, love me
Love me like you used to.
When I'm gone,
The last gold dollar's gone.

Suddenly she stopped.

"I've just sometimes got music in me," she said. "And again I ain't. Can't do much with these hands."

Maybe it was because she has been shut up all winter, knowing that music-makin' folks were gathering here and there and she couldn't join in.

"Broke my hip about a year ago," she said. "Can't get out like I used to, and I can't clog any more. But come spring. . . ."

Yes, come spring and she'll be out with her fiddle and her banjo. And the rafters will ring.

Bear-Huntin' Men Know the Feeling

Sunset Farms

ALONG ABOUT THIS TIME OF YEAR, ED BUMGARNER GETS the figets.

And when he does, he starts feeding his hounds corn pone and hardening them for the trail.

The fidgets and the corn pone diet are sure signs that bear-hunting time is near.

Ed is more restless than usual, for word has come out of the Blacks, the Snow Birds and the Balsams that the mountains are alive with bear—big, black fellers, vicious as catamounts and game as cold water trout.

"The word is," Ed said, "that there's more bear moving this year than old-timers can ever remember, and I'm anxious to get after them."

Ed was sitting on the porch of his log lodge here in the hills above the Tuckaseigee River and he was eyeing his pack of hounds. The dogs were shiftless after a long, lazy summer, and he was fretting whether they'd be in shape when it come time to hit the rhododendron jungles.

"It's a feeling I get every year about this time," he said. "But they're always ready when the time comes to start running. Some of 'em are trailers and some of 'em are only fighters. The fighters follow the trailers. They couldn't smell ham and eggs, but they'll fight a buzz-saw."

Ed is one of the bear-huntin'est men in all the land and wherever bear-hunting men congregate his name is legion and legend.

"It's the greatest sport there is," Ed said. "Show me a bear hunter and I'll show you a man who knows how to live."

Ed isn't the only hunter who is getting restless and chomping to hit the trail. Talk with Dr. Wayne McGuire, Harry Ferguson,

Realus Sutton and others of their clan, and the talk is of bear hunting these days.

Bear hunting gets in a man's blood, they will tell you, and it never gets out.

Men and dogs hunt the bear in the fall when the bear are hungry and mean, and it's necessary to hunt them early, for they hibernate after the first snows sweep the mountains.

Already the old hunters of the hills are watching the gaps for bear trails and scouting where the best hunting will be.

Pretty soon word will go out and sportsmen will gather at a cabin with their packs to take up the trail of the big, black fellers.

When the season opens most of the hunters will be rangy mountain men with steady aim, quick trigger-fingers and what it takes to follow the hounds when the chase become hardest.

Each will be armed with a heavy rifle, for a bear's hide is thick and tough. The hunters wear heavy shoes—most of them hobnailed. That's to keep from slipping on the rocky ledges in the highlands when the fight nears an end.

A big part of the fun in bear hunting is lolling about the cabin waiting for the hunt to begin, where the hunters tell whoppin' yarns that no one believes.

A few—usually the tenderfeet—generally take a swig or so from a jug, but the tried hunters leave it alone, for bear shooting and corn liquor don't go together.

Granville Calhoun, one of the old-time hunters, prohibited liquor on his hunts.

"If we found a feller with a jug," be said, "we sent him packing or else made him stay at the cabin."

On a typical hunt, the dogs are set down at break of dawn where a bear has been feeding. Sentries are posted in nearby gaps.

"Bears always run up-hill when the dogs jump them," Ed explained. "So, when a trail is struck dogs and men and bear head for the highlands.

"If the bear runs through the guarded gap he usually gets it in the neck. A feller has got to be steady and quick. He's got to shoot fast and sure. Some fellers get excited and miss, and then they've had it. You can tell by the sound of shots when a man kills a bear. You'll hear a shot and then another in about ten or twenty seconds. That usually means a man has got himself a bear. The second shot is to make sure the bear is not just wounded.

"Now, if the bear misses the gap and heads for the roughs, it means a chase, and that's something to be in on. That's where the men and boys are separated.

"The dogs string out behind the bear, baying like coon dogs. It's pretty music and their cries ring for miles. The dogs are cagey. They are born to taunt rather than fight. They nip the bear's flanks but avoid his razor-sharp paws. Sometimes the foolish ones get reckless and the bear slaps them dead or rips them to pieces. It's not a pretty sight.

"He'll tree when he's crowded, and the dogs will bunch at the base of the tree and howl in rage. But the bear snoots them, climbs to the top of the tree and watches the mountains. When the hunters come into view, he will calmly descend, slap down any dog that gets in his way and then race higher into the hills.

"The chase can go on for hours. Men and dogs fall by the wayside, just plumb tuckered out, for it takes strong men and strong dogs to endure the hardening, terrific pace.

"Often the big fellers get away. They know the mountains and the rough places. Few men and dogs can follow them into the rhododendron jungles which are so thick that you have to crawl through them.

"Once a bear gets into a rhododendron jungle he is usually safe. Men have been known to get lost in the jungles. The bear always heads for the jungles high in the reaches of the hills. Sometimes he has a den in a rock cliff, and when he heads there he is pretty safe. I've helped smoke out bears that have got themselves into a rocky den. And you'd better watch out when they come a-running. They are mean-mad. And anything that gets in their way is sure to feel the storm."

One of the most famous of the old-time bear hunters was Wid Medford over in Haywood County. He was a story-teller, too.

"I memorize one time," he related years ago, "that I was in a tight box. It was down on Pigeon where the laurel is too thick for a covey of partridge to rise from. There was one straight trail, and I was in it. My gun was empty.

"I heard the dogs a-comin' and knowed without askin' that the bear was afore 'em. I never had no objection to meetin' a varmint in a square stand-up fight—his nails again my knife, you know, so without thinkin' on gettin' out of the way, I reached for my sticker. The knife was gone, and there I was without a weapon big enough to skin a boomer with.

"I run along lookin' at the laurel on both sides, but there wasn't a place in it for a man to get one leg in. Ticklish? You're sound there. I didn't know for certain what to do, and I got all in a sweat, and drawin' nigher, nigher up the windin' trail, I heard the varmint a-comin.'

"Well, I dropped on my elbows and knees square across the narrow path, so narrow that I had to hump myself into a kind of dead-log. I squinted out one side to see the procession, you know. It come!

"A big monster brute, with a loose tongue hangin' out, and red eyes. He was trottin' like a stage-hoss. He never stopped to even sniff, but, puttin' his paws on my back, as though I was a log, he just leaped over me and was out of sight in a jerk.

"The dogs was close on his heels, a-snappin' away and every one of them jumped over me careless like as him, and raced along without ever stoppin' to so much as lick their master's hand."

Now, after a bear chase, the hunters gather back at the cabin, treat the dogs' wounds and start yarning. Then they cook a bear steak, maybe.

"It's pretty good eating if a fellow is real hungry, but it's course," Ed will tell you. "After being chased a day or so, a bear loses so much fat that the meat gets stringy. But to a fellow that likes bear meat there's nothing like it."

Some folks say the way to cook it is to drop several red hot rocks in a pot of boiling water with the meat, boil the meat for several hours and throw the meat away and eat the rocks.

Be that as it may, Ed Bumgarner likes his bear meat and bear hunting.

That's why he's getting the fidgets and feeding his hounds corn pone.

Origin of Mountain County Names

Newland

THERE'S A HEAP OF UNFAMILIAR HISTORY BEHIND THE names of the counties that form Western North Carolina.

Strangely enough, these names are as familiar to us as their origin and meaning are unfamiliar, and the search for their source and significance reflects images of past people.

Most folks native to the region can reel off the names of our nineteen mountain counties with the ease of a second grader reciting his letters, but when it comes to identifying them with the men they honor there's a scratching of heads.

Except for geneologists and historians, chances are not one person in a hundred can identify the county named for a man known as "Old Bunk," or the county honoring "Pleasant Gardens Joe."

If you know the county named for a man who could have kept Andrew Jackson out of the history books, go to the head of the class.

But we will give odds you'll never guess the name of the county which would bear a different one if the man it honors hadn't quarreled with his family and left Ireland.

With these as teasers, let's take the nineteen counties and give a source and a significance to their names.

To begin with, we are writing this column from the county seat of Avery which was the 100th and last county created in North Carolina (1911). And Newland, incidentally, is the highest county seat in the state, possibly in Eastern America, with an altitude of 3,589 feet.

Avery was named for Colonel Waightstill Avery, Revolutionary patriot and first attorney general of North Carolina, who, challenged to a duel by young Andrew Jackson, allowed the young red head to fire and then marched up to lecture him on his hot-headedness.

Buncombe, formed in 1892, once extended to the western boundary of the state and was named for Col. Edward Buncombe who came from St. Kitts in the West Indies to Tyrrell County in 1766 where he built a mansion of fifty-five rooms called Buncombe Hall. He was a Revolutionary War figure, wounded at Germantown and died of his wounds while on parole in Philadelphia.

Burke, formed in 1777, extended to the Mississippi River and was named for Thomas Burke who emigrated to America because of a family quarrel. He was governor of the state from 1781 to 1782 and is buried near Hillsboro.

Cherokee, formed in 1839, was given its name from the Indians whose lands the county encompassed.

Clay, formed in 1861, was named in honor of Henry Clay.

Graham became a county in 1872 and was named for William A. Graham, U.S. Senator, Governor, Secretary of the Navy and Confederate States Senator. Incidentally, Robbinsville, its county seat, is nearer to the capitals of six other states than to its own.

Haywood, formed in 1808, was named for John Haywood, State Treasurer from 1787 to 1827, and Waynesville, the county seat, was named for General "Mad Anthony" Wayne of Revolutionary fame.

Henderson, formed in 1838, was named for Leonard Henderson who served as Chief Justice of the State Supreme Court from 1772 until 1833. Upon his death, his successor was chosen by the toss of a coin.

Jackson, formed in 1851, was named for Andrew Jackson and the first county seat was at Webster which lost out to Sylva in 1913 when the railroad bypassed it. Incidentally, the present county seat was named for a wandering Dane, William D. Sylva, who paused there briefly.

Macon, formed in 1828, was named for a statesman who argued that five dollars a day was ample pay for a Congressman and who had a rule while in Congress that "if a measure did not arouse great enthusisam in any one section of the nation" he would consider voting for it, but not otherwise.

His name was Nathaniel Macon. He was a Jeffersonian Republican and sat in Congress for thirty-seven years, believing that government should be a policeman for the protection of life and property and nothing more.

Macon was a fancier of wine made from the scuppernong grape, and when sending Thomas Jefferson a couple of bottles in 1819, he described it as "the best in America."

Madison, formed in 1851, was named for President James Madison.

McDowell, formed in 1842, was named for Colonel Joseph McDowell who appended "P.G." to his signature and was called "Pleasant Gardens Joe" to distinguish him from his cousin "Quaker Meadows Joe."

Mitchell, formed in 1861, was named in honor of Dr. Elisha Mitchell, a scientist and professor at the University of North Carolina, who measured the peak now known as Mount Mitchell in 1835 and discovered it to be higher than Mount Washington, N. H., then considered the highest peak in Eastern America.

Polk, formed in 1855, was named for Colonel William Polk of Revolutionary War fame.

Rutherford, formed in 1779, was named for General Griffith Rutherford who led an expedition against the Cherokee in 1776 and wiped out sone 30 towns in the first scorched earth policy on the American continent.

Swain, formed in 1871, was named for the first lawyer of Buncombe County and who had two nicknames—"Old Warping Bars" and "Old Bunk."

His name was David Lowrie Swain. He was the state's youngest governor, taking office when he was thirty-one years old. Later he became president of the University of North Carolina where students bestowed upon him the name "Old Bank," since he came from Buncombe County.

When Sherman's army entered without resistance in April, 1865, Swain, as president of the university and in the absence of the governor, delivered the keys of the Capitol to the victorious Union general.

Transylvania, formed in 1861, derived its name from a couple Latin words meaning "across the woods," which is quite appropriate since much of its territory is in forests and beautiful mountains and laced with waterfalls.

Incidentally, back in colonial days the high hat industry flourished in Brevard and a tax was levied on those who wore the "beavers" made in the now Transylvania County seat.

Watauga, formed in 1849, was not named for an Indian tribe as some historians argue, but for a Creek word meaning "broken waters."

Yancey, formed in 1833, was named in honor of one of the first men in the state to favor public schools for all people.

His name was Bartlett Yancey. He was an eloquent orator, many times a member of the legislature, speaker of the State Senate, and a member of Congress.

Burnsville, county seat of Yancey, was named for Captain Otway Burns of Beaufort who won fame in the war of 1812 against England, and when his statue was erected in the town square somebody asked:

"Is he an Indian?"

Yes, there's a heap of unfamiliar history behind the names of the counties that form Western North Carolina.

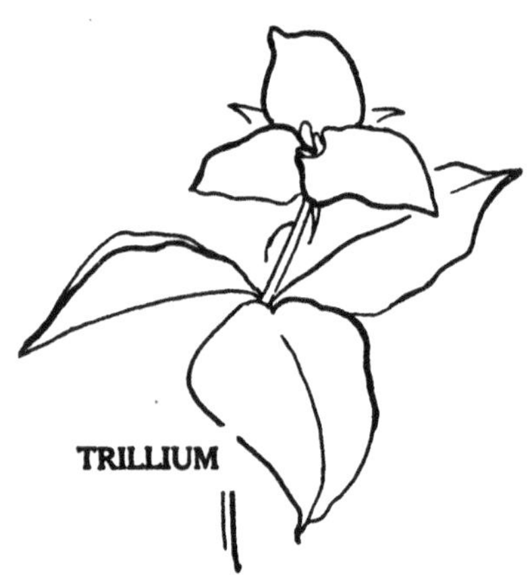

Prophet of the Long Trail

Mount Sterling

THE PROPHET OF THE LONG TRAIL CAME THIS WAY SOME one hundred and fifty years ago on a religious crusade that gave birth to the circuit riding preacher.

His real name was Francis Asbury, the first bishop of the Methodist Church in America.

For a dozen years he roamed the mountains of Western North Carolina winning new converts and entrenching the church over a wide area of the new nation.

This was a wild and uncharted wilderness then, a frontier that tried the souls of hardier men than Asbury whose health was poor but whose zeal was a burning, living thing that pushed him ever onward in the mission he had set for himself.

It is still a wild and beautiful country, and much of the route that Asbury followed in crossing the mountains sixty-three times from Western North Carolina to East Tennessee is now in the Great Smoky Mountains National Park.

So that posterity might know the route that Asbury followed, the Methodist Historical Association began a movement several years ago to designate this trail officially as the *Francis Asbury Trail.*

The route originally was an old Indian trail which mapmakers designated long ago as the Cataloochee Trail.

In the early days of the Republic it connected the eastern seaboard with the Tennessee Valley.

Appropriately enough, the Lake Junaluska Assembly of the Methodist Church is situated on or near the Cataloochee Trail, a few miles from Cove Creek Gap where it enters the Great Smoky Mountains National Park.

The trail used by Asbury, who also was known as the "Bishop on Horseback," connected the Big Pigeon River area of Haywood

County in North Carolina with the region around Cosby and Newport, Tennessee.

It roughly paralleled the present N. C. Highway 285 and Tennessee Highway 32.

The section runs from Cove Creek in North Carolina, by way of Cove Creek Gap, the mouth of Little Cataloochee Creek, Scottish Mountain, Mount Sterling Gap, Mount Sterling Post Office, and Davenport Gap, to an undetermined point on Cosby Creek.

Of the trail, Asbury wrote in his journal in November, 1810:

"Friday our troubles began at the foaming, roaring stream which hid the rocks. At Catahouche I walked over a log. But O, the mountain—height after height, and five miles over! After crossing other streams, and losing ourselves in the woods, we came in, about nine o'clock at night, to Vater Shuck's. What an awful day.

"Saturday, December 1. Last Night I was strongly afflicted with pain. We rode, twenty-five miles, to Buncombe."

Vater Shuck's, where Asbury found shelter, is known as the Shook House and still stands at Clyde, where markers have been placed by the Methodist Historical Society.

Asbury's preaching place in Buncombe County was the Killian house near Asheville, which has been similarly marked.

According to research done by Hiram Wilburn of Waynesville, well-known historian and former employee of the National Park Service, a part of the old road followed by Asbury lies within the boundaries of the Great Smoky Mountains National Park.

This is a stretch of six or seven miles between Cove Creek Gap and Mount Sterling Gap, which skirts the extreme edge of the park.

From Mount Sterling Gap the trail runs by way of Mount Sterling Post Office and Davenport Gap to Cosby Creek and lies slightly outside the park.

There is no road or scarcely noticeable trail there now, albeit more than half of the old foot-beaten trail is identifiable and deeply indented in the ground.

It winds through the woods and brush and in most instances is thickly covered with laurel and other brush.

In seeking to have the trail restored and appropriately marked, the Methodist Historical Society pointed out that no other person of such importance is known to have passed this way and by naming it the "Francis Asbury Trail" no historical tradition would be affected.

When the trail has been so designated and appropriately marked, the society pointed out, it will become a mecca for thousands of persons each year and an area of great scenic beauty will be turned into a useful recreational and inspirational purpose.

Back in 1846, an attempt was made to build a road over the trail.

The State Legislature of that year passed an act creating the "Jonathan Creek and Tennessee Mountain Turnpike Company" which was to construct a road from Waynesville to the Tennessee State Line.

Specifications called for a road twelve feet wide and not steeper than one foot vertical to eight feet horizontal which would be a grade of twelve per cent.

When the road should be completed according to specifications the company would have the right to erect a toll gate and collect the following rated toll:

A six-horse wagon; seventy-five cents; a five-horse wagon, sixty two and one-half cents; a four-horse wagon or coach, fifty cents; a three or two-horse wagon or carriage, twenty-five cents; a one-horse wagon, cart, or carriage, twenty cents; man or horse, ten cents each; hogs and sheep, one cent each.

But the company failed and the road was not built.

Another attempt was made by the legislature in 1851 for construction of a four-foot road, but there was difficulty in deciding on the best and most practicable route.

The final location was almost exactly along the line of the old Indian trail.

In his travels through Western North Carolina, Asbury first tried making his way through the mountains by chaise but had to resort to horseback, which was not easy either.

He first came into the mountain area in 1800. He was so encouraged by the religious hunger he discovered in the coves that he continued his visits until November, 1813.

When he first visited Hot Springs in November, 1800, he wrote in his journal that "my company was not agreeable here—there were too many subjects of the two great potentates of this Western World, whisky, brandy. My mind was greatly disturbed."

He continually complained of the cold and heat and roughness of the roads and trails.

There was both ardor and anger in his writings.

After stopping at Thomas Foster's he wrote that "we must bid farewell to the chaise; this mode of conveyance by no means suits the roads of the wilderness."

"Coming to Laurel River," he wrote, "we followed the wagon head of us—the wagon stuck fast. Brother O'Haven mounted old Gray—the horse fell about midway, but recovered, rose, and went safely through with his burden."

Sometime later he preached at Fletcher and "gave them a good sermon and an exhortion."

On November 14, he wrote "we took our leave of French Broad—the lands flat and good, but rather cold. . . . We had no labor getting down Saluda Mountain."

The following year in October "we made a push for Buncombe Courthouse: man and beast felt the mighty hills" as he rode in from Hot Springs.

Once on a trip to Rutherford County from Buncombe, he wrote that "one of the descents is like the roof of a house, for nearly a mile. . . . I rode, I walked, I sweat, I tumbled, and my old knees failed; here are gullies, and rocks, and precipices . . . bad is the best."

Without any established home, Asbury traveled on horseback approximately 275,000 miles during his crusade for Methodism.

Appropriately enough, there is a monument to him in Washington showing him sitting astride a horse.

Perhaps sometime in the near future he will be memorialized here in the mountains where he labored long and hard in the vineyards of the Lord.

Perhaps it will not be too long until there will be markers along the trail up here to show that the Prophet of the Long Trail came this way.

In Calvary Churchyard . . .

Fletcher

THERE'S A WIND THAT BLOWS BETWEEN THE WORLDS and riding it are sounds that tease the imagination.

It gives a voice to the long dead and weaves a picture of events in time out of memory.

But to recognize the sounds and the voices you must know what took place on yonder mountain, or along the valley there, or here in the churchyard of Calvary Episcopal parish.

For those with an uncommon ear, the wind that whispers in the tall pines that stand like sentinels in the churchyard conjures up scenes of a colorful and eventful period along the old Buncombe Turnpike.

So come along to the churchyard of Calvary and wander along the twisting paths beneath the pines in the blue of twilight.

Perhaps you will hear the voices of General George Stoneman and his Yankee raiders, for they came this way during the turbulent years of the War Between the States.

Listen sharp for the whinny of blown horses, the rattle of mess kits, the mumbling, grumbling of men who wanted to be home.

Stoneman's raiders camped here one night and, as they dismounted, the general was drawn into the sanctuary.

Perhaps he went to see what he could plunder, or perhaps his conscience was bothering him and he went to pray.

For behind him lay a country he had laid waste, looted and plundered.

But he was so impressed with the beauty of the sanctuary and its quiet atmosphere of reverence that he gave orders that no part of the church was to be molested.

He did allow his men to sleep inside and nothing was harmed.

Next morning before leaving, his men begged for the church carpet to be used as saddle blankets.

The general at last gave in and the raiders were seen going south on the turnpike that day with red church carpet fluttering from the backs of their horses.

Listen and you will hear other voices in the wind, the voices of men who wore Confederate gray and fought for a forlorn cause.

For the churchyard was the meeting place of volunteers from the surrounding mountains and valleys to the Confederate army.

The church itself was used at one time as barracks by Confederate troops.

There are echoes in the wind, too, of carriages passing down there on the turnpike and turning in the drive.

These were the carriages of the people from the low country who organized the parish almost a century ago, merchants and rice planters of Charleston—summer residents of this region—who, wanting to attend church services of their own faith, had to travel to Flat Rock over the rough miles of the turnpike.

Perhaps the voices in the wind that whispers in the pines are the voices of Edmund Molyneux, Alexander Robertson and Alexander Blake.

They were responsible for organizing the parish whose quaint sanctuary has been described as one of the most beautiful country churches in America.

At a dinner party at The Meadows plantation of Blake one evening early in 1857 the subject of rough roads and the need for a church came up.

One of the most enthusiastic advocates for the church was Molyneux, an Englishman who had been serving as a consul from his country to America at the time he began coming to North Carolina.

Within a matter of minutes that night more than five thousand dollars was subscribed for a building fund and Blake donated four acres of land for the parish.

A Charleston architect was employed to build the church. The brick for the structure was made here in Fletcher by slave labor.

The church was consecrated on August 21, 1859 by the Rt. Rev. Atkinson, bishop of the diocese of North Carolina.

For the first year or so after its completion, the church was kept open only during the summer months and services were held by visiting clergymen.

Among them were the Rev. Dr. J. S. Hanckel and the Rev. Toomer Porter of Charleston.

Then the Rev. N. Collin Hughes, rector of St. James Church in Hendersonville was called to take charge of Calvary parish. He officiated two Sundays each month during the winter of 1860-61 and while the War Between the States was in progress he held services on many occasions.

Fire destroyed the original structure in 1935.

But the edifice was rebuilt and enlarged less than three years later and was consecrated on the 79th anniversary of the consecration of the original church.

Brick from the old church was salvaged and used to veneer outside walls, thus preserving some of the appearance of age.

Pause there in the churchyard by the grave of Edgar Wilson (Bill) Nye, the famous humorist, and listen to the wind in the pines.

Perhaps the wind will send his voice whispering out of time.

Nye was one of the most beloved of those who have been associated with Calvary Church and its grounds.

During the years the Nye family lived at Buck Shoals, near here, they attended services at Calvary Church and Mrs. Nye sometimes served as organist.

Sometimes the wind is high and keen. When it is, there is a sound like the stagecoach bugle echoing along the old Buncombe Turnpike in the days when events flowed and ebbed around Calvary Church.

Yes, there are voices in the wind that plays through the tall pines in the churchyard of Calvary parish.

For it is a wind that blows between the worlds and riding it are sounds that tease the imagination.

Listen sharp the next time you stand beneath the tall, whispering pines in Calvary churchyard when the blue of twilight is upon the land.

Tinkle of Bell Teams Fades

Highlands

THE DAYS OF RIDING THE SHAKE-GUTS AND THE TINKLE of bell teams have faded into the limbo of an epic pageant of wheels.

Gone are the lurching gig, the antiquated shay, and the spring wagon.

The hitching rack and the boot scraper have been destroyed.

The trucker has replaced the romantic wagoner with his six-horse team, and the livery stable has gone the way of the old stagecoach inn.

Homespun and calico have bowed out to satin and silk.

Gee and haw, the nigh side and the off side, these were familiar terms until thirty years ago, but now almost incomprehensible.

There are those who remember the freight horses, with brass-studded collar housings and tinkling bells, and still around are a few old-timers who held the reins when hacks, surreys, buggies and wagons provided the only transportation for folks here in the mountains

The six Potts brothers remember, and well they should, for they nursed many a horse-drawn vehicle up and down the mountains between Highlands and the South Carolina and Georgia market towns.

Their father started the business in 1895, and for almost twenty years the boys hauled everything from tourists to silver dollars.

The Potts livery service was one of the most famous in all the mountains. It was known for its fast horses and fast service.

Stables were operated here and at the South Carolina towns of Walhalla and Seneca.

"When we had stables in South Carolina," recalled Charlie

Potts, who is now postmaster here, "we even pitted out stagecoaches against the trains, and outrun 'em, too.

"We had a stagecoach on the run between Walhalla and Seneca that used four to six horses, and they were fast steppers. Kentucky-bred and fast, running fast.

"It was our boast that we could get folks from Walhalla to Seneca faster than the train. And we did. Made the nine-mile run in thirty minutes. Got so folks would ride the stagecoach instead of the train."

During the summer when freight hauling and tourist travel was the heaviest, the Potts kept between fifty and sixty wagon, carriage and saddle horses. They cut the number down to twenty in winter.

They bought their saddle horses in Tennessee and Kentucky in the spring, used them during the summer, and took them in the fall to South Carolina where they sold them to planters.

"The roads were pretty bad in those days," said Charlie Potts. "Actually you couldn't hardly call them roads. They were rough and got mighty muddy and sticky when it rained.

"I used to do mostly freight hauling, though I worked hacks and carriages and stagecoaches. In hauling freight from Walhalla it used to take me three days to make the round trip, a distance of sixty-four miles there and back. Naturally, you could make it quicker in a carriage, a day to go and a day to come.

"Our passengers found it pretty rough riding sometimes. They got shaken up a bit, but we always managed to bring them up here and take them back. I can't remember of a horse ever failing to come through."

Before 1907, all visitors to Highlands had to go either to Walhalla or Lake Toxaway, the nearest railway points, and come the rest of the way in a horse-drawn vehicle.

But in 1907 the Tallulah Falls Railroad extended its lines to Dillard, Ga., which is about half the distance it was to Walhalla.

So the Potts brothers brought most of the visitors up from that point, the Dillard-Highlands run requiring only about five hours.

For these runs, they used five types of passenger vehicles—buggies, two-seated surreys, three-seated hacks, three-seated surreys, and four-seated hacks.

"All of them had fringed tops and curtains that could be pulled down or up," said Charlie Potts. "They had steel-wire wheels and brakes.

"Trunks and other baggage and supplies were brought in by wagon from Walhalla, Dillard or Lake Toxaway."

The Potts brothers also had a mail route.

They picked up the mail at Russell's Wayside Inn, which was half way between Walhalla and Highlands. They carried both mail and passengers by way of Grimshawes in Whiteside Cove.

"The postoffice at Grimshawes was named for an Englishman by that name who also kept boarders during the summer," Potts said. "Once he fussed with the feller bringing the mail and passengers from Walhalla to Russell's, claiming that he was purposely being slow so folks headed for Grimshawes would have to spend the night at Russell's.

"The feller on that end of the run was named Houtchins, and Grimshawes told him if he didn't get the folks through in one day he was going to route them by Sapphire.

"That caused old man Russell to pipe up and say he didn't care if he routed them by hell-fire."

Potts said during the years they ran the livery service they hauled into Highlands everything except feeds, which were raised here.

"All the groceries and hardware that the town had to have we hauled," he said. "We even hauled in money for the merchants and for the bank. It was mostly silver. We never did seem to have enough on hand for transactions, and still don't.

"We would take an empty cotton-seed hull box, put the sack of money in it and then cover it with hulls. No, nobody ever tried to hold us up. We never lost a cent in all the years we hauled silver into the town. I guess we were pretty lucky."

Potts began driving a team when he was six and made a career out of it for some fifteen years. He is sixty-one now.

"We got our wagons and hacks and buggies from different sources," he said. "R. H. Brown at Cashiers made wagons and he had a shop at Highlands, too. We also bought wagons from Jim Palmer in Franklin. Then we had Studabakers and Nissens.

"The carriages came from the Rock Hill, S. C., Buggy Company and were called Rock Hill Buggies.

"We used two horses to a buggy because one couldn't pull all day over the rough roads.

"Beck and Bill were the best team of wagon mules we ever had. I reckon the best horse we ever had was one named Nellie, a beautiful bay from Kentucky.

"And Mollie, another bay, was one of the meanest, most contankerous horses that ever lived. Anybody who drove Mollie had to keep his eye on her and keep a strong hand on the reins."

While spring and summer were busy months for the livery service, there was the job of hauling freight right on through the winter.

Maneuvering a big wagon drawn by skittish horses or mules over the snowy, often slushy and icy mountain roads, was a task that kept the driver busy all the way.

Contrary to popular belief, mountain teamsters walked more than they rode.

Freighting demanded strong wagons, sturdy harness and stout horses. The team was the center of interest always. Wagons were made only to be pulled, and harness was only harness, but the horse was a living thing.

Strangely enough, wagoners had no trouble getting up hills, but the trouble was getting down with a heavy load. A feller could wear out a set of tires if he had to lock his wheels.

Yes, the days of riding the shake-guts and the tinkle of bell teams are gone, but there are a few left like Charlie Potts who can remember how it was and the feel of the reins in their hands.

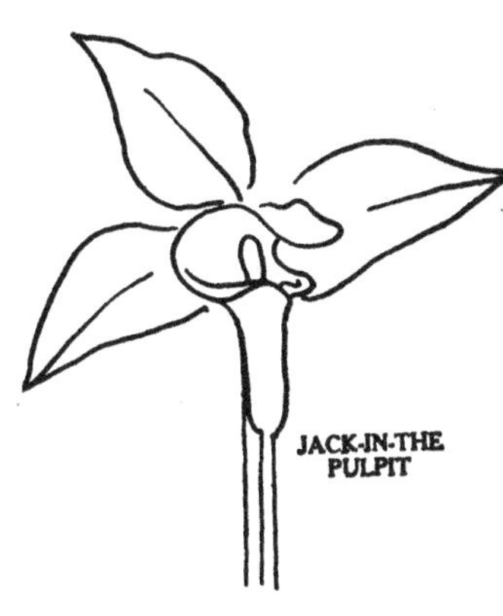

The Legend of Tom Collins

Balsam

THEY SAY TOM COLLINS REALLY LIVED.

He has been haunting me for twenty-five years, and I still don't know if he was a man or a legend.

My grandfather, who has seen the trees come to leaf two score plus man's allotted span upon the earth, is inclined to believe that Tom Collins actually lived.

"Where there's smoke," says my grandfather, "there is fire."

Legend says Tom Collins was fire.

He was a clansman, a feudal lord of the Carolina hills.

The only monument he ever got is a drink which bears his name.

That is part of the legend.

There is a ballad, too.

A ballad about Tom Collins and his keen eye and quick trigger-finger and how he could drink his fill of corn whiskey, which was a heap.

There are some who say the ballad was about George Coggins, another mountaineer.

But George appeared on the scene long after Tom Collins was a name from New York to London, San Francisco to Singapore.

The Collinses were among the first settlers in the wilderness of Western North Carolina.

They blazed a trail for others to follow.

They sought wingroom and a place where a man could spit without hitting a neighbor. They staked a claim in the Great Smokies long before other white men discovered the venerable temple of the world's oldest mountains.

One of their kinsmen has carried the story of Tom Collins around the world.

I grew up with him, and he knew the spring from which Tom dipped up a gourd of water to mix his famous concoction that many swear is the granddaddy of today's famous drink.

Some folks say Tom Collins grooved together a cabin here and tarried a while, because of a bubbling spring that years later was to make this a famous resort, and then moved on to the Great Smokies.

I first heard the story of Tom Collins around a campfire high in the Smokies. It was told by a boy named Collins. He's a Commander in the U. S. Navy now.

We were kids then, part of a troop of Boy Scouts exploring a virgin wilderness, in the days when the Smokies were a jungle that had felt the feet of few white men.

There was a mountain in that jungle that had been named for one of his kinsmen.

It wasn't Tom, but perhaps it should have been.

I don't know if he ever got that far.

You see, Tom died when he was quite young.

At least that's what the legend says.

I'm a skeptic and a sentimentalist, one and at the same time.

But I would like to believe that Tom Collins really lived.

For I have a hunch that he did.

And when I have doubts, I remember what Stephen Vincent Benet wrote:

"It's always seemed to me that legends and yarns and folk tales are as much a part of the real history of a country as proclamations and provisos and constitutional amendments."

A dozen years had passed when the late James Street, a history buff, reintroduced me to Tom Collins. Another dozen years passed when I next heard of the fabulous mountaineer.

A soldier in Harry's Bar in Paris, learning I was from the North Carolina mountains, brought up the subject of Tom Collins and said he had heard of the ballad about him. He didn't remember the lines.

I've never found anyone who knew the ballad, and all I've ever been able to collect are bits and pieces, along with the legend of Tom Collins.

They say Tom Collins was born with a rifle in his hand and hate in his heart. At three days old he swore to wipe out the English single-handed.

My grandfather said he never believed the story.

Anyway, the story goes that Tom's folks came to America after the Battle of Culloden when the Scotch had been crushed to submission and swore never to bear arms against the British.

Any man with an English name, they said, was a prime target for Tom's rifle as he lay in the rhododendron thickets and watched the trails, nipping at the jug that was always close by.

They say Tom could knock a squirrel's eye out at fifty paces, clip at least two birds from a covey and reload before they hit the ground.

Tom ambushed his enemies one day, wiped off the leader of the opposing faction and got a bullet in his lungs as final payment.

He went to a neighbor's house and drank his fill of corn. Then he went home and died.

The ballad says:

Tom Collins came home one Saturday night
And he lay him down and died.

And when he had been laid out for burial, they say his sweetheart sang:

Turn back, turn back that carfin' lid
And lift them silks so fine
And let me kiss those dear sweet lips
Which never in life kissed mine."

There's nobody around today who remembers Tom Collins or where, if he was ever more than a legend, he is buried.

But even if he was born on the wind, there's a monument to Tom Collins.

It's the drink that bears his name.

Many folks believe it's the educated descendant of Tom's favorite mixture, which was a jigger of corn whiskey, sweetened spring water, and a dash of bitters made from the squeezings of elderberries.

The Sisters of Loneliness

Cashiers Valley

SHE WAS A STRANGER TO BUTTONS AND BOWS, BUT SHE was queen of the wild frontier.

She was the axeman's woman, the pioneer's wife.

She had no name, yet she had many.

She was Daniel Boone's Rebeccah and Davy Crockett's Polly.

She was your great-great-grandmother, and mine.

She was a Biblical wife, and she told her husband:

"Your sorrows will be my sorrows, and your joys will be my joys."

She gave him her heart and her hands and children.

The gold band on her finger encompassed a lifetime's fidelity.

She came this way before there was a light or a hearth or a roof.

She knew the meaning of suffering and travail, and she was a sister to loneliness, yet she never complained.

She was a heroine who, for the most part, was passed up by the history books, because the things she did were the things expected of her.

She fought Indians, defended her home and her children, hefted an ax, sometimes followed a plow, stood at a spinning wheel.

She was a shoemaker, a tanner, a dressmaker, a miller, a farmer, a trapper, a nurse, a preacher, an undertaker, or anything else that the occasion might demand.

Her hands were hardened with toil and browned from exposure.

She hunted greens, picked wild berries, and gathered nuts for the winter's store.

She made candles and soap.

She told time by the shadow falling through the open door on the puncheon floor.

Her calendar was the mantlepiece, notched and re-notched.

She remembered the years by a death, or when the big snow came, or by a birth.

She had no time for dreaming, albeit all women dream.

She drew her satisfaction from the things she did for her family

Her day began at the first cock's crow and ended long after darkness.

She knew her Bible from "kivver to kivver."

She read from it nightly, gathering her flock about her, setting aside a few minutes of her precious time so her children would not be ignorant of the word of God.

She knew the old ballads that had been fetched over from Scotland and England and Ireland, and these she sometimes sang, if she wasn't too tired.

She sang of fair ladies and bold knights, of fine silks and satins, this woman who only knew homespun and calico.

And in time, there were ballads about her, too.

She was a legend.

Her name lives in a thousand stories and a thousand tales.

Some of them, a few, you will find in the history books.

But most of them have been handed down by word of mouth.

This queen of the wild frontier was a woman named Polly Stepp, and another named Mary Norton. She was also Fannie Stepp, the courageous, and Lydia Whaley, who preached her own husband's funeral.

Mary Norton lived right here in the valley.

She followed her husband here, and stood by while he chopped down trees to build their cabin of pine. They had no nails, so they used wooden pegs.

In time, children came along. And they prospered in a modest way, with cattle and hogs.

One night when her husband was away from home, she was awakened by the squealing of hogs at the nearby hog-pen.

The night was cold and she had no time to clothe herself, but rushed from the cabin in her nightdress and with bare feet. She snatched up an ax and hurried to the hog-pen where she saw a large, black bear.

The bear was in the act of killing one of her pet "fattening hogs."

She aimed a blow at the bear's head and split it from ear to chin, and they had bear meat for breakfast.

Fannie Stepp was one of the first pioneer women to settle in what is now Polk County.

Once when her husband was away, Indians surrounded her cabin, then took her and her children captive and started with them through the woods.

The Indians stopped to cut some lead from a spot on one of the mountains. For some reason they got scared. One of them hit Fannie in the head with a tommyhawk, then scalped her.

Another of the Indians hit little Polly, the baby, then picked her up and dashed her head against a tree. But she wasn't killed.

Even though half dead, Fannie was fighting mad.

They tied her to a tree.

Then they took her little boy—they had scalped him, too—and told her they were going to burn him to death.

They piled up brush and set fire to it and started toward the fire with the boy.

Fannie passed out when she saw them laying him in the flames.

When she regained consciousness, the Indians were gone. The fire had died down, and she couldn't find any sign of the boy.

She never did.

She finally got loose from her bonds, took Polly in her arms and made her way back to her home.

Polly grew up and had her go with the Indians.

She was middle-aged when an attack was made on the fort at Point Lookout.

The Cherokee were led by a chief called Big Injun.

After several rounds of shots had been fired, Polly, who had been molding bullets and running them for the men, picked up a rifle and moved over to one of the loopholes. She stuck the rifle through and took dead aim, pulled the trigger.

When the smoke cleared, she let out a whoop.

"I've killed the Big Injun," she shouted. "Damned if I ain't killed the Big Injun."

When Polly wasn't fighting Indians she was seeing to the wants of her family, making shoes for the children, canning and drying fruits and vegetables, and sometimes taking in a bit of sewing.

She received a dollar for making a man's coat and vest, and fifty cents for a pair of breeches. She made dresses for women and children for as low as twenty-five and fifty cents.

She and her sisters never knew what it was to be idle.

The pioneer woman was a swapper, too.

Aunt Lydia Whaley once traded two pairs of homemade and homegrown socks to an Indian medicine man for a pipe and some medicine secrets.

The frontier woman and the frontier have long disappeared. There are only memories of them.

But Aunt Mollie Fisher down at Cullowhee can tell you how it was. She remembers what her mother and her grandmother told her, and she knows a bit what it was like, for as a girl during the Civil War, when the menfolks were off fighting, she hoed corn and did the planting.

My grandfather remembers, too.

"They just don't grow 'em like your great-grandma any more," he says. "Times have changed and we don't have such womenfolks now-a-days, else the Lord would raise 'em up like he did back then."

The Beef Shoot

Cataloochee Ranch

MOUNTAIN MEN WHOSE MARKSMANSHIP IS LEGEND ARE limbering up their muzzle-loading rifles and smartening up their aim.

They are getting themselves all primed for an event that had its origin back in the days of the American Revolution when the long rifle talked independence and argued well for John Sevier's mountain boys.

It is the traditional "shooting for the beef," commonly known as a shooting match, a custom that blossomed into a crackerjack sport because of such famed rifle-crackers as Daniel Boone and Davy Crockett.

Only in those lean days it was called a "rifle frolick," and the shooting was for liquor, beef being scarce on the frontier. That's where the term "rifle-whiskey" was born.

Like the hoedown, the Elizabethan ballad and the Plott bear hound, the old-time muzzle-loading beef shoot has survived the swift inroads of modern civilization here in the mountains of Western North Carolina.

And come next Wednesday the seventeeth annual Cataloochee Beef Shoot will draw mountain rifle-crackers here to Tom Alexander's ranch atop mile-high Fie Top Mountain, reached by a three-mile gravel road connecting with U.S. 19 at Maggie.

As practiced here, the beef shoot is one of the unique sporting events in America. It is really the only truly authentic muzzle-loading rifle shooting match in the nation.

Only the muzzle-loader or Kaintuck rifle is used, and a fellow caught using a "peep sight" on his hog-rifle will get thrown off the mountain.

"We're going to keep this meet authentic," Alexander explained recently. "No where else in America has the old muzzle-loading rifle been preserved as here in the Smokies and we are not going to let other types of rifles, even copies of the old ones, be used.

"Makes no difference where a man is from. If he's got one of the old muzzle-loaders or Kaintucks he can step out and lay his aim on the line with the boys from hereabouts."

The colorful contest—held each August—usually attracts upward of 100 marksmen of all ages, and a large crowd of spectators who watch the shooting, listen to fiddle-music and maybe join in a bit of square-dancing.

The mountain men will begin to drift in about the time the sun slips over the mountain laurel.

They'll come from over the ridges of the Smokies by foot and by mule and horse and car and truck.

They'll be carrying their long-barreled muzzle-loaders in their arms, powder horns and bullet pouches slung across their shoulders.

Maybe they'll pause down behind the barn, tip a jug. They'll be sure to scan the sky, wet a finger to the wind to get a bearing on how they must aim their shots. The wind can play havoc with their shooting.

Their talk will be rifle-talk, of failing eyes and the infirmities of age, of crops, and the precious price of black powder.

They'll build a fire and melt lead and mold bullets for their ancient rifles.

And then they'll do some shooting here on the flat tableland of Fie Top Mountain which looks away to Tennessee and Carolina's Balsams and Smokies and Blue Ridge.

Just across the ridge is Happy Valley. That's where John Sevier gathered his mountain boys and struck out for a place called Kings Mountain with their long rifles. The British casualties were shocking.

And it wasn't too far from here that Andrew Jackson practiced law and Davy Crockett hunted bear with his famous old Betsy gun on whose stock was carved: "Be sure you are right, then go ahead." That was the same gun that almost wrecked Santa Anna's army at the Alamo.

Across the ridge to the south is where Tom Collins lived and feuded and died. He was a pretty good man with a muzzle-loader, too, until he tried to take on too many fellers at one time and got a bullet in his chest.

The shooting will begin about midmorning.

And they'll be shooting for one of Alexander's prize beeves.

There will be five prizes—a quarter of the beef will go to each winner in an individual age group, and the fifth prize will be the hide and tallow.

The old-timers go about winning deliberately. Some take as long as three minutes to aim, and hours in preparation, which includes measuring powder charges—some use a hollow bear's tooth—and molding their bullets by hand over an open fire.

Of course, there are some who will depend on Charlie Cagle from over at Hemphill to do their bullet molding for them.

Charlie is sixty-four. His eyes went bad on him several years ago and forced him to hang up his muzzle-loader for good.

"Got so I couldn't see the target," Charlie told us. "So about six years ago I started running bullets fer them that didn't hanker to make their own. It was a sad come-down. I'd been shootin' on to forty years when my eyes went bad."

Charlie is an expert at running bullets. Let him explain how he molds them for the muzzle-loaders.

"First," he says, "you build a roarin' good fire of hickory sticks. Hickory makes a hot fire. Then you take your lead and put it in a ladle. You put the ladle on the fire and melt the lead. Then you pour that hot lead into a mold and you've got a bullet. Your mold is whatever size the bore of your rifle is. Mold and rifle bore have got to match, or you've got mean trouble."

Wadding for the bullets is made mostly from bed ticking.

All of them make their own targets—a charred hardwood board, against which a white sheet of paper is tacked. From the center of the paper, the mountain men cut out a diamond about two and a half inches high.

That exposes a black, diamond-shaped bullseye.

In the center of the diamond, they scratch a cross with a knife. The point where the lines cross is dead center. And it is from there the bullet holes are measured by the judges.

The beef shoot rules are simple.

The range is sixty yards, and it takes good shooting to put a lead ball into a three-inch square.

But these mountain rifle-crackers can do it.

Each man gets three shots at the target which, incidentally, is the same type Daniel Boone shot at when he was the first rifleman of these hills.

He pays two dollars for his target and the right to shoot. He can buy as many boards and shoot at as many targets as he sets up, and as long as his cash holds out

The event is non-profit, and the money that is collected from the contestants goes to help Alexander bear the expenses of the meet.

Most of the shooting is done from a prone position. A log or other rest may be used. Any amount of assistance may be obtained, such as shading the sights or breechlock from the sun's glare.

Actually, the shooting is a test of rifles.

Some of them have "cranky ways," known only to their owners. For example, with the sight on dead center of the diamond, the shot may rise a little. Another may pull to the right, or the left.

The rifles range in weight from ten to fifteen pounds on an average.

Throughout the day, there are lively discussions of the merits of favorite rifles, which often have names like *Granny*, *Skinner*, *Old Fetchem*, *Betsy Gal*, *Mister True*, *Little David*, *Squirrel Barker*, *Fire-And-Be-Damned*, or *Smokie Joe*.

The actual makes are the Lancaster, because they were made in the Pennsylvania town of Lancaster, and the Lewin, which was made in an Ohio town by that name.

Mountaineers call the muzzle-loaders "hawg rifles." Pioneer sharpshooters used them to kill wild hogs in the Smokies.

Many of them were made here in the mountains.

The Messers of Cataloochee were a renowned family of gunsmiths.

Then there were the Beans—Russell and William. Also the Wards, the Hopkins, and the Gillespies.

In some cases, folks in the Smokies bought the barrel and the firing mechanism from outside and supplied handhewn stocks from native hardwood. Sometimes the stock was ornamented with inlays of brass, German silver, or even coin silver.

Among the old-timers who have been participating in the annual beef shoots and who are expected to be on the line when the firing starts Wednesday are 83-year-old E. L. Horton of Democrat and Daniel Boone Arrington of Balsam, who is seventy-four.

If 64-year-old Robert Lee Wallin of Big Laurel is still alive and able to sight a gun, he will be there to defend his sharpshooting title as the best shot in the Smokies, which he plucked last year with his "Little Lewin."

There's some speculation whether the Suttons and the Riches and the Messers will be there to resume their bloodless feud.

They stayed away last year, just when everybody was primed to see them go at it tooth and nail.

If they do show up, while the other rifle-crackers are shooting for the beef, they will be laying family pride of marksmanship along the sites of their muzzle-loaders.

The feud between these families started here several years ago when the judges awarded the Suttons first prize after much deliberation and much careful measuring.

The Riches and the Messers made no bones about their displeasure with the decision. The Suttons didn't help matters with a little boasting.

In 1953 while they were carrying on their own shooting match, an old-timer named Bill Bradley of Waynesville stepped in and out-shot everybody to grab the title.

The Riches, the Messers and the Suttons all agreed the old man had done some pretty fair shooting, and then retired back of Alexander's corn crib where they tilted a common jug.

So, if you want to see a rare event and the kind of shooting that won this country, come on up to Fie Top Mountain where the ghosts of Daniel Boone and Davy Crockett will be hanging around.

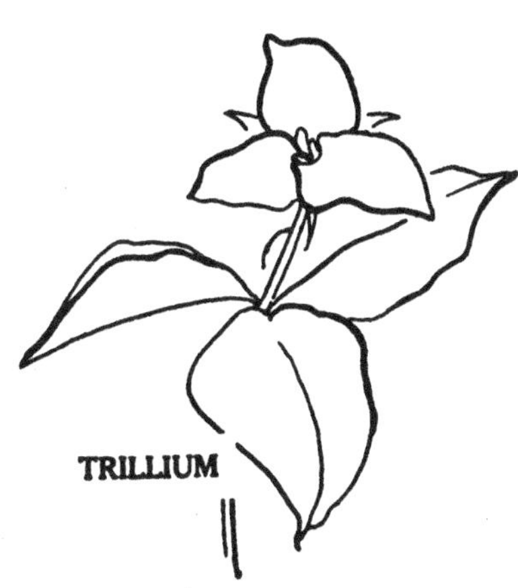
TRILLIUM

The Ballad of Tom Collins

Patton Mountain

THE GHOST OF TOM COLLINS—HE OF THE DEMIJOHN, THE fiddle and the rifle—can rest easy now.

I have found the long-lost ballad that his death inspired.

And now perhaps mountain fiddlers once again will play and sing the ballad of Tom Collins.

It is the story of a clansman of the Great Smokies, who took his pleasure in feudin', and a mountain girl named Mary, who pined away for the love she couldn't have.

A 25-year search for this elusive ballad came to an end a few days ago here on Patton Mountain just at daydown, in the pink of evening, as the long shadows moved down across Asheville toward the faraway peaks of the Smokies.

From the big picture-window in the home of Bob and Margaret Bunnelle we stood gazing off toward the Balsams and the Smokies and the subject of Tom Collins came up.

Somebody wrote a ballad about Tom, I said, although there are some who say it was about George Coggins, another mountaineer. But even so, I said, I can't find anybody who knows the words of the song which I had heard so long ago and forgotten.

But I knew the story. How Tom ambushed his enemies one day, wiped off the leader of the opposing faction and got a bullet in his lungs as final payment.

Tom went to a neighbor's house and drank his fill of corn. Then he went home and died.

"Why, I know the song you have in mind," said Bob. "Heard it on a trip out to Balsam Gap about twenty-five years ago. But it was sung about George Coggins."

And then he began singing the words of the ballad I had known as the ballad of Tom Collins, and Margaret joined him.

George Coggins come home one Saturday night
Laid down on his bed and he died
And his own true love in the very next room
Sat sewing them silks so fine.

That's it, I told him. Just as I remembered it . . . his true love in the next room sewing her trousseau for a wedding she had hoped would turn Tom from his feudin' and drinkin'.

When she heered George Coggins were dead
She folded them silks so fine
She weeped, she moaned, she moaned, she weeped
She weeped and she moaned and she cried.

Bob and Margaret sang it as it should be sung—in a sing-song cadence, more wails than rhythm.

Oh, Mary, Oh, Mary, git up from there
And dry your weeping eyes
There are other young men a'hangin' around
A'watchin' you weep and cry.

No, Mother, No, Mother, I know there are other young men
A'hangin' round
But I followed George Coggins through this life
And I'll follow him to the ground.

Then, as the story goes, when the clansmen filed past his bier, she sang:

Lay back, lay back them coffin lids
Fold up them silks so fine
And let me kiss them dear pale lips
That never in life has kissed mine.

To one and all, and to the dead sweetheart, Mary sang her requiem, just as Bob and Margaret sang the words from out of long memory:

Then as a dove who moans for his love
And flits from pine to pine
I'll weep and I'll moan and I'll moan and I'll groan
For I in this life have lost mine.

In the gathering shadows the story of a feudal lord and his sweetheart, his death and her love for him, came alive.

Whether the story and the ballad are about Tom Collins or George Coggins, I don't know.

Could be that they were one and the same.

When I first heard it more than twenty-five years ago, the story and the ballad were about Tom Collins.

Then later, I heard it sung about George Coggins.

None of the old-timers who could have known either are still around.

For legend has it that Tom Collins lived in the Smokies when this was still wilderness.

At any rate, the ballad is no longer lost.

And until I can meet up with his ghost, I'll let Tom Collins remain the hero of the ballad.

[Editor's Note: James S. Lane of Enka says the version his family has been singing as long as he can remember has as its hero's name, neither Tom Collins nor George Coggins, but rather a combination of the two—George Collins.]

Chestnuts: Only Memories Stand

Burningtown

THEY STAND LIKE GAUNT, WHITENING SKELETONS AMONG the living giants of our mountain forests.

And the old man grows nostalgic and a bit sad when he looks upon them, for they remind him of his lost youth and of something that will not come again in his time—if ever.

A part of the sadness stems perhaps from the knowledge that his great-grandchildren have been deprived of a birthright.

For when he was a boy, and even in his grandson's youth, there was no finer sport than to go hunting for chestnuts on a crisp fall morning when frost had opened the big burs and spread their fruit among the fallen leaves.

The only reminder of that era are the whitening skeletons of the chestnut trees which survived the ax only to die under the whirlwind ravages of a mysterious blight.

"The only chestnuts you see now," said the old man, "are a few brought in from some foreign country and they're not like the kind that grew here in the hills.

"But when I was a boy, and up to thirty years ago, chestnuts were a right common thing here in the mountains. Folks even had chestnut orchards, same as you have apple and peach orchards today.

"They were a form of specie. Why, I've hauled many a bushel to the South Carolina markets to trade for sugar and salt and green coffee."

He paused a moment, then pointed with his stick toward the grassy meadow back of the old homeplace here in the Macon County hills.

"Right over there," he said, "over there where there's nothing but grass now, was where we had our chestnut orchard. There were two acres all in chestnut, with the under brush cleared out. We used it as our calf lot.

"Why, I remember in the fall when the chestnuts started falling, I'd go out there every morning while my wife was getting breakfast and pick up two gallons before she got the coffee on the table.

"Reckon the most I ever took to market at one time was twelve bushels. Got a dollar and a quarter a bushel for 'em, which I took out in trade. Now, that was a lot of money back in those days.

"Everybody hunted chestnuts back then. Folks who didn't have chestnut orchards would get up parties and get a covered wagon or two and go off into the hills where there was a good stand of chestnut. They would camp out and be gone two or three days, coming home when they had got their wagons filled up.

"Them that wasn't sold would furnish goodies for the children and the grownups. We'd serve them up boiled and roasted or just eat 'em plain. If you boiled 'em you could keep 'em a long time."

One of the ancient dishes of the Cherokee Indians was chestnut bread. It was still made by them here in the mountains until the last of the chestnuts disappeared several years ago.

And of course there are those who remember when the Thanksgiving turkey was stuffed with chestnuts and how in the fall the chestnut vendors, like Ira Barker, sold them on the street corner of a Saturday or when court was in session.

Some pasture chestnuts were more than eighty feet tall. They were about as broad as they were tall, spreading their arms in a great umbrella of shade on the town square or over the village smithy's shop.

While youngsters prized the great tree for the nut crop it produced, the lumberman looked on it with high favor for other reasons. Besides making the best beams, it was rich in the tannin used in the tanning industry.

Back in the days when there were only dirt roads, hundreds of wagons hauled cord after cord of chestnut from throughout the region to the big mill at Sylva which manufactured and shipped out tanic acid.

The nut crop also was a big factor in furnishing a proper diet for the bear population in the mountains, and the old-timers will tell you that bears on a chestnut diet were fatter and that their meat had a better taste.

But the nuts are gone and so are the trees. Only the skeletons remain, and these are being cut down and carted off. For a use has been found of the dead trees. That's where wormy chestnut panelling comes from, and it has grown quite popular during the past ten years.

The blight that struck the American chestnut is believed to have come into this country on Chinese chestnuts, which despite a high percentage of infection show too a degree of resistance to it.

No immunity existed in our American tree, which was one of the giants of our sylva when De Soto came this way.

From the time the blight was first detected in 1904 in the New York Zoological Park, it spread like wildfire, sweeping across New Jersey and Pennsylvania and into all parts of the country.

Every effort was made to control the malady. Even the federal government joined in. But nothing could stop the destruction or the spread of the blight.

Eventually, every spot where chestnut grew was infected and devastated.

Sometimes you will notice little sprouts coming up from the blight-killed trees, and you perhaps get the idea that the chestnut is going to return to its former glory.

But they never become more than saplings, even though a few have been known in recent years to put out burs and have a few nuts. But they die, too, for the infection is still in the stumps of the old trees and is still taking its toll among the sprouts and saplings.

Some efforts have been made recently to develop a new blight-resistant strain. This has been done by scientists of the U. S. Department of Agriculture through crossing the Japanese chestnut with the chinquapin.

Apparently, it has a chance to succeed, for there have been some plantings here in the mountains and this fall there were a few chestnuts from this new type of chestnut.

But it is not our true American chestnut.

My grandfather is dubious. He doesn't believe the chestnut ever will return to the mountains.

"Not in my time or your time," he said, "and probably my great-grandchildren's children won't even see it. Maybe there will be a few, but there won't be any chestnut orchards like we had when I was a boy."

He looked off toward the high hills where the gaunt, whitening skeletons stand, and shook his head.

Yugwilu, the Magic Bait

Big Witch Creek

IF YOU WANT TO REALLY CATCH FISH, GET YOURSELF A horsehair fishing line, a bone hook, a piece of red cloth, and some yugwilu.

Then learn an old Indian formula which must be chanted to the fish who only understand Cherokee.

Once you have mastered the technique of these simple trappings you can throw away your fancy rods and gaudy bait and buy a larger deep-freezer.

This is all apropos to the opening of the fishing season this week when men will take to the hills and wade in streams that watered rhododendron an eon or so before Nubian slaves built tombs for the Pharaohs.

Thousands of fishermen will greet the dawn Tuesday on hundreds of trout streams throughout Western North Carolina for it has been a long winter.

And here in the high reaches of the Cherokee Indian reservation descendants of the first people to fish the cloistered streams of the Great Smokies will be luring trout to disaster with tried and true methods few white men ever heard of, much less used.

In the early days before the white man made fishing a sport, the rivers and streams of the mountains abounded in fish such as perch, croakers, bass, catfish, garfish, trout and even sturgeon.

The Indians had some novel but effective fishing methods, and it seems strange that the white man did not appropriate them, for he took most of the things that belonged to the red man and turned them to his own use and benefit.

The Cherokee first used the "grappling" method.

He would wade into a stream and search for the rocks where

the fish hid. He would make a pass at the fish with his hand. He had to be quick. Particularly with the wily trout.

But if he could ever get his fingers on the stomach he had a catch. A trout can't stand to be tickled and he will flop over and call it quits when you rub him in that sensitive place.

Later, when the white traders came into the mountains and sold them red cloth, they devised another unique method.

They would seek out places in the river or stream where there were rocks standing over the deepest parts.

There they would pull off their red breeches, or their long slip of Stroud cloth, and wrap it around their arm so it would reach the lower part of the palm of their right hand.

Then they would dive under the rock where catfish or trout shelter from the scorching beams of the sun and watch for their prey.

Seeing the red cloth, the fish would seize it and try to swallow it. And that was when the diver opened his hand, seized the fish by his tender parts and brought it out.

Many of the Cherokee methods have been outlawed by the white man.

But time was when the Cherokee ground up horse chestnuts and certain roots into a fine powder which they put in the streams. The powder stupefied the fish but did not kill them.

Actually, the powder made the fish drunk and they would float to the surface, bellies up, where they were gathered into baskets.

The more fancy Cherokee fishermen of early days used hook and line.

Hooks were made of bone, usually the tines of the deer which is easily carved but is strong.

The first fishing lines were made from bark fibers meticulously woven into thread.

When horses were introduced among the Cherokee, they took the hairs from the tail and wove them into fishing lines.

Actually, a horsehair fishing line is the greatest thing that ever came the fisherman's way.

It has a stretch of a couple inches to over five feet, and it won't break.

For fishing mountain trout streams where it is difficult to cast because of overhanging branches it is the answer to the fly-caster's dream.

A horsehair fishing line will bounce off a limb. It won't wrap around a limb or bush like nylon or linen.

There are only a few Cherokee today who know the art of making horsehair fishing lines.

George Owl is one, but because it is a long, tedious process he doesn't make many.

Seven strands of horsehair go into the process. These seven strands are plaited into one thin thread.

"Besides," George explained, "horses are scarce now, and it is difficult to find the proper length of horse hairs."

It was George who told me about yugwilu, which is Cherokee for the plant we know as Venus flytrap.

And that's where the ancient Cherokee formula comes in, too.

First, the fisherman must chew a small piece of yugwilu and spit it upon the bait and also upon the hook.

Then, standing facing the stream, he recites this formula, talking to the fish:

"Listen! Now you settlements have drawn near to hearken. Where you have gathered in the foam you are moving about as one.

"You Blue Cat and the others, I have come to offer you freely the white food.

"Let the paths from every direction recognize each other (meaning let the fishes, who are supposed to have regular trails through the water, assemble together at the place where the speaker takes his station).

"Let them (your and my spittle) be together as we go about.

"They (the fish) have become a prey and there shall be no loneliness (meaning there shall be an abundant catch).

"Your spittle has become agreeable (a wish that the fish may prove palatable).

"I am called Swimmer. Yu!"

Then the bait is put on the hook.

According to the old-time medicine men, the yugwilu is put on the bait because it will enable the hook to attract and hold the fish just as the plant itself seizes and holds insects in its cup.

If you wonder if yugwilu really works, then think a spell on this:

Did you ever know of an Indian coming home with an empty creel?

Then grab yourself a horsehair fishing line, a bone hook, a piece of red cloth, and some yugwilu.

And learn that Cherokee formula.

Frog Hunting

Ela

TWILIGHT PASSED AND THE BULLFROGS BEGAN THEIR nocturnal ballads.

It was a symphony being repeated from hundreds of lakes and ponds and along the rivers and in the swamps of the Western North Carolina highlands.

The music had lured us into the night and onto the river to try our hand at a sport old as man's craving for food.

This is by way of saying it is frog-hunting time.

And from now until fall many a man will join the twilight-to-dawn procession where the waters are still and the jumbos cry.

It is a fascinating sport that is getting a big play from men who never owned a rifle or ever suspected there could be fun in matching wits with a bullfrog on a moonless night.

The introduction of novel methods in knocking off the bassos of the lake and river opera has given a new impetus to the sport.

The gig and the pine torch are as obsolete as the block-buster bomb.

Not long ago some amateur psychologist gave a new twist to the sport. He discovered a weakness in the bullfrog's behavior that has been the ruin of many another creature.

And now vanity and the spotlight are bringing humiliation and death to the kings of the lakes and rivers, ponds and swamps.

Hunters are killing the big fellows with rifles and torches because the pop-eyed kings of the marshes are so dumb and vain they'll preen and bellow when a light dances in their face.

It's an exacting sport—shooting bullfrogs at midnight without even a moon to guide the hunter.

Some men who hunt just for the legs use gigs or small-caliber rifles.

But the sportsmen who want to give the frogs a chance use air rifles.

It's necessary to shoot them in the eye, for the skin will turn air rifle shot.

Hunters, equipped with spotlights and .22 calibre rifles loaded with hollow-point shells, lounge around the river banks until twilight passes and the chorus of frogs begin their nocturnal ballads.

Then each hunter lies prone in a flat boat and paddles softly along the edges of the river or pond listening for the love song of a green, slimy bullfrog.

Finally the romantic thing bellows—a deep, roaring plea that rolls across the river and the swamps in a weird echo.

Fully a thousand other jumbos take up the cry.

The hunter turns on his light—the best ones are those you can strap to your forehead—just as the symphony reaches its height.

And usually sitting on a log nearby will be a big fellow, his eyes blinking in light, his throat full with the notes of his song.

He won't jump—he just sits there and looks at the light.

An expert can hit him in the eyes with the little shot.

If he misses, the bullfrog will leap—sometimes clean over the boat, sometimes in it, and sometimes into the reeds along the bank.

Usually you get only one shot. Then you paddle on.

It takes a Davy Crockett or a Daniel Boone to be expert with the air rifle.

The bullfrog's eye looks mighty big when spotlighted but it's a deceptive target when you're sighting along the barrel of an air rifle.

But the hunters who really bag the big fellows are those who use the small caliber rifles and hunt the pop-eyed kings for their legs.

The king of this class hereabouts is Carol White of Bryson City who is giving the jumbos along the waters of the Oconaluftee River above Ela quite a fit these nights.

His partner is Barney Rentz who can snap off a shot that would do justice to the memory of Annie Oakley.

They discovered they could bring home more frog legs if they used hollow point shells in their rifles.

"The hollow point busts up the frog," White explained, "and keeps him from sinking. All you've got to do is pick him out of the water. But shoot him with a regular bullet and he'll sink."

White and Rentz prefer the lakes and ponds to do their frog hunting.

"That makes a boat necessary," White said, "and cuts out all the walking and stumbling in the swamps."

But sometimes they go on foot into shallow water.

Sometimes when one jumps the wrong way and lands on the bank they hold him spellbound with their spotlight and then have some fun.

For just such an occasion, White carries a pocketful of loose shot.

With the frog sitting there high and dry and bathed in light, White starts rolling the little shot toward the big fellow and he begins lapping them up.

"First thing you know," White said, "he's got a pound of lead in his stomach and he couldn't jump an inch for all the prodding in the world.

"Funny thing but frogs just seem to love to lap up lead shot. They'll lap it up until its running out of their mouth."

White figures the idea of feeding bullfrogs shot originated with Mark Twain back in the days when frog-jumping derbys were all the rage in Texas.

Back then many an unscrupulous man with a packet of greenbacks on a jumper managed to demobilize the favorite by feeding him shot when his owner wasn't looking.

Frog legs are quite a delicacy and more and more folks are learning just how good they are when properly prepared.

Some two million frogs are used in America annually for food.

In Europe, frog farming is an established industry.

There are many ways of preparing frog legs, most of them bad.

Our favorite recipe is one we picked up from a Frenchman.

This is it, and it should adequately serve eight guests:

Take a dozen pair of frog legs, six finely chopped spring onions, one-fourth clove of crushed garlic, one cup of chopped button mushrooms, salt and cayenne to taste, four ounces of butter, three tablespoons of tart white wine, two cups of cream sauce, one tablespoon of chopped parsley, two bay leaves and two tablespoons of sherry or Marsala wine.

Dip the frogs' legs in milk, dust with salt and cayenne, dip in a little flour. Heat butter, turn in onion, garlic and bay leaves, chopped mushrooms, and then brown frogs' legs to a delicate gold.

Take them out and serve on a hot plate.

Add wine to saucepan, simmer up, poach frogs' legs five minutes longer. Put this cooking sauce through a sieve, after taking out the mushrooms. Stir into hot cream sauce and put mushrooms back again. Stir in the sherry or Marsala.

Serve with sauce poured over frogs' legs, and dusted with chopped parsley for garnish.

Try it once and you'll be lost forever to the twilight-to-dawn brigade who know where the jumbos cry.

Old-Timy Recipes

Highlands

SINCE DANIEL BOONE'S REBECCAH FOLLOWED HIM INTO the wilderness, mountain women have demonstrated their resourcefulness in supplementing the family larder.

From the beginning, they turned their imagination toward figuring how to add spice to a steady meat-and-bread diet whose sameness could have wrecked a nation.

They were quick to discover the wild fruits and berries, the herbs and nuts, which grew in profusion in the highlands and were free for the gathering.

These provided in-season dishes—a spring-to-fall changing table that made it easier to spin out the long winter months on just meat and potatoes, maybe some dried beans and dried pumpkins.

In time, however, the mountain women learned the art of canning and preserving. When they did, they opened up an adventure in good eating.

The fruits and berries, which until then had to be eaten when picked or else they spoiled, went into jellies and jams and preserves to be served any time during the year.

This also resulted in a lot of experimenting with the various wild fruits and berries, and pretty soon the mountain women—swapping the formulas of their discoveries—had a dozen different ways of turning a particular fruit or berry into a mouth-watering dish.

Strangely enough, these native recipes for the most part were not written down but passed on from mother to daughter and neighbor to neighbor by word of mouth.

These recipes still remain outside the pages of the cookbooks, but in recent years a few enterprising mountain women have been "putting up" a few choice jams and jellies and preserves for folks from the outside.

And now the old-timy recipes are being used to establish a business with a strictly mountain flavor.

Many a mountain woman is discovering there is a booming market for the things that grow wild which for a century have been common in most farm homes.

Mrs. Elizabeth Edwards here in Highlands has probably done as much as anyone in the mountains to develop this new industry which is still in its infancy but is catching on with folks who never bothered to pick more wild fruits and berries than needed for their own use.

"It seemed a shame to me," Mrs. Edwards said, "that visitors and folks in the city couldn't have wild strawberry preserves or wild crabapple jelly like our mothers and grandmothers had made. So I started doing something about it."

Actually, she started her canning and preserving business as a hobby. That was eight years ago. Now it has grown into a booming full-time job.

Folks from all over have got to know what real mountain flavor is like in grapes, strawberries, blackberries, rhubarb, plums and gooseberries, to name a few.

Mrs. Edwards is probably the busiest woman in all the mountains. Each year she cans and preserves hundreds of jars of jams, jellies, preserves, conserves and marmalades. She has only one helper in her canning kitchen, which is right in her home.

And even though she has a hundred or more mountain folks out gathering wild fruits and berries, for which she pays excellent prices, she roams the woods and fields herself with bucket and basket.

"We've got things growing here in the mountains a lot of folks never heard about, much less eaten, and they were just going to waste until I started asking that they be brought to me," she said. "Take grapes, for instance. There are coon grapes, possum grapes, fox grapes and wolf grapes. I take them all and fix them the old-timy way."

Perhaps the greatest contribution Mrs. Edwards has made in this new field is to the economy of her mountain neighbors. For many a mountain family is finding a new source of income by gathering the wild things that grow all around them.

"One day I was out in a berry patch with two or three families, when all at once a little boy began jumping up and down and hollering for joy. 'Ma,' he yelled, 'I've figured how many quarts I've picked and we've got enough to make the last payment on the cow.'

"Another time I was out roaming about looking for new sources of fruit and berries when I saw a woman coming up the road with a bucket in her hand. I stopped and asked her what she had. She told me she had a gallon of wild strawberries. She said she wanted 25 cents a quart for them. I told her they were worth more than that a quart. I told her I would give her sixty cents. She started crying.

"When I finally got her to stop crying she told me that it was because she was happy. 'The Lord done sent you to me today,' she said. 'My man's dying. Got no money for the doctor. He ain't movin,' he ain't lookin'.' She told me she had more berries back home a-ways that she had picked but couldn't carry.

"So we got in the car together and drove to her house and I bought all the berries she had. They came to fourteen dollars."

Some days later, Mrs. Edwards saw this woman and asked about her husband.

"He's up and is goin' to be all right," she told Mrs. Edwards. "I took that money I earned from you and got to a telephone and called the doctor and he come and gave him some medicine and got him well. Charged me ten dollars, but he got my man well."

One thing you learn in dealing with folks who sell wild fruits and berries, Mrs. Edwards has discovered. And that's you come to know those that are honest and those who are dishonest.

"There are those who will give you good measure and those that don't," she said. "But I trust them all and take their word for how many quarts they say they've got. That's the way it's done.

"Once I paid a man for twenty quarts of berries when he only had a ten-quart bucket. He told me he had twenty quarts and I didn't even think to argue with him. My husband called my attention to it. I told him they were capped berries and there were more of them. Of course, he told me it didn't make any difference if they were capped or not, that a ten-quart bucket would hold only ten quarts no matter how you figure it."

One of her most faithful providers of wild fruits and berries is "Aunt" Albie McCall. She is 88 years old and lives on Clear Creek at the foot of Bushy Place, which is four miles from Highlands.

"From home to home again is eight miles," Mrs. Edwards explained, "and Aunt Albie walks it about twice a week in summer. She comes in on her visits before we get up. That's about seven o'clock. And she brings two baskets on each arm. Sometimes she has blackberries, again it's wild strawberries, and another time it's buckberries.

"She walks straight as a die and like a deer. Doesn't wear glasses, and does her own picking down there around her farm where a heap of wild things grow."

During the season as the wild fruits and berries mature and are fetched to her home, Mrs. Edwards works day and night. She's up at seven and usually never gets out of the kitchen until well after midnight.

"You have to make up things that are in season now so they will go through the next season," she explained. "You're always working on stuff for a year ahead."

Some of the unusual things she makes are wild elderberry jelly and jam, quince jam and jelly, artichoke pickles, pickled okra, beet relish, corn relish, preserved carrot sticks, and pomegranate jelly.

And, when she's busy, she has a habit of whistling.

Folks around Highlands call her "The Whistler." It's a thing she does unconsciously.

"Reckon when I've got things on my mind and know I've got a lot to do I just whistle," she said. "There have been times I've busted out whistling in places where I shouldn't. Didn't realize I was until somebody mentioned it."

But her mountain neighbors love her and her whistling and hope she never stops, for as long as she whistles that means she's doing things that will bring more money to all of them.

The Fairy Crosses

Brasstown

EVEN THE FAIRIES IN THE GREAT SMOKIES WEPT WHEN Christ died.

And the tears they spilled turned to stone and formed tiny crosses—symbols of the Crucifixion.

That is the story the old Indians tell.

For the skeptical, the Cherokee will show you the tiny crosses to prove the story they tell—a story that has been handed down through almost 2,000 years of telling.

No human hand carved these crosses, which lie scattered upon the earth near here.

And nowhere else in all the Cherokee land will you find them except at this one spot in the Clay County hills.

I first heard the story of the fairy crosses many years ago, but it was only recently that I went searching for the spot where the strange miracle occurred.

A friend of mine, Lynn Gault, led me to the spot and I have a hundred or more of the tiny crosses which I picked up to prove they do exist.

But unless you know what you are seeking you probably would never notice them, for they are the color of the earth and at first glance look like so many pebbles.

The little crosses only become significant when the story about them is told.

And the story the Cherokee tell is a story that rightfully belongs in the treasury of world folklore and myth and legend.

"My people," said Arsene Thompson, "have told the story through the ages about the crosses. It is a beautiful story."

Arsene is a Cherokee Indian preacher who plays the role of

Elias Boudinot, the Indian missionary, in the Cherokee Indian drama, "Unto These Hills."

Arsene's people have always had a reverence for the supernatural.

And the original Cherokee attitude toward the "Great Mystery" —the Eternal—was quite simple.

The Cherokee had no temples, no shrines, no idols.

The Sun and the Moon and the Stars—they were his Trinity.

The lightning and the wind, the thunder and the rain provoked both reverence and fear.

For these were only messengers of the Great Man Above.

So it is not difficult to see how the Cherokee would accept the story of the crosses and how they came to be.

"Yes," said Arsene, "it is a strange story. And this is what the old men told me when I was a boy.

"When the world was young there lived in these mountains a race of little people. They were spirit people. Like the fairies you read about.

"Now, one day when these little people had gathered to dance and sing around a pool deep in the woods, a spirit messenger arrived from a strange city far, far away in the Land of the Dawn.

"But soon the dancing and singing stopped, for the messenger brought them sad tidings.

"The messenger told them Christ was dead.

"The little people were silent, then they were sad.

"And as they listened to the story of how Christ had died on the Cross, they wept and their tears fell upon the earth and turned into small stones.

"But the stones were neither round nor square.

"Each was in the form of a beautiful little cross.

"Hundreds of tears fell to earth and turned into tiny stone crosses, but the little people were so dazed and heart-broken they did not notice what was happening.

"So, with the joy gone from their hearts, they wandered away into the forest to their homes.

"But around the spot where they had been dancing and singing, where they had stopped to shed their tears, the ground was covered with these symbols of the death of Christ."

What happened to the little people? I asked. Are they still here in the mountains? Has anyone ever seen them?

"No one knows for sure what happened to them," said Arsene. "I first heard the story when I was a boy and the old men of the tribe who told it to me said that after that day the little people were never seen again.

"But the old men said that on still nights you could hear them whispering along the river and that when there was a gentle breeze their sighs could be heard in the tall trees."

There is a wealth of stories in Cherokee mythology about the crosses.

But they all originate with how they came into being.

There was one belief among the Cherokee that the crosses had the power to render the owner invisible at will.

The Nunnehi, according to one story, were told where to find the stones as a reward for their goodness and kindness to all people.

The Nunnehi were the immortals who dwelled in the fastness of the mountains. They had their townhouses under the Cherokee mounds and under the hills.

They were spirit people who could make themselves invisible at will after they had become the possessor of one of the tiny crosses.

In some instances, the tiny crosses were supposed to give the owner the power of diving into the ground and then coming up again among the enemy to scalp and kill with sudden terror and destruction.

The crosses have found their way into rare collections of gems and artifacts.

Several years ago an Asheville jeweler displayed a small collection of these crosses, which are not much larger than those on a rosary.

In some instances, they have been polished and ground to beautiful symmetry and mounted in gold and used as watch charms or good luck emblems.

Ghosts of Yesterday

Sylva

OUT OF THE LONG AGO, LIKE SOME HALLOWEEN GHOST returning to earth, comes the voice of a little man with a gargoyle face to guide us on a journey into yesterday.

On winter nights, when the logs on the fire simmer and hiss, the hollow whispers of his ghostly tales return to prod the memories of the old man and his grandson.

This being Halloween Eve, the memories conjured up ghosts and witches and a host of supernatural beings which the little man had come to collect over the years and dwell upon as his special interest in life.

"Tell me a ghost story, Uncle John," I would say, then crawl upon my father's lap, and listen while he swapped ghostly tales with my father and my grandfather.

The three of them were personally acquainted with ghosts in one form or another, and the tales they spun were told for the truth.

As a boy of eight, they peopled my imagination with cats big as a man and bigger, cats that talked like a human, and with headless men and ladies in gray walking in the moonlight.

They so filled my mind with the eerie and the macabre that for years I would shut tight my eyes and hold my hands to my ears when we went abroad at night.

For in time, there was hardly a place in the region, especially on the road to Webster and to Savannah, that I did not associate with some ghostly tale.

In the night I expected to see the headless man my father had seen as a boy, or the lady in gray walking beside the road that my grandfather had spoken to, or hear the rattle of chains on the bridge or the thump-thump of the dragging, booted feet in the old house where my grandfather lived.

I never did know exactly the location of the house where Uncle John tangled with the cats that were as big as a man and talked like a human.

But I remember the story and how he sat in front of our fire and spun it out until I never again saw a cat that I didn't expect to hear it speak right out.

"I was on my way to market in Walhalla," he would begin. "I had got a late start and night come on when I was on a lonesome section of the road. It had started to rain and I knew I had to find shelter.

"Pretty soon I made out a house just off the road. There was a barn, too. I drove off the road and up to the house. There was just enough light left to see that nobody lived there.

"So I put the horses in the barn, then took my axe and got some wood and went in and started a fire in the fireplace. I brought in some rations and a couple blankets.

"After I ate supper, I spread my blankets out in front of the fire and lay down. About that time a cat walked into the room and got between me and the fire. I never paid much attention to it, for it was just an ordinary cat. But a few minutes later another came in and it was bigger than the first. A third came in and it was about a foot high. I roused up a bit and said to myself that these were big cats.

"Before I could get the thought out of my mind, a fourth and a fifth and a sixth cat walked in, each a little bigger than the other. Then a seventh came in and it was as big as a man. They were all lined up there between me and the fire.

"I was getting uneasy by this time, so I reached down and got one of my shoes and drew back to throw it. I figured they would get out of there and leave me be. But just as I drew back my arm, the biggest cat spoke up just as plain as a man and said, 'Where you from?' and 'What are you doing here in our house?'

"Well, I knew I had to get out of there. So I started easing on my shoes. By that time, when I looked around, there were a dozen or more cats in the room and some of them were standing between me and the door.

"Funny thing, I didn't have a gun with me. When I left home I forgot it, and didn't think of it until now. Funny thing, too, it was the first time I'd ever forgot my gun.

"Well, I eased to where I could get my hand on a piece of wood.

I grabbed it and threw it at that big cat. He jumped and then everything began happening. I started for the door and cats began coming down the stairs, screaming like a woman. There was cats all over the place. Some how I got to the door and got it open. I made a beeline for the barn.

"But I was no sooner outside than everything got just as still as could be. None of them cats followed me outside. I got in the wagon and spent the night there. Never slept a wink. When it was daylight I got out of there. Left my blankets and rations in the house. I never did go back for them.

"About three miles down the road I come to a store and I stopped and I told the feller that run it what had happened. He said nobody had lived in the house long at a time for twenty years.

"Seems like everybody that lived there had trouble with cats at night but never could find one around during the day. This feller told me that years before a man and woman lived there and the woman kept a lot of cats and was always nagging her husband.

"Well, one night he killed all the cats and then took his axe and killed his wife."

My grandfather would then light up his pipe which had gone out and tell about the woman in gray.

He swears he saw her on several occasions, but the time he likes to recall was once when he had driven over in his hack from Webster to meet an eccentric aunt who had arrived in Sylva by train.

She had come in on the night train and they were driving through Love Field when my grandfather startled his aunt by saying, "Howdy, lady. Ain't it late for you to be out all alone?"

"Now what in the world has got into you, Riley?" his aunt said.

"Why, I was just speaking to the lady walking there beside the hack. Don't you see her?"

His aunt looked all about, didn't see a thing.

"Why there's nobody there," she said. "It's just the devil after you, Riley."

The old man shakes his head when he tells about it.

"But I saw her plain as day," he said. "She never answered me. Had on a long gray dress that drug the ground. She walked alongside the hack for a quarter of a mile, I reckon, then stepped off the road and went walking across a new plowed field. I could see her good because the moon was shining and it was as light as day.

"I come back the next day and looked all around. Went to that new plowed field. There wasn't a sign of a track anywhere, except them I made walking across the field.

"Over the years other folks saw her, too.

"I remember that Fred Hooper who runs the drug store here saw her one night back just about the time we was getting into World War I.

"He drove into town and got a bunch of fellers and they all went out there and looked every place but couldn't find her or her tracks. He saw her walking across a plowed field, too.

"That was the last time I ever heard of anybody seeing her."

The headless man at the swinging bridge on the Tuckaseigee River was another one seen by more than one person. My father saw it, and so did a bunch of young fellows who were there at the time.

It happened late one afternoon. My father was heading home from Dillsboro when an electric storm came up just as he reached one end of the swinging bridge.

As he got half way across he saw this thing.

"I saw a man without a head walking through the bushes into the river at the other end of the bridge," he told me when I was a boy. "Lightning was flashing and thunder was rolling. Just at the other end of the bridge was a great shelf of rock where we fellows used to gather and play cards or just talk. There were six or seven of the boys there.

"They saw the headless man about the same time I did and began shooting at it. The headless man kept right on walking and went right into the river and disappeared.

"We all got down there and searched the bushes, looking for blood or tracks. We couldn't find a thing. The sand there at the edge of the river was just as smooth and unruffled as it could be.

"I never did believe in such things, but I certainly saw something."

There were lights that used to play in the night around his grandfather's house, after his grandfather had died. Some folks said they were guarding the money the old man hid and which nobody ever did find.

So, this being Halloween Eve, the old ghosts are gathering, and in many an old house there are the ghostly sounds that only old houses know.

If you go there you can hear their hollow whispers, drifting like the wind through the empty shells of the houses long since forgotten.

Yellow-Jacket Soup

Cherokee

IF YOU THINK THE FRENCH AND THE CHINESE ARE FANCIERS of strange and exotic foods, then you should talk to Aggie Lossiah, the Cherokee epicurean, and learn about yellow-jacket soup and fried locusts.

For the Cherokee Indians bow to no people when it comes to serving rare and unusual foods which they have been preparing for a thousand years and more.

Many of the old recipes were disappearing until Aggie Lossiah put them down on paper a few years ago and saw them printed in the first and only Indian cookbook, *To Make My Bread.*

Aggie is 74, granddaughter of the famous chief John Ross, and they call her "the bread-maker of the Cherokee," which is like saying Oscar of the Waldorf.

If you are around Oconaluftee Indian Village any day at pre-lunch time you will find Aggie preparing some of the Cherokee dishes over an open fire either inside one of the cabins or outside near the fish pond.

"Why, child," she will say, "the only way to cook is over an open fire, and the old dishes are the best, food that you and most of my white friends turn away from because the names don't sound appetizing."

Aggie likes to tell about a white friend who dropped in on her one day at her own home and stayed for lunch, which included a clear soup.

"She sipped away at the soup without a word but you could tell she was enjoying it," Aggie recalled. "Finally she said, 'Aggie, this is heavenly; what is it?' And when I told her it was yellow-jacket soup she all but dropped out of her chair. She wouldn't eat another bite."

Aggie's eyes danced with a mischievous sparkle and she chuckled at the memory.

"Folks are peculiar," she said. "They'll eat things that have no taste if the name sounds appetizing. But give them a real tasty dish like blood pudding or fried locusts or lye dumplings and they won't eat it if they know what it is.

"I can't understand why folks are so squeamish about what they eat. If they'd been brought up like I was they'd be thankful for anything they could get.

"I remember," she recalled, "when I was a little girl and we had to hide out in a cave over in Tennessee, we lived off berries and whatever we could scrounge in the woods."

Aggie will tell you that America is rich in foods that are going to waste because folks are squeamish about what they eat and won't eat.

"My people," she says with pride, "learned in the beginning that there was a use for everything God put upon the earth. My people have always accepted these gifts of God and that's why they can get along on what some folks think it so little."

Unless you are fortunate enough to be invited to a Cherokee home for a specially prepared feast, you will never know what Cherokee food is like, for, strangely enough, there is no restaurant here that features even a single Indian dish.

It seems to me the Cherokee restaurateurs are missing a golden opportunity by not including a few of their people's unusual dishes on their menus, if for no other reason than their originality and as food conversation pieces.

For people like to talk about the rare and strange foods they have eaten, even if they are reluctant to admit they didn't enjoy them.

Until a few years ago, Samuel E. Beck of Asheville, who used to own the Museum of the Cherokee Indian here, sponsored an annual Cherokee Indian feast to which he invited his friends.

The festive board was loaded with a variety of original Indian food that made a Stockholm smorgasbord look like a fat man's diet, what with roast bear and venison, roast bison, speckled trout, turkey, raccoon, eight different vegetables, six kinds of bread, and a choice of three drinks, to name a few.

But missing were yellow-jacket soup, fried locusts, blood pudding, lye dumplings, baked groundhog, crayfish, leather breeches, slick-go-downs and ramps.

For a dish that belies its name, slick-go-downs is nothing more than mushrooms boiled and served with corn meal mush.

And then there are "knee-deeps," which are really only bull-frogs. But if you sit down to a dish which the Cherokee tell you is frogs, then you'll be eating those we know as toads.

For a potent drink, there is the one made from hominy corn which you drink hot or wait until it sours and drink cool.

Sumacade is an appetizing pink colored drink, which contrary to popular belief is not poison.

But for pure nectar, the honey locust bean provides a treat that rates just ahead of one made from ripe field apricots.

There are a couple of dishes known as sochani and wanegidun, which I have never been able to identify.

The sochani is a plant that is picked young, parboiled, washed and fried in grease.

Wanegidun is also a plant and it is picked when tender, par-boiled, fried and served with eggs and bread or just bread.

Hominy soup, as prepared by the Cherokee, is of such strength that if your stomach can hold it you'll never have to worry about trying any dish yet concocted.

It is stored in a pottery jar after being cooked and served only after it has turned sour. Four days is the limit for keeping it, such is the taste and aroma as it ages and ferments.

About the only dishes the white man has come to know with any degree of familiarity are bean bread and chestnut bread which can be had at the annual Cherokee Indian Fair.

These are only a few of the many rare and strange foods of the Cherokee.

And, incidentally, Cherokee men are quite handy in the kitchen.

Fact of the matter, many a Cherokee woman will admit that she learned what she knows about cooking from her husband.

So, if you've got a yen for yellow-jacket soup or fried locusts, maybe you can get Goingback Chiltoskie or William Crowe to play host one of these days.

As Aggie Lossiah says:

"Child, you don't know food until you've tasted Cherokee food fixed in the old way."

Hog-Killin' Time

Cartoogechaye

THE BUSK MOON IS PASSING, THE HARVEST MOON WASTING, and old-timers are arguing a theory as old as the hills.

The argument has been going on since man first looked to the moon for a sign to guide him through seed-time and harvest-time.

It revolves around the all-important question of when folks should do their hog killing.

From the high coves of Watauga and Yancey to the rolling valleys of Cherokee and Clay, the argument is as sharp and crisp as a November morning.

Some folks argue a man must do his hog killing on the "shrinking of the moon." Others are just as insistent the butchering should be done on a "growing moon."

The "shrinking moon" faction contend a hog killed when the moon is wasting will prevent the bacon and lard from shrinking.

My grandfather, who is 96 and who has butchered many a hog, holds to this theory with a persistency that rules out all argument.

"The proof," he says, "is in the meat. So there ain't no room to argue. When a hog is butchered in the dark of the moon, the meat will shrink in the pot and yield its juicy goodness.

"Now, if a feller kills his hog in the full light of the moon, the meat won't give up its fat. It'll just grow bigger and tougher the longer it's cooked in a pot.

"Show me a piece of bacon and I'll tell you right off when the butchering was done. It's the easiest thing in the world to tell. All you've got to do is put a piece of it in a pan and start frying it.

"If the bacon curls up, you know for a certainty that it was butchered in the light of the moon. Meat butchered on the dark of the moon flats out and you get a heap of grease."

There are others, however, who argue that unless you do your hog killing on the full of the moon there won't be as much grease and fat.

Be that as it may, a lot of folks are now butchering their hogs, for this is a time when the moon is wasting and the nights are darker.

They have until November 15th to get in their butchering on a waning moon, for the following night the moon will start to grow.

My grandfather's brother-in-law, Carl Donaldson, is of the "shrinking moon" faction and he's doing his butchering right now.

He is known in these parts as a super prime hog killer and butcher.

He is one of the few old-timers still around who used to kill hogs by cracking their skull with the flat side of an axe.

"Back when I was a boy," he says, "gun powder and shot was too scarce and too hard to come by. But it was right smart of a chore to kill a hog with an axe. The fellers holding it had to be strong and the man swinging the axe had to have a good eye and a hefty pitch."

Hog killing usually begins when the first heavy frost hits the valleys. That is, it begins if the moon is right. Of course, the weather must be cold and crisp and clear.

In many sections of the mountains, neighbors gather and make hog killing a sort of community affair.

It is about the only thing left of the old-time customs where neighbors gather to help each other.

"Neighbors come in and help me with my killing and butchering," Donaldson says, "and then I go help them. When hog killing time rolls around I'm a busy man. Keep busy right on into January."

Joking and laughing are a part of hog killing. They are mere manifestations of the excitement and anticipation that accompanies the first fresh meat of the fall and winter.

The actual days of hog killing are lean eating days for all concerned with the task. It is such a demanding job there is little time for eating.

But each man and woman participating in the hog killing knows that later on there will be good eating—fresh pork, sausage and livermush.

However, it will be next March at the earliest before the new hams will reach any proper degree of curing.

Hog killing time spells steaming pots of backbones and ribs, wedges of tenderloin, and stacks of crisp, brown "cracklin' bread," lumpy and glistening with the jewels from the lard vats.

The menfolks do the killing and the butchering. The womenfolks stick to the kitchen where they cut and grind the lean meat into sausage.

Then the women cook the sausage and sirloin and can it in glass jars.

They make liver pudding or liver mush and souse meat from the feet and ears. Some of them pickle the feet.

As for chitterlings—most womenfolks don't like them, won't have anything to do with them.

Sometimes they use the chitterlings in stuffing sausage in the cases, although most womenfolks prefer cloth bags.

Just as the men folks are particular about when they do their hog killing, so are the women particular about the way they prepare their sausage.

It's pretty difficult to find any two women who make sausage the same way.

But Mrs. Donaldson says the main thing is to get it seasoned just so with just the right amount of fat to make it cook well in the pan, and no more.

The approaching Thanksgiving and Christmas seasons, with a barn full of fresh meat, spells fine feasts and every appetite is geared to just that.

The coming holiday feasts may spell turkey on the tables of urbanites, or baked goose along the Carolina coast, but they mean fresh pork to the rural folks of the mountains.

Yes, the busk moon is passing, the harvest moon wasting, and old-timers are killing hogs and arguing a theory as old as the hills.

Before Sutter's Mill

Brindle Town

SAM MARTIN CAME THIS WAY AS A TRAMP AND LEFT IN A plush carriage with a fortune in gold.

And thereby hangs a tale that was legend when Sutter's Mill made its pitch for the history books.

For it was here in the Burke County hills that a rich strike was made twenty-one years before the California gold rush.

This led to the establishment of the only privately-operated mint in the country down the road a piece at Rutherfordton where the first gold dollars were coined.

But this is Sam Martin's tale, this is his tune.

And if the California gold rush and old man Bechtler and his gold dollars get mixed into it, that's because they are a part of the tune.

Some men see the beginnings and never stick around to see the endings.

Sam Martin was one of these, a man always on the edge of chance.

It was chance, and nothing but chance, that brought him to Brindle Town in 1828.

No man alive remembers his coming, and the history books passed him by for a man named John Sutter, but his tune lives on because men still dig in the hills for the thing he discovered by chance.

Sam Martin was about as low in spirit as a man can get when he came shuffling along the dusty turnpike leading into the hills that day 167 years ago.

Behind him were the lost and frustrating years of searching for gold in South and Central America. He had worked his way aboard ship to a port in Alabama and then struck off across country for his home in Connecticut.

He was broke, living on hand-outs along the road and trusting to the generosity of folks along the way for a place to lay his tired body.

The day was young when he passed through Rutherfordton and headed up the Cane Creek road which led to Morganton and the north and home.

When he reached the Brindle Town community he stopped at the home of a shoe cobbler named Anderson.

The Anderson family took him in and fed him, and Martin tried to repay them that night as they sat around the fire with stories of his travels to far-away places and of the strange and wonderous sights he had beheld.

Naturally, Martin talked of his long search for gold and the golden touch that had eluded him.

Apparently, the wanderer caught the fancy of the Anderson family, for he was invited to linger a while and Anderson told him maybe he would like to dig a bit in the hills.

The following morning Sam Martin stood outside the Anderson cabin drinking in the mountain air and watching a brilliant sun warm the land.

As he turned to go back into the cabin his eyes were attracted by a glitter from the clay in the wall of the mud-daubed house. Maybe he was wrong. Maybe everything he looked at now had the color of gold.

But quickly he pulled out his pocketknife and dug some of the glittering particles out of the clay.

He was excited. This was gold! But he didn't want to shout out his discovery. Could be fool's gold. Besides, he had no way of knowing where Anderson had got the clay.

So Martin went on back in the cabin and, after a while, he asked Mrs. Anderson to let him have the use of a dish pan for a little prospecting.

A stream flowed nearby and that is where Martin went. From the stream bed he began to sift sand and clay.

And what he had searched for through the long years he found.

Gold! The cry welled up in his throat. He danced a jig. He whooped. The Andersons came running. Gold! He said it over and over, again and again.

The word spread throughout the state.

Brindle Town became a bustling, feverish community of gold miners.

Folks searched the hills while Martin and Anderson panned the yellow stuff from the creek and from the area about the cabin.

Martin taught Anderson all he knew about mining gold.

In return for the knowledge and the discovery, Anderson made Martin a partner in the venture.

The partnership arrangement lasted six months.

Sam Martin, born to be a wanderer, got itching feet again and decided to move on, for he could go home in style.

And, too, he had the money that would provide another try at the hidden gold of South and Central America.

Sam Martin wanted a golden city, which legend persisted lay somewhere in South or Central America.

That was his dream, just as it had been the dream of Cortez and DeSoto and a million more down through the centuries.

So Sam Martin made his decision.

He had come to Brindle Town broke and downcast.

He was leaving in style and with the confidence of a man who has found the golden touch.

His boots mirrored the sunlight the morning he took his leave from the Anderson home. A black hat sat atop his head. The cut of his broadcloth suit marked it as expensive.

He shook hands with Anderson, then stepped into a handsome carriage drawn by four sleek horses.

His bags were loaded with gold. Nobody ever knew just how much, albeit it was estimated "in excess of $10,000," which was a fortune, to say the least.

Sam Martin took up the reins, spoke to his horses, and the carriage rolled off up the turnpike toward Morganton and on toward home.

Cobbler Anderson stood in the door of his cabin and watched him until he was out of sight.

That was the last he ever saw of Sam Martin.

Where he went and where he ended up is a mystery.

But he left behind him a legend.

Folks have been mining gold here off and on ever since.

There are some who say that more than a million dollars in gold has come out of the Burke County hills since Sam Martin made his discovery.

Be that as it may, however, Brindle Town never has become a Sutter's Mill.

It's still only a community, but it has its memories and once it had its glory.

And folks still talk of Sam Martin who came this way as a tramp and left in a plush carriage with a fortune in gold.

The Mountain Dulcimer

Little Savannah

PLAY ME A TUNE, THE BOY WOULD BEG, PLAY ME A TUNE on the dulcimer.

And because my father at eight was the apple of his grandmother's eye, she would take down the rare, old instrument hanging over the fireplace.

Then, in the firelight of the winter night with the chant of the trees an obbligato, she would pick out the old, old tunes which her own grandsires had fetched from over the seas.

The boy grown to man remembered and told his son how it was when he sat at his grandmother's feet and listened to her play the dulcimer, picking out the tunes with a plectrum made from a goose quill.

She was no longer young. She and the dulcimer were old, and both were part of an epic that has come to live again because the old stories really never die, albeit the years nibble away at them and blur many of the details.

A boy of eight remembers many things, but only the things that catch his imagination, and so it was with my father and the dulcimer.

Perhaps the memory stayed with him through life because the dulcimer was the first musical instrument he ever knew and because it led him into making fiddles, then banjos.

The memory of his grandmother and the dulcimer was stirred years later on winter nights before the fire when his son would echo an old refrain:

Play me a tune, the son would beg, play me a tune on the banjo.

And that is how he come to pass on the story of his grandmother and the dulcimer that hung over the fireplace.

His grandmother's father had been a man who could make things with his hands. He could groove together a cabin, make chairs and tables, fashion a spinning wheel for his wife, and he made a dulcimer from out of memory of one once seen.

As a girl, my father's grandmother listened to the old songs her mother sang. She learned them by heart and she learned to play the dulcimer. In time, the dulcimer became her own and when she married she carried it with her and hung it above the fireplace.

But with children coming on, she had less and less time for playing and singing and the dulcimer gathered dust, but she never forgot how to pick out the old tunes on it.

And when she was old and alone and sat by the fire, her grandson would ask her to play him a tune, play him a tune on the dulcimer.

When she died the dulcimer disappeared. No one, my father said, seemed to know what happened to it. It just disappeared, as things will when a house becomes empty.

In his own mind, he had a picture of it and so he took a knife and a piece of glass and tried to duplicate it, but without success.

Somehow, he said, the instrument he made just didn't seem to be right. So he borrowed a fiddle from a neighbor and duplicated it.

He never again saw a dulcimer.

I was reminded recently of his story of my great-grandmother and the dulcimer when Fess Parker, more familiarly known as Davy Crockett, dropped by the house and wondered out loud if I knew somebody who could make him a real mountain dulcimer.

Fess is a collector of old folk songs and old ballads and he believes that those from our mountains should be sung only to the accompaniment of a dulcimer.

There are only a few mountain dulcimers still in existence and still fewer dulcimer makers.

The dulcimer is one of the rarest musical instruments in the world.

It is a quaint, plaintive, oblong instrument that seems to have been created in the Southern Highlands.

As known in the mountains, there is little resemblance to the instrument of the same name described in dictionaries and encyclopedias.

They describe the dulcimer as a hollow triangular box strung with wires of varying lengths, which are struck with a little hammer held in each hand.

The word dulcimer, incidentally, is used to translate a Hebrew word rendered in Greek by *symphonia*, which was applied to a kind of bagpipe.

The mountain dulcimer more nearly resembles the zither. It has from two to six strings, sometimes eight, but more often three.

A plectrum of wood or a goose quill is used to strum the strings.

Allen H. Eaton, who is probably the world's greatest authority on handicrafts of the Southern Highlands, says the first dulcimer of the mountain type probably was an adaptation from the German zither.

Along with making dulcimers, folks of the Southern Appalachians made other musical instruments such as fiddles and banjos.

Some of the earliest homemade fiddles were made from gourds.

Banjos were made with cat-skin heads.

My father became quite an accomplished fiddle and banjo maker.

The first fiddle he ever made he used only a pocketknife and a piece of glass. He carved the throat out of maple. The bottom and sides were of white pine.

It wasn't much better than his attempt at making a dulcimer.

However, in time he made some fine fiddles that brought a fancy price.

But he was really a banjo-man.

Perhaps his heart lay there because it was the nearest thing to a dulcimer he could make that would play and on which he could pick out tunes.

Unlike the disappearing dulcimer when his grandmother died, the banjo—or one of the banjos—he made has been saved.

It was the banjo he used to play when I was a boy, picking out *Old Joe Clark* and *Skip To My Lou.*

It was the banjo that forged a link with the past and the long-remembered words that a boy of eight spoke to his grandmother on a winter night as she sat before the fire:

Play me a tune, play me a tune on the dulcimer.

A Christmas Long Ago

Sylva

• AUNT EDE'S GRANDSON NELSE RODE UP IN HIS WAGON just at dusk with the big water-soaked hickory stump.

Grandpa Parris used to say there was nothing like a water-soaked hickory stump for a Yule log. Grandpa knew, for he was a mountain man. When he was a boy it was his job to fetch in the Yule log, and later when he had sons it was their job to search out the hickory stumps on Little Savannah.

By the time I came along we were living in town and our fireplace had a grate and we couldn't have a hickory stump. But Dad always took me to Grandpa's during Christmas, and there was the big hickory stump blazing and simmering in the big fireplace where Grandma did a lot of her cooking.

Looking at the stump Nelse had fetched down from the mountain, I thought that somehow it didn't look as big as the stumps remembered at Grandpa's as a little boy.

I said, "Nelse, you sure this is the biggest hickory stump you could find?" and he looked at me and then at the stump.

"Why, that stump'll burn for a month of Sundays. It'll be all right. I reckon my grandmammy would've been proud to see such a stump as that. I've heard my mammy say back in olden times when her mammy was a slave that it was the custom for everybody to just rest and fold their hands long's the Yule log burned. The white folks lit it on Christmas Eve and sometimes, my mammy said her mammy said, that ol' Yule log'd burn for two whole days, maybe three. Times shore have changed, and that's a true fact."

Yes, times have changed, I said, thinking on the size of Grandpa's logs and sitting around his hearth on Christmas day listening to him tell about the Christmas he was snowed in and the other

Christmases, some that sounded like fun and others that sounded pretty grim, even to a ten-year-old boy.

"Reckon I'll be gettin' on toward home," said Nelse. "It looks like it's fixin' to weather-up."

While we had stood there, flurries of snow had started blowing down from the peaks that towered dark above the valley.

"If this keeps up," said Nelse, "I reckon we will have us a shore 'nough white Christmas. My ol' bones start achin' when it snows."

I watched Nelse climb up into the wagon and ride off. The clop-clop-clop of the mule and the squeak of wheels were only a whisper from down the road when finally I picked up a couple of logs from the stack beside the door and moved on inside to mend the fire.

In the last few minutes darkness had come on with a suddenness, and the only light in the paneled room was that from the big fireplace. I tossed the logs on the fire, then sank down into a chair. Sitting there I watched the flames dance along the logs of birch.

The birch tossed flames to which you could attach a face, a figure, even a voice. And suddenly the flames etched into life a scene from out of the long ago. . . .

It was a snowy Christmas and Grandpa was eighty-seven. Mother and Dad and I had driven the eight miles out from town and parked the Model-T under the apple tree across the creek from Grandpa's. We carried presents for Grandpa and Grandma, who lived all alone since their sons had grown up and moved into town.

Standing by the Model-T while Mother heaped my arms with packages, I looked over toward the house which wore a shawl of snow and, watching the blue wood smoke curl up from the chimney, asked Mother did she think Grandma would bake me some johnnycake on the hearth and Mother said she guessed she might if I was real nice about it.

When we got to the house we found Grandpa sitting by the fire, all hunkered over the flames, and he said he couldn't seem to get warm. "Been havin' chills all day," he said.

Even before I took off my coat I went over to him and handed him a little package all done up in red paper and tied with a piece of green ribbon. He took the package and laid it down beside his chair but I said he was supposed to open it right then. He reached down and got it and opened it and smiled at me as he held up the pocketknife I had picked out all by myself. He gave it to Grandma and told her to lay it on the mantel.

For a moment he just sat there staring into the fire and was all quiet, not like he usually was when I came to see him. Then he pulled me to him like he always did and hugged me and a little later he reached into his pocket and took out a bright, shiny silver dollar.

"I've been so poorly, son, I couldn't get into town to get you anything for Christmas. This is the best I can do."

And then he took my hand and put the silver dollar in it and closed my fingers around it. I thought it was the finest present I had ever had. I knew right then I never would spend it.

Grandma said she was about to fix supper and, of course, we would stay, but Mother said the weather was so bad we would have to get back before dark. Grandma said then why didn't we spend the night but Mother shook her head and said Santa Claus wouldn't know where I was and Grandma smiled and ran her hand through my hair.

Then Grandma said how would I like some johnnycake and sweet milk, knowing all the time I would, and I looked at Mother and she nodded and I said, please, then asked, "Would you bake it on the hoe like you sometimes do, Grandma?" and she said, "Why, bless you, honey, I will."

While Grandma was gone back to the kitchen to mix up the batter, Grandpa said this was the first time since he and Grandma had been married that they hadn't had a Yule log.

"It don't seem like Christmas," he said, and Dad nodded his head but didn't say anything.

Mother looked at Dad but he wasn't looking at her; he was staring into the fire.

And Grandpa said, "I'm not as young as I used to be and I've got no one to go out and fetch me a hickory stump," and he paused and looked at Dad, then went on, "Boy, remember them big hickory stumps you used to drag in?" And Dad nodded again, still not saying anything.

Then Grandpa was quiet, and he reached down and picked up a little bitty hickory log and tossed it on the fire.

Finally, Dad said, "Pa, has the mule been fed?" and Grandpa looked at him and said, "I reckon. Jim Pott's boy has been lookin' after him for me, though he's not been by the house yet."

"Think I'll have a look," Dad said, and I said I would go with him but he shook his head and went on back through the house toward the back door and the path that led out across the branch to the barn.

"Now why do you suppose he got interested all of a sudden in that mule?" said Grandpa.

Mother shook her head.

About that time Grandma came back. She had a bowl of batter in one hand and a hoe in the other.

Grandma said, "Where's John?" and Grandpa said, "Went to see about the mule."

Then Grandma bent down and dipped her hand into the batter and spread some of it on the hoe blade. With the edge of the hoe turned toward the fire she leaned the handle against the top of the fireplace. The batter started steaming and simmering and turning gold-like.

Grandma went back to the kitchen to fetch me a glass of sweet milk and when she came back the johnnycake was all brown. She handed me the milk, then bent down and broke off a hunk of the johnnycake for me. It was almost too hot to eat. I would take a bite of it and then a swallow of the milk to cool it off.

While I ate, Mother and Grandpa and Grandma talked about this and that, stuff that didn't interest me. Once Mother said she wondered what was keeping Dad, and then they talked about Grandma's other sons and their children and by that time I had stuffed down all of the first johnnycake and Grandma had cooked me another one.

By this time it was beginning to get dark and Dad had been gone over most an hour, Mother said, remarking that she was a little concerned. Grandpa said maybe he was talking to Jim Pott's boy and had plumb forgot the time. Mother said if he didn't come soon we would never get home. Then they went back to talking about something else.

Grandpa's clock on the mantel struck five and Mother said she was going out to see what had happened to Dad, but just then we heard a clomping and a stomping on the porch and the door opened and there was Dad, all covered with snow from head to feet.

Mother took one look at him and said, "Where've you been?" and Dad sort of grinned and shook the snow from his shoulders.

"Doing something that I used to do," said Dad, grinning again.

He called me to him and told me to hold the door open for him and then he went back outside. Grandma came to the door and said, "Land sakes!" and Grandpa said, "What is it?" and Mother started to get up but by that time Dad was backing through the door saying, "Easy does it."

Dad had ahold of one end of a big log and Jim Pott's boy had ahold of the other end. They toted it right into the room and right up to the fireplace and then they eased it down into the fire where the other logs had just about burned out.

"There's your hickory stump," said Dad, looking at Grandpa. "Now don't say you haven't got a Yule log. Of course, it's not like the ones I used to fetch when I was a boy but I didn't have much time to look around and in this snow besides."

Grandpa seemed to perk up for the first time and he smiled at Dad, then lowered his head and got out his handkerchief and blew his nose. "Reckon that hickory stump'll heat up this place and cure my cold," he said.

Dad gave Jim Pott's boy a dollar and told him to see that the mule was put up in the barn, and then we were all laughing and talking at once and watching the hickory stump begin to catch fire.

Mother said we'd better be going and Dad said he guessed so. She got up and helped me into my coat. Dad held open the door for us and it was dark as we said "Merry Christmas" to Grandpa and Grandma.

Both of them had come to the door and both of them were smiling and Grandpa said he already felt better. Then we were out in the night, tramping through the snow to the Model-T.

Dad cranked up the Model-T and got in and Mother said to him, "You probably got your death of cold," but her voice wasn't sharp. There was something proud in it. She reached across me and touched Dad's arm and then looked back toward the house where Grandpa and Grandma sat before the fire that now was eating into the hickory stump Dad had fetched, like he had when he was a boy.

It had stopped snowing as Dad backed the Model-T out into the road and headed her for home. . . .

The scene faded from the flames of my own fire as Dorothy came into the room and said, "Asleep?" and I laughed and said, "Just dreaming."

"We'd better have some light," she said, and I said, "I guess so."

But before I got up and walked over to the wall switch, I said, "Nelse brought our Yule log but it doesn't look as big as the ones Grandpa used to have."

And then I felt in my pocket and my fingers caressed a silver dollar.

John Parris was a Sylva, North Carolina native. He was a brilliant writer and dedicated newspaper man from the tender age of 13 when he began writing for the local weekly, *The Jackson County Journal*, and working as a correspondent for *The Asheville Citizen-Times*. In 1934, he accepted a job in Raleigh, NC, working with United Press for two years. In 1936 he moved to New York and became a bylined feature writer, and was subsequently transferred by United Press to London in 1941 where he covered the diplomatic run until 1944. He took a brief time out from his work in London to cover the North African invasion where he landed with the GIs at Arzew. Shortly thereafter he joined the Associated Press in London, holding the post of diplomatic correspondent until 1946 when AP transferred him to New York to cover the United Nations. For his work with the Belgian underground he was decorated with the order of Chevalier of the Order of Leopold II.

By 1947, Parris was ready to return to his beloved mountains in Sylva, NC, devoting the rest of his life to creative writing. In 1951, he became director of public relations of the Cherokee Historical Association and later began writing his popular "Roaming the Mountains" column for *The Asheville Citizen* and *The Citizen-Times*. Their immense popularity resulted in this book's first publication in 1955.

Retrace the roots of our storied mountains with one of North Carolina's greatest storytellers and folklorists.

CPSIA information can be obtained
at www.ICGtesting.com
Printed in the USA
FSHW021550040919
61565FS